THE BEST OF TIMES,
THE WORST OF TIMES

Maritime Security in the Asia-Pacific

THE BEST OF TIMES,
THE WORST OF TIMES

Maritime Security in the Asia-Pacific

Editors

Joshua Ho
Catherine Zara Raymond

Institute of Defence and Strategic Studies,
Nanyang Technological University, Singapore

World Scientific

Institute of Defence and Strategic Studies

Published by

Institute of Defence and Strategic Studies
Nanyang Technological University, Block S4, Level B4
Nanyang Avenue, Singapore 639798

and

World Scientific Publishing Co. Pte. Ltd.
5 Toh Tuck Link, Singapore 596224
USA office: 27 Warren Street, Suite 401-402, Hackensack, NJ 07601
UK office: 57 Shelton Street, Covent Garden, London WC2H 9HE

British Library Cataloguing-in-Publication Data
A catalogue record for this book is available from the British Library.

THE BEST OF TIMES, THE WORST OF TIMES:
Maritime Security in the Asia-Pacific

ISBN 981-256-321-0
ISBN 981-256-332-6 (pbk)

Typeset by Stallion Press
Email: enquiries@stallionpress.com

Printed in Singapore by World Scientific Printers (S) Pte Ltd

Foreword

In Southeast Asia, maritime security has, over the last 20 years, taken on much greater importance, due in part to the 1982 UN Convention on the Law of the Sea (UNCLOS) and its archipelagic state and Exclusive Economic Zone (EEZ) regimes. Regional seas contain rich marine resources, major sea lines of communication (SLOCs) and a range of non-conventional threats such as piracy, illegal migration, arms smuggling and maritime terrorism. Economic development has provided the resources for maritime expansion amidst growing reliance on foreign trade and energy. There is greater dependence on long and vulnerable SLOCs in a region not without instability and the risk of conflict.

Whilst military spending in Europe declined as a result of the peace dividend from the end of the Cold War, military spending has increased in the Middle East and Asia, reflecting continuing concerns over security threats. Much of this military spending has gone into improving and expanding maritime security capabilities. This emphasis on maritime security has resulted in new building programmes for the Chinese Navy, continuing investment in naval capabilities by India and recent naval expansion programmes by countries such as Taiwan, Burma, Thailand, Malaysia, Indonesia and Singapore. Competition for resources and strategic access may increase the potential for conflict in maritime zones, especially in disputed areas of maritime jurisdiction that may include SLOCs and choke points. Multilateral security cooperation is thus required to manage emerging security threats in both the traditional as well as the non-traditional domains.

This volume is a product of a conference organised by IDSS on "Maritime Security in the Asia-Pacific". The volume begins by taking a look at the regional maritime environment, from there it then examines the maritime challenges that the regions faces, followed by an examination of the prospects for regional cooperation. Both traditional and non-traditional security matters are addressed in the volume. We hope that the analyses presented in this volume will spark further debate among policy-makers and scholars, debate that could generate policy alternatives and possible solutions to emerging security issues.

The Institute of Defence and Strategic Studies is pleased to have been involved in this volume and the excellent contribution of the 12 scholars is also gratefully acknowledged. We look forward to further collaboration with scholars and other interested parties in studying the maritime security issues of the Asia-Pacific.

Barry Desker
Director
Institute of Defence and Strategic Studies

Contents

III. Prospects for Regional Cooperation

List of Contributors

Rommel C. Banlaoi is professor of political science at the National Defence College of the Philippines (NDCP) where he serves as Course Director of Political Dimension of National Security. He is presently on special assignment at the Philippine Department of National Defence as a consultant. Rommel served as Vice President for Administrative Affairs at NDCP from 1999 to 2002 and as Assistant Vice President for Research and Special Studies in 1998. As a political science practitioner and political analyst, he provides consultancy services for the League of Municipalities of the Philippines (LMP) and Lady Municipal Mayors Association of the Philippines (LMMAP). As a defence and security analyst, Rommel is the Executive Director of the Strategic and Integrative Studies Center, Inc. (SISC) and was a Vice President of the Center for Asia-Pacific Studies from 1998 to 2002. Rommel has to his credit various local and international publications, which include, to date five books, two monographs and 35 articles on various issues related to politics, international relations, terrorism and regional security. His articles appeared in *Contemporary Southeast Asia, Parameters, Foreign Relations Journal, Asia Pacific Journal* and *National Security Review*, among others.

Sam Bateman retired from full-time service in the Royal Australian Navy with the rank of Commodore (one-star) in 1993 and became the first Director of the Centre for Maritime Policy at the University of Wollongong in New South Wales where he is now a Principal Research Fellow. His naval service as a surface warfare officer included four ship commands (including a frigate and a destroyer), 5 years in Papua New Guinea and several postings in the force development and strategic policy areas of the Department of Defence in Canberra. Current research interests include regional maritime security, the strategic and political implications of the Law of the Sea, and maritime cooperation and confidence building. Sam completed his doctorate at the University of New South Wales in 2001. He has written extensively on defence and maritime issues in Australia, the Asia-Pacific and Indian Ocean. He is Co-Chair of the Council for Security Cooperation in the Asia-Pacific (CSCAP)

Working Group on Maritime Cooperation and a member of the International Sea Lines of Communication (SLOC) Study Group, as well as a member of the National Oceans Advisory Group (NOAG) established by the Australian Government to advise on the implementation of Australia's Oceans Policy.

Robert Beckman is an Associate Professor and the Vice-Dean (Academic Affairs) at the Faculty of Law of the National University of Singapore (NUS) where he has taught since 1977. He has a J.D. from the University of Wisconsin, Madison, and an LL.M. from Harvard. He currently teaches Ocean Law and Policy, International Maritime Law and International Legal Process. He has also taught Public International Law and Space Law and Policy. Robert's areas of specialisation are public international law, law of the sea, maritime law and marine environmental law. He has a special interest in the international regulation of shipping and in the legal issues relating to maritime security. He is an advisor to the Maritime and Port Authority of Singapore (MPA) and to the Legal Committee of the Singapore Shipping Association (SSA), and he has been representing CSCAP Singapore in meetings and workshops on maritime security. Robert also specialises in training students for international moot court competitions, and he has coached NUS law students who have participated in the various international moot court competitions, including the Philip C. Jessup International Law Moot Court Competition in the United States.

James Boutilier is the Special Advisor (Policy) at Canada's Maritime Forces Pacific Headquarters in Esquimalt, British Columbia. He is responsible for advising the Commander of Maritime Forces Pacific on matters of defence and foreign policy and maritime security in the Asia-Pacific region. Prior to his appointment at MARPAC, James spent 24 years on staff at the Royal Roads Military College in Victoria as Head of the History Department and then as Dean of Arts. During his time at RRMC, he was instrumental in establishing the military and strategic studies degree programme at the college and taught courses on naval history, contemporary Asia, the history of the Pacific and strategic issues. He is also an adjunct professor of Pacific and Asian Studies at the University of Victoria and the President of the Maritime Awards Society of Canada. James specialises in Asia-Pacific defence and security, particularly with regards to maritime issues. He has published widely on international defence and security issues, including *RCN in Retrospect* (1982), and articles in professional monographs as well as the *Asia-Pacific Defence Reporter* and

Canadian Institute of International Affairs journals. Some of his recent lectures have focused on the Canadian Navy's role in the Asia-Pacific, the new Asian security architecture, Northeast Asian security issues and the new naval order in Asia.

Rupert Herbert-Burns is a senior consultant at the Maritime Intelligence Group (MIG) in Washington, DC, specialising in maritime security, terrorism and asymmetrical threats in the maritime domain, and piracy at sea. He joined MIG in March 2003, where he has since consulted for the US Government (Departments of Homeland Security, Justice, and Defence), the US Coast Guard and the New York Police Department (NYPD). Prior to joining MIG, Rupert, following graduation from Britannia Royal Naval College in England, served at sea as an officer in the Royal Navy in operational theatres worldwide, including deployments to the Atlantic, Barents Sea, Mediterranean Sea, Pacific and the South China Sea. Ensuing service also included appointments as a platoon commander and regimental intelligence officer with the British Army's Brigade of Gurkhas, with tours in Brunei, Hong Kong, Nepal and the United Kingdom. Rupert has a BSc (Hons.) in International Relations and Politics from the University of Plymouth in England, an M.Litt. in International Security Studies from the University of St Andrews in Scotland (Centre for the Study of Terrorism and Political Violence — CSTPV), and is currently a second-year PhD candidate at the University of St Andrews, writing a treatise on geopolitical theory and the security of maritime and terrestrial modes of conveyance of oil and natural gas worldwide.

Peter Cozens is the Executive Director at the Centre for Strategic Studies, Victoria University of Wellington, New Zealand. He was educated at the Duke of Yorks Royal Military School in Dover England between 1954 and 1962. He chose a career at sea and joined the British India Steam Navigation Company Limited after leaving school. During those years he sailed in the Company's cadetship, cargo, passenger and cruise liners, sailing and trading around the orient but left in 1972 to join the Royal New Zealand Navy. During his career in the RNZN he enjoyed a wide variety of postings and a stimulating career and retired in the rank of Commander in 1993. A highlight of his naval vocation was his time as Aide de Camp to His Excellency the Governor General of New Zealand Sir Denis Blundell. His research interests include maritime strategy, oceans policy, the United Nations Convention on the Law of the Sea and Chinese and Indian maritime development. Peter is a graduate of Victoria University of Wellington (BA in History and MA in Economics) and the Royal Australian Naval Staff College.

Derek da Cunha has MPhil and PhD degrees in the field of International Relations from Cambridge University, and the Australian National University respectively. He is a Senior Fellow at the Institute of Southeast Asian Studies (ISEAS) in Singapore where he is Coordinator of the Regional Strategic and Political Studies (RSPS) programme, and between August 1992 and December 2002 was also Editor of the journal *Contemporary Southeast Asia*. Derek's research interests ranges from a focus on defence and security issues related to Southeast Asia and the wider Asia-Pacific, to the impact of globalisation on Southeast Asian societies, to Singapore politics and society. In the area of defence and security, his publications include the edited volumes, *Southeast Asian Perspectives on Security* (ISEAS, 2000, 204 pp.) and *The Evolving Pacific Power Structure* (ISEAS, 1996, 261 pp.). In the area of Singapore society and politics, his publications include the book, *The Price of Victory: The 1997 Singapore General Election and Beyond* (ISEAS, 1997, 149 pp.); and the edited volumes *Singapore in the New Millennium: Challenges Facing the City-State* (ISEAS, 2002, 281 pp.), and *Debating Singapore: Reflective Essays* (ISEAS, 1994, reprinted 1996, 173 pp.). His forthcoming publication is the volume he is editing entitled *Globalisation and its Counter Forces: Multidimensional Aspects from Southeast Asia*. Derek is a member of the London-based International Institute for Strategic Studies.

Seema Gahlaut is the Co-director of the South Asia Program at the Center for International Trade and Security, University of Georgia. She also teaches courses on *American Government and Politics, Political Economy and National Security in Southern Asia* and *Politics of Trade and Security Policy* at the School of Public & International Affairs at the University. She is in-charge of the India and Pakistan sections of the Center's *Global Evaluations of Export Control Development* project. She regularly briefs government officials in India and the United States on export control issues. She has appeared on *CNN Talk Back Live* and often contributes to *Voice of America, Radio Free Asia* and the *BBC* (Hindi Service) as an expert. She is the co-editor of *Engaging India: US Strategic Relations with the World's Largest Democracy* (Routledge, 1999) and co-author of *To Supply or to Deny: Assessing Nonproliferation Export Controls in Six Supplier States* (New York: Kluwer, 2004), *Reforming Multilateral Export Controls* (CITS Report, February 2004), *Strengthening Multilateral Export Controls* (CITS Report, November 2002) and *FAQs on Proliferation* *from Pakistan* (CITS Report May 2004). She has contributed articles on challenges for nonproliferation regime after 9/11, Proliferation Security Initiative, Russian perspectives on South Asia, the future of the Australia Group and India's policies regarding chemical weapons, export controls, intangible technologies and Pakistan.

Hideaki Kaneda is a Special Research Advisor for The Okazaki Institute and Mitsubishi Research Institute, and a member of the Policy Proposal Committee of the Japan Forum for Strategic Study. He is a retired Vice Admiral of the Japan Maritime Self Defence Force and was a Senior Fellow of Asia Center and J.F. Kennedy School of Government of Harvard for the last two years. He became a Guest Professor of the Faculty of Policy Management of Keio University from September 2002. He is the author of many published books and articles about security, such as *Proposal for Maritime Coalition in East Asia and West Pacific Region*, IMDEX, Germany, November 2000, *Theater Ballistic Missile Defence for Japan*, Okazaki Institute, Tokyo, December 2000, *Changing Situation of China's and Japan's National Security*, World and Japan, Tokyo, September 2001, *Role of JMSDF in Peace Time*, Securitarian, Tokyo, August 2001, *US/China Power Game in Maritime Hegemony*, JIIA, Tokyo, March 2003, *BMD for Japan*, Kaya-Books, Tokyo, March 2003, *Immediate Threat of Nodong Missile to Japan*, Bungei-Shunju, Tokyo, June 2003 and *Maritime Coalition in Asia-Pacific Region*, Okazaki Institute, Tokyo, January 2004.

W. Lawrence S. Prabhakar is a Visiting Research Fellow at the Institute of Defence and Strategic Studies and an Associate Professor of Political Science, Madras Christian College, Chennai (Madras), India. He graduated with MA and MPhil degrees in Political Science from the Madras Christian College. His doctoral work was on *"Strategic Thought in India Since 1971"* in which he earned a PhD from the Department of Defence & Strategic Studies, University of Madras. Lawrence is Consultant to the Directorate of Net Assessment Office of the Chiefs of Integrated Defence Staff, Chiefs of Staff Committee, Ministry of Defence, Government of India, on two projects: *"The Role of the Dragon: Strategic Role and Posture of China in the India-Pakistan Conflict Spectrum"* in the Simulation-cum-Scenario Development Exercise: India–Pakistan Conflict Spectrum Under the Nuclear Backdrop at the Army War College, Mhow, February 2003; and *"Extra-regional Naval Presence and Posture: Implications for the Indian Navy"*, July 2003, in the project, Regional Maritime Balance in Indian Ocean 2020. Both projects were commissioned by the Directorate of Net Assessment, Office of the Chiefs of Integrated Defence Staff, Ministry of Defence, Government of India, New Delhi.

Stanley B. Weeks has since 1990 been a Senior Scientist with Science Applications International Corporation (SAIC) in McLean, Virginia. His current work includes port and CB defence support for US Central Command. Recent work include support of the SAIC-led multinational team's Layered TBMD Feasibility Study for NATO, providing support to the Office of the Secretary of Defence in analysis of current Asia-Pacific security issues (including Taiwan TMD, multilateral security cooperation, ASEAN Regional Forum (ARF), Theatre Missile Defence, Korean and other proliferation concerns, regional maritime security cooperation and Russian relations with Japan and the Pacific region). Stanley has supported USCENTCOM cooperative defence/counterproliferation work. He has also supported Commander, US Pacific Fleet, with an assessment of the implications of theatre missile defences, and supported Commander, US Naval Forces Europe, with an analysis of Allied interoperability in sea-based missile defence. He has also supported the US Pacific Commander's new Asia-Pacific Center for Security Studies (APCSS) in the thematic preparation and conduct of the first two Biennial Conferences for regional security leaders. He has supported the US Navy's Strategy and Policy Director in developing new naval strategies, concepts and force structures to address regional and proliferation threats. Other work at SAIC has included corporate strategic planning for commercial Latin America business.

Editors

Joshua H. Ho is a Senior Fellow at the Institute of Defence and Strategic Studies, Singapore. He obtained a B.A. and M.A. in Engineering from Cambridge University, U.K. on a SAF (Overseas) Scholarship, and also holds an MSc (Management) (Distinction) from the Naval Postgraduate School, California, where he was awarded the Graduate School of Business and Public Policy Faculty awards for Excellence in Management, given to the top student in the faculty, and Outstanding International Student. Joshua is a serving Naval Officer with 18 years of service and currently holds the rank of Lieutenant Colonel. He was trained as a Principal Warfare Officer and completed his command and staff training at the Royal Australian Navy Staff College and the Singapore Command and Staff College. He has served in various shipboard and staff appointments including the Command of a Missile Gun Boat and stints in the Naval Operations, Plans and Personnel Departments as well as a short attachment to the Future Systems Directorate, MINDEF. He has held concurrent appointments of Honorary Aide de Camp to the President, Secretary to the Naval Staff Meeting, and Secretary to the Policy and Strategy Meeting chaired by the then Second Minister for Defence, Mr Teo Chee Hean.

Joshua's commentaries have been published in Singapore's leading broadsheet newspaper, *The Straits Times*, as well as in Singapore's leading free daily, *Today*. He has also published in well known local and overseas journals like *Defence Studies, Australian Army Journal, Journal of the Australian Naval Institute* and *Pointer*, and presented papers at conferences organised by the *Center for Strategic & International Studies, Washington D.C.*; the *Observer Research Foundation, New Delhi; National Institute for Defence Studies, Tokyo;* the *Norwegian Institute of International Affairs (NUPI), Oslo*; as well as by local conference organisers *Defence Directory* and *Defence IQ*, a local subsidiary of *IQPC*. He has lectured at the Singapore Command and Staff Course as well as the Home Team Command and Staff Course.

Catherine Zara Raymond is an Associate Research Fellow at the Institute of Defence and Strategic Studies (IDSS), Nanyang Technological University, Singapore. She is currently involved in research into maritime terrorism and piracy, under the Institute's Maritime Security Programme. She was previously an analyst at the Centre for the Study of Terrorism and Political Violence, St Andrews University, Scotland. At the centre she was responsible for briefing senior staff on terrorist trends, with particular emphasis on Southeast and Central Asia. Her research has been used for a book on the Al Qaeda terrorist network, British Ministry of Defence reports and the latest edition of the Jane's Counter Terrorism Manual. She has carried out research for Security Risk Management Consultancies and has conducted profiles on terrorist groups for governmental and non-governmental bodies. Zara has an MSc in International and European Politics from Edinburgh University and an MA in International Relations from St Andrew's University, Scotland.

Introduction

The Shifting of Maritime Power to the Asia-Pacific

Much has been written and said about the 21st century being the Asia-Pacific century as the region is expected to experience phenomenal growth rates unprecedented in the history of world development. Projections that have been done by both US intelligence agencies and wealth management institutions seem to point to an inescapable conclusion: that we are already witnessing the beginnings of an Asia-Pacific century.

Currently, the combined 2002 GDPs of China, India and Japan are already half that of the United States in nominal terms.[1] By 2015, the CIA's long term growth model has forecasted that the combined GDPs of China, India and Japan would surpass that of the United States and the European Union at US$ 19.8 trillion, US$ 14 trillion and US$ 11.6 trillion, respectively, in 1998 dollars.[2] By 2050, Goldman Sachs has projected that the situation will become even more astounding when the combined GDPs of China, India and Japan will be slightly more that twice that of the United States and about four times that of Russia, United Kingdom, Germany, France and Italy combined in 2003 dollars.[3] In 2050, the largest economies in the world will be China, United States and India, respectively, with Japan at a distant fourth. In the short span of time of only one generation, the economic centre of gravity would have shifted to Asia.

As the economic centre of gravity shifts to the Asia-Pacific, it is natural and inevitable that maritime power also shifts to the Asia-Pacific due to the importance of the sea to the regional economies. Again, the shift in maritime power may have already started by observing current trends in three areas: (1) the increasing trade flows into and within Asia, (2) the increasing energy demand in Asia, and (3) the increasing strength of the merchant fleets in the region. Let us look at each trend in turn.

1

Trends Indicating a Shift in Maritime Power

The first trend is that intra-Asian trade flows have increased and Asian trade with the United States and Europe is also increasing. In particular, China's trade expansion has remained outstanding, as its exports and imports have risen by 30 percent between 2000 and 2002 even as world trade stagnated.[4] In fact, China's trade expansion is so broad based that she has become the fourth largest merchandise trader in 2002, and across the globe, China has become a major supplier and a major export destination for many countries including ASEAN, South Korea, Japan, Taiwan, India, the European Union and the United States. As most of the intra- and inter-regional trade is conducted via sea routes, an increasing reliance on sea transportation will ensue as a result of increasing regional trade.

The second trend is that resource demand, particularly energy demand, in Asia is rising in tandem with its economic development. Asia as a whole currently uses about as much energy as the United States. By 2020, Asia will have the same energy consumption as North America and Western Europe combined. However, Asia is only close to self-sufficiency in coal. For natural gas, Japan, South Korea and Taiwan already consume most of the region's methane supply. To support the expected increase in consumption in natural gas, the region will have to turn to Russia as well as the Middle East. As the absolute demand for oil rises, Asia has also to import oil from outside the region, particularly from the Middle East.[5] This increased energy demand will mean an increasing reliance on the sea as most of the energy is transported by sea.

The third trend is that the strength of the merchant fleet in Asia has been increasing relative to the proportion of the world's fleets to meet both the increasing demands for trade as well as the demands for energy. By July 2003, Asia owned about 40 percent of the merchant fleets amongst the Top 20 owners in the world, and 41 percent by tonnage. If we include the United States, then the Asia-Pacific owns about 46 percent of the merchant fleets and 48.1 percent by tonnage and the figure looks set to increase in the future. Already construction of the world's largest shipyard with a frontage of 8 km is underway in Shanghai, China.[6] This development will further consolidate East Asia's position as home to the world's largest shipbuilders with Chinese, South Korean and Japanese shipbuilders having 12.8, 36.2 and 28.8 percent, respectively, of the global order book in terms of tonnage currently.[7]

Alternative Regional Futures

The trends of increased trade flows, increased energy demands and increased strength of merchant fleets all point to the shift of maritime power to Asia. As maritime power in the region increases, the ability of the regional countries, as well as extra-regional powers like the United States, to manage the power politics that emerge will be a key determinant of stability. But what kind of possible future scenarios are we looking at? In the National Intelligence Council's sponsored study on global trends by 2015, four alternative future global scenarios have been postulated based on outcomes of the globalisation process, which can be inclusive, pernicious, or result in regional competition and the creation of a post-polar world.[8]

In three of the four scenarios, the possibility of internal conflicts is postulated, and in three of the four scenarios, there is a possibility of internal conflicts spilling over to its neighbours with one scenario of a regional conflict. Hence, the ability to manage and resolve conflicts that arise will become a key determinant of regional stability if we want to allow the wealth effects from regional economic progress to spread and for the majority of the people to benefit from globalisation. In the maritime arena, the two main challenges are:

- to ensure the security of the sea lanes in order to ensure the continued unimpeded flow of resources and goods, and
- to prevent maritime conflicts between states due to resource and trade competition as the region and their navies grow.[9]

The chapters in this volume attempt to address the twin challenges of ensuring the security of sea lanes and the prevention of inter-state maritime conflict in three parts. The first part looks at the maritime environment in the Asia-Pacific by examining the regional force modernisation as well as commercial maritime trends globally, in Northeast Asia, Southeast Asia, and South Asia. The second part examines the maritime challenges that the region faces as a result of the trends identified. In particular, topics like maritime boundary and territorial disputes, the modernisation of naval forces in the Asia-Pacific, piracy and maritime terrorism are covered. In the final part, the volume examines the prospects for regional cooperation that present themselves as responses to address some of these challenges. The responses include the proliferation security initiative, export control measures, new initiatives for maritime cooperation and maritime "regime" building. The volume is based on the proceedings of a conference on maritime security conducted by Institute of Defence and Strategic Studies from 20 to 21 May 2004 in Singapore. What follows is a summary of the chapters in the volume.

The Regional Environment

The title of **James Boutilier's** article — *The Best of Times, the Worst of Times: The Global Maritime Outlook 2004* — gives a clear signal as to the findings of the chapter, which is essentially a review of the global maritime outlook, with particular focus on the Indo-Pacific region. Boutilier examines the maritime sector from the perspective of six main themes: the growth of navies and merchant fleets, maritime theatres of operation, maritime roles, information, technology and regulatory regimes. Under each theme he provides a "snapshot" of current conditions and outlines significant trends. Boutilier concludes that the global maritime outlook is in "a paradoxical state of affairs". On the one hand, the Indo-Pacific region is witnessing an impressive growth in seaborne trade and shipbuilding, with naval expenditure also on the increase. On the other hand, the shadow of maritime terrorism looms over the maritime community and shifting theatres of operation in the maritime security environment pose new challenges in the areas of maritime roles, technology and the management of information.

In his chapter, *Regional Maritime Security Outlook: Northeast Asia*, **Hideaki Kaneda**, offers a valuable summary of the challenges facing the Asia-Pacific region at the beginning of the 21st Century. Kaneda, draws attention to seven factors that have a potential to cause, or are currently causing, instability in the region: the proliferation of weapons of mass destruction and ballistic missiles from Northeast Asia to the other regions of the world; the rise of the specter of international terrorism in the region; the rapid build-up of Chinese military power, in particular its naval and air power; the confrontational military structure, which originated in the Cold War and still remains in the Korean Peninsula and the Taiwan Strait; territorial and ethnic disputes that have plagued the region for decades, most of which centre around conflicting claims to the various resource-rich islands in the region; the confrontation over oceanic interests, caused mainly by Chinese naval activities; and finally, the increase in international and organised illegal activities, in particular the problem of piracy. Kaneda goes on to provide a refreshing examination of the prospects for regional cooperation, which he argues is essential in the solution to the challenges faced by the region. He also makes recommendations as to how the regional community should proceed with the formation of a regional framework of cooperation.

Rommel Banlaoi mentions in his *Maritime Security Outlook for Southeast Asia* that maritime security encompasses such a broad concept that it is difficult to come to grips with it. Notions of maritime security include maritime safety, port security, freedom of navigation, security of the Sea Lines of Communication (SLOCs), security from piracy attacks including armed robberies against ships and security from maritime terrorism. But despite the lack of a workable definition, the importance and growing concern on maritime security have led participants to issue the *Statement on Cooperation Against Piracy and other Threats to Maritime Security* at the 36th ASEAN Ministerial Meeting and the 10th ARF Post Ministerial Conferences. Hence, as a maritime region, maritime security is an integral component of the regional security agenda and discourse. The chapter describes the maritime security outlook for Southeast Asia in the areas of piracy and maritime terrorism and analyses these issues in the context of shipping and force modernisation trends in the region. The chapter contends that piracy and maritime terrorism in Southeast Asia have root causes and addressing these root causes is crucial to promoting regional maritime security. The root causes include pervasive regional poverty, weak governance, huge coastlines and weak port security, relatively weak maritime forces, underpaid staff of regional maritime security forces and limited instances of maritime security cooperation in the region. The chapter concludes that defence development in the form of extra-regional powers aiding in the force modernisation of regional countries is imperative to increase the capacity of Southeast Asian countries to surmount the huge challenges to maritime security in the region.

In *Regional Maritime Dynamics in Southern Asia in the 21st Century*, **Lawrence Prabhakar** states that the regional maritime dynamics of Southern Asia are governed by the geo-strategic maritime space of the South Asian littoral, the adjoining Indian Ocean maritime space and China, the hinterland of Afghanistan and the Central Asian Region with its convergent foci on the Indian Ocean. It is also dependant upon the role and dynamics of the regional navies of South Asia that are characterised by their colonial heritage and regional rivalries, and the intervening profiles of the extra-regional navies in the Indian Ocean region.

This analysis of Regional Maritime Dynamics is based around the following parameters: (a) the salient trends of the Regional Maritime Dynamics evident in the evolving missions and roles of the regional and extra-regional navies; (b) the nature of alliances and coalitions in the region that have emerged from the inter-regional naval rivalries and the role of the extra-regional navies in the region; (c) the role and status of nuclear weapons in the region;

their implications in a maritime context; and the responses generated by the extra-regional navies, which is evident in new deployment doctrines and the emergent technologies of sea-based missile defences; (d) the accents of cooperative security in bilateral and multilateral aegis with emphasis on Maritime Confidence Building Measures and Risk Reduction; in particular, the bilateral and multilateral cooperation in the maritime economic domain; proactive security measures with regards to counter proliferation, involving the maritime based interdiction of the transfer of technologies for Weapons of Mass Destruction, known as the Proliferation Security Initiative.

The Regional Maritime Challenges

As the title suggests, the chapter, *Some Reflections On Maritime Boundary and Territorial Disputes in the Asia-Pacific with a Focus on the South China Sea*, by **Peter Cozens**, traces the emergence of boundary disputes in the Asia-Pacific. The chapter begins by giving a brief account of the historical process leading up to and including the creation of Exclusive Economic Zones (EEZs) in the region. EEZs being an area of 200 nautical miles extending from the coast of a state, in which that state has exclusive use of the sea. According to Cozens, the creation of EEZs "has opened a sea of troubles that today manifest as maritime and territorial boundary disputes". China's claims in the South China Sea are then examined, from the perspective of contemporary Chinese maritime history. The conclusion of this examination is that despite various efforts at resolving boundary disputes though cooperative measures or agreements of conduct, boundaries will have to be drawn for there to be any long lasting benefit to all those concerned.

According to **Derek Da Cunha**, in his chapter on the *Modernisation of Naval Forces in the Asia-Pacific: A Focus on Three Northeast Asian Navies*, defence spending in the Asia-Pacific region on naval forces capabilities has outpaced that of the other component arms of the military forces since the early 1990s. Derek accounts for this trend of the modernisation and expansion of naval forces, and then goes on to examine the process in three North Asian states: China, Taiwan and Japan. Derek Da Cuhna breaks from the norm of what he calls "simple bean counting" in his examination of the modernisation of naval forces, and provides an important account not just of "the upgrading of equipment or the induction of new platforms" into navies, but of the changes to operational concepts that will affect the theatre of operations in which the navies will be operating. The chapter concludes with a brief analysis of the challenges faced by the regional navies despite their continued advancement.

Rupert Herbert-Burns offers a valuable overview of *Terrorism in the Early 21st Century Maritime Domain*. He begins by examining the maritime environment in which terrorist groups operate, drawing our attention to the "enormous scope, variety and 'room for manoeuvre'" that the maritime arena has to offer. He then goes on to make a critical assessment of the commercial shipping industry, which he argues provides an "ideal operational and tactical cover" for terrorist groups. The source of the threat — international terrorism — is then addressed, through the examination of a number of case studies, which are used to highlight the number of ways in which the maritime realm can be harnessed by terrorists. The author uses the findings of his investigation to make an informed assessment of future threat scenarios. He concludes his chapter with a discussion of various counter-terrorism strategies that could be used to mitigate the terrorist threat. According to Herbert-Burns, the solution lies in the "fusion of intelligence, international and transnational cooperation, and risk assessment".

The chapter *Maritime Terrorism, A Risk Assessment: The Australian Example* by **Catherine Zara Raymond** investigates the extent of the threat posed by maritime terrorism to Australian commercial ports and shipping. It focuses in particular on the threat from the terrorist groups located in Indonesia and the Philippines and the vulnerability of Australian vessels passing through Southeast Asia's strategic sea-lanes. In her analysis, Catherine Zara Raymond finds that there are inherent weaknesses present in the Australian maritime transport industry, and that there are terrorist groups in the region with maritime capabilities who possess the motives to target Western economic interests. Thus, according to the author, this necessitates the conclusion that maritime terrorism is a threat to Australian commercial ports and shipping. The chapter then goes on to describe how the extent of the threat from maritime terrorism has increased in recent years, especially since the terrorist attack against the United States on 11 September 2001. Finally, the author briefly discusses the potential consequences of a maritime terrorist attack and possible counter-measures and risk-treatment options.

Prospects for Regional Cooperation

Robert Beckman in his chapter on the *Legal Implications of the Proliferation Security Initiative* asserts that the terrorist attacks on 11 September 2001 resulted in a "two-pronged" approach by the United States to counter what was perceived to be the new threat from maritime terrorism, and in particular the transport of weapons of mass destruction (WMD) by sea. The two approaches are: to work with the relevant international organisations and encourage them to adopt new counter-terrorism measures, and gain cooperation in the form of bilateral and multilateral agreements on new measures through the use of its power and influence in the international community.

In his paper, Beckman discusses these two approaches in the context of the proliferation of WMD. First, the Proliferation Security Initiative (PSI) is examined, which as Beckman states is an effort by the United States to deal with the issue of the proliferation of WMD through the establishment of a coalition of willing partners, outside of the institutions and regimes governing the law of the sea. Second, the efforts of the United States to work with the UN Security Council and the International Maritime Organisation to change the legal regimes governing the proliferation and transport of WMD, principally through the creation of a new protocol to the 1988 Convention for the Suppression of Unlawful Acts Against the Safety of Navigation (SUA Convention) are examined.

In the chapter on the *Political Implications of the Proliferation Security Initiative*, **Seema Gahlaut** mentions that the Proliferation Security Initiative (PSI) is an initiative to develop political commitments and practical cooperation to help impede and stop the flow of weapons of mass destruction (WMD), their systems and related materials to and from states and non-state actors of concern. But since its launch by President Bush in May 2003 critics have identified at least three major weaknesses in the structure and functioning of the PSI. These weaknesses include the contention that: (1) PSI's operations are likely to violate the established treaties and conventions like the UN Convention on the Law of the Sea (UNCLOS); (2) the PSI is an informal agreement among a small group of self-selected countries, who appear to be more interested in safeguarding their own commercial and security interests rather than in upholding international or regional security; and (3) PSI has no clear legally acceptable means to define and identify dual-use technologies that it will target for interdiction. Seema assesses whether the PSI, despite its legal and political shortcomings, and despite the current opposition to it, is likely to survive beyond its current hyperactive phase. She does this by using the example of the multilateral export control regimes, which share many of the weaknesses of the PSI, to make the case that PSI's chances for survival are very good.

Stanley Weeks, in his chapter on *New Initiatives for Maritime Cooperation*, mentions that after the end of the Cold War, and especially in the last few years, there has been noteworthy progress in improving transparency in the maritime arena, particularly in various bilateral contexts. However, he emphasises that there is a need in the coming years to increase Asia-Pacific maritime cooperation to deal with the growing threats posed by maritime terrorism and other maritime challenges. In particular, he says that Asia-Pacific nations would have to move beyond the previously successful focus on maritime confidence-building measures, which have been mainly in the form of transparency measures, and start emphasising Maritime Operational Cooperation as the ultimate in "Security Building" against the common new threats of maritime terrorism.

Stanley suggests that initial attempts at Maritime Operational Cooperation would logically consist of patrols of sea lanes and choke points, which are at greatest threat from maritime terrorists and violent piracy at sea, and this will include the western to the eastern entrances to the Straits of Malacca. He also suggests four paths that could be used for Maritime Operational Cooperation. The first path could be through the Council for Security Cooperation in the Asia-Pacific (CSCAP) Maritime Cooperation Working Group, the second path could be through the Western Pacific Naval Symposium (WPNS), the third path could be through Track One forums like the ASEAN Regional Forum (ARF) Intersessional Meeting on Confidence Building Measures and, finally, the fourth path could be through the new Regional Maritime Security Initiative (RMSI).

In his chapter, *Maritime "Regime" Building*, **Sam Bateman** makes a critical assessment of maritime regime building in East Asia. Present and previous attempts at maritime regime building in the region are outlined and their progress traced. Bateman describes how these current and past experiences can be instructive as to what might be possible in the future. The idea of a maritime regime is then situated within the wider context of regime theory itself. Bateman argues that the key to establishing order, in the largely anarchic maritime environment of the *high seas*, is the development of a more stable regional maritime regime. The relationship between cooperation and regimes is discussed. Bateman contends that the assumption of cooperative arrangements being a prerequisite for the formation of regimes needs to be investigated further. The chapter then goes on to examine some of the main issues and problems associated with building a maritime regime, such as sovereignty and national interest. Bateman looks briefly at the European and South Pacific experiences of building a regional maritime regime to highlight the importance of existing political frameworks to regime building. Bateman concludes his chapter by outlining a number of issues that need to be addressed in order to improve the prospects of establishing a regional maritime regime.

Notes

1. The 2002 GDPs of the United States, China, Japan and India are US$ 11,145 bn, US$ 1299 bn, US$ 3986 bn and US$ 501.2 bn, respectively, in nominal terms. See Economic Intelligence Unit, *Country Report: United States of America* (London: November 2003), p. 5; "Country Forecast: China", *Economic Intelligence Unit*, November 2003, p. 11; "Country Forecast: Japan", *Economic Intelligence Unit*, November 2003, p. 12; and "Country Forecast: India", *Economic Intelligence Unit*, November 2003, p. 12.

2. National Intelligence Council, *Global Trends 2015: A Dialogue About the Future with Nongovernment Experts* (Washington, DC: National Intelligence Council Publication, December 2000), pp. 34–38.

3. The forecasted 2050 GDPs of China, United States, India and Japan are US$ 45 bn, US$ 35 bn, US$ 27 bn and US$ 7 bn, respectively, in 2003 dollars. See Dominic Wilson and Roopa Purushothaman, "Dreaming with BRICs: The Path to 2050", *Goldman Sachs Global Economics Paper No. 99*, 1 October 2003, p. 4.

4. World Trade Organisation, *International Trade Statistics 2003* (Switzerland: World Trade Organisation, 2003), p. 2. Available at http://www.wto.org/english/res_e/statis_e/its2003_e/its03_toc-e.htm.

5. Ibid, p. 192.

6. "Shanghai to Build 'World's Biggest Shipyard'", *The Straits Times Interactive*, 30 December 2003. Available at http://straitstimes.asia1.com.sg/.

7. Sam Chambers, "Special Report — China: Nation's Shipbuilding Ambitions Laid Bare", *Lloyd's List International*, 27 November 2003, p. 13.

8. National Intelligence Council, pp. 83–85.

9. Nazli Choucri and Robert North, *Nations in Conflict: National Growth and International Violence* (San Francisco: Freeman, 1975), pp. 283–284.

I. *The Regional Maritime Environment*

Chapter 1

The Best of Times, the Worst of Times: The Global Maritime Outlook 2004

James Boutilier

Introduction

The oceans of the world have gained greater and greater prominence in the post-Cold War era. Globalisation has stimulated worldwide trade, most of which moves by sea. Increasingly, major powers like China, India and Japan have embraced Mahanian visions of seapower, using their navies to project their influence abroad. These same powers have an insatiable appetite for energy and this has spurred the growth of tanker traffic. The export-driven economies of Asia have created a huge demand for containers and container ships, much of it met by the region's burgeoning shipyards. At the same time, the War on Terrorism has acquired a maritime dimension, making every ship and port a potential target. This is particularly true for the megaports of East Asia. Combating the terrorist threat has meant utilising the full range of maritime agencies and assets. Navies have been drawn more deeply into constabulary work. The counter-terrorist campaign has highlighted the complexity and inadequacy of oceanic regulatory regimes. Furthermore, it has placed a premium on what the practitioners call domain awareness; that is to say the development of a comprehensive picture of everything that moves on the world's oceans. Domain awareness is central to the War on Terrorism, not only in the conduct of naval operations but also in the provision of maritime and port security. Thus, exploiting the latest technologies to collect, analyse and manage maritime knowledge has become an overarching priority for those engaged in prosecuting the war and dealing with piracy, smuggling, illegal fishing, human trafficking and the flow of weapons of mass destruction (WMD).

This chapter analyses the global maritime outlook. It provides a snapshot of current conditions and highlights trends. Its primary focus is on the Indo-Pacific region although examples are drawn from elsewhere. The region is demonstrably the world's most dynamic in terms of maritime trade, ship construction, naval growth, competing maritime ambitions, contested oceanic claims and terrorist activity. Six broad themes will be addressed: information, technology, theatres of operation, regulatory regimes, maritime roles and the growth of navies and merchant fleets. These themes are inter-related in complex ways with ship owners, naval captains, international lawyers, information technicians and a host of other marine interests contributing, in aggregate, to the global maritime outlook. When we review their activities and set them in an oceanic context we can only conclude, as Dickens once did, that this is the best of times and the worst of times in the oceans of the world.

Growth

The first thing that strikes us when we look at the Indo-Pacific region is the phenomenon of growth; growth set over and against the vital role that maritime commerce plays in facilitating the global economy. The statistics are both telling and impressive. Seaborne trade has doubled every decade since 1945 and shipbuilding tonnage worldwide has doubled since 1990. Roughly 5.7 billion tons of cargo are shipped annually in 93,000 merchant vessels bound for 8200 ports.[1] The world's largest trading nation, the United States, exports and imports about one-fourth of global merchandise, by volume, each year. This amounted to US$ 2 trillion in 2000. The largest part of that trade — over 1.2 billion metric tons — was moved by sea. Projections suggest that US foreign trade may grow to four times its present value and almost double its current tonnage by 2020.[2]

When we turn to worldwide energy flows — with much of the demand originating out of East Asia — we see that the future order book for tankers is "exceptionally strong" with shipyard availability "severely limited" until 2006.[3] The demand for tankers is the result of two factors. First, seaborne oil movements have increased by an average of 2.3 percent per year since 1990. China accounts for much of this sustained growth. The People's Republic of China became a net importer of oil in 1993. China's crude oil demand in 1990 was 2.3 million barrels per day (bpd). By 2000, it was 4.6 million bpd.[4] With China's crude oil imports expected to treble over the next decade, the shipping routes or sea lines of communication (SLOCs) from East Asia via the South China Sea, the Straits of Malacca and the Indian Ocean to the oil-rich Gulf states are becoming increasingly important, commercially and geo-strategically.[5] Second, following the loss of the tanker *Erika* in December 1999, the International Maritime Organization (IMO) reacted to demands for the revision of the MARPOL Convention, including the accelerated withdrawal of single-hulled tankers. This decision was reinforced by the break-up and sinking of the *Prestige* off the Iberian peninsula in November 2002.[6]

East Asian trade has increased "nearly twice as fast as world trade in general [over the past 20 years] and has already surpassed that of North America".[7] Asia controls and operates over 40 percent of the global commercial fleet while over one-quarter of the world's trade and half of its oil and LNG pass through the Straits of Malacca everyday.[8] China is expected to be the "greatest single factor influencing the world's shipping industry over the next two decades".[9] China's maritime economy grew 17 percent per year in the 1980s and 20 percent per year in the 1990s. China contributes to two major trade flows: trans-Pacific and intra-Asian. Asian shipping companies announced recently that they expect to carry between 10 and 12 percent more cargo from Asia to the United States in 2004 than forecast earlier.[10] Container traffic was up 16 percent from China to the port of Vancouver in the first 6 months of 2003 and overall trade between these two destinations more than doubled from 1999 to 2002 (1,588,000 metric tons to 3,569,000 metric tons).[11] That said, intra-Asian trade is growing more quickly than trans-Pacific trade, In 2003, for example, South Korea's trade with China surpassed its trade with the United States for the first time. Indeed, more and more Asian states are re-orienting their trade flows towards China. This phenomenon reflects the power and attractiveness of the China market, the general recovery of East Asian economies in the period after 1997 and the emergence of trade facilitation agreements between China and Southeast Asian states.[12]

Regional statistics underscore this demand. Japan's ship exports doubled in 2003 to a post-war high, with almost 600 ships being exported from Japanese yards. The boom is attributed to the dramatic growth in China with shippers scrambling to keep pace with China's voracious appetite for imported grain, wheat, iron ore, oil and cement.[13] While these are bulk cargoes, container ships carry an increasing proportion of Asian trade. The production of freight containers in 2003 reached 1.6 million TEUs (twenty-foot equivalent units), an increase of 25 percent over the previous year.[14] Dry freight containers constituted the bulk of this production and made up 80 percent of the total; China dominated container production with 87 percent of the market share.[15] Similarly, UNCTAD figures reveal that while the global tanker fleet increased by 6.6 percent in 2003, the container fleet outpaced it, increasing by 7.4 percent.[16] When one looks more carefully at these figures we see that the trend is not so much towards more container ships but to bigger ones. Vessels with a capability in excess of 3000 TEUs made up 67 percent of the total deliveries in 2002. More significantly, vessels with that capacity made up 79.8 percent of the ships on the order book.[17] The growth in the number of containers and the number of container ships is reflected in regional statistics. Shanghai, for example, is now the world's third-largest container port and the fourth-largest port in the world.[18] Association of Southeast Asian Nations' reports tell a similar story with ASEAN container traffic rising from 26,307,000 TEUs in 1997 to a projected 68,100,000 in 2010.[19]

If mercantile activity, global and especially in the Indo-Pacific region, has been impressive, naval growth has been equally dramatic in the same region. This contrasts with a marked decline in three of the world's major navies, although the third, the Chinese Navy, must be treated as somewhat of an exception. In 1987, as dreams of a 600-ship navy were fading, the US Navy stood at 376 major surface (and subsurface) combatants (for a total tonnage of 4,782,500). Ballistic and attack submarines constituted 139 of the 376 vessels. By 2003, the figures had declined to 200 (73 ballistic and attack submarines) and 2,643,000 tons. The really significant losses were among the mid-sized combatants, destroyers (down from 69 to 55) and the workhorses of the fleet, the frigates (down from 115 to 32).

It could be argued that the Russian Navy was, or is a very special case. The navy's decline is sobering in the extreme. In 1985, the Soviets had 506 ships with an overall displacement of 4,871,100. By 2000, the figures stood at 124 and 1,198,850. Destroyer numbers fell from 74 to 26. That said, President Putin seems intent on rebuilding the Russian Navy and the Navy adopted a master plan in 1998 for the "long term development of its maritime potential".[20] The objective is "the transformation of the country back into a leading naval power".[21] In pursuit of that goal, the Russians deployed about ten warships from the Pacific and Black Sea fleets to the Indian Ocean during April to June 2003. This was the largest out of area deployment in more than a decade; a Herculean and exhausting effort in view of the beleaguered condition of the Russian Navy, but a harbinger of things to come. The figures tell a somewhat different story when it comes to the People's Liberation Army Navy (PLAN). The PLAN had 163 submarines, destroyers and frigates (the only major combatants in the Chinese Navy) in 1985, amounting to 317,910 tons. By 2000, the figures stood at 123 and 311,905 tons. Significantly, the number of submarines was down from 117 to 66 while the frigates and destroyers were up by about 16 percent (31 to 36) and 25 percent (15 to 21), respectively. What this bold picture does not reveal is the move toward more sophisticated conventional (Russian Kilos) and nuclear (indigenously designed and constructed) boats. Similarly, while the command and control elements in the latest Chinese mid-sized surface combatants are considered, in some quarters, to be old-fashioned, the newest destroyers and frigates (supplemented by a growing number of powerful Russian Sovremennys) exhibit an increasing array of innovation and capability.[22]

Although the US Navy has suffered from profound budgetary disarmament over the past 15 years, the US Defence Budget for Fiscal Year 2005 foresees the maintenance of a 300 ship navy (all classes), the allocation of almost half a billion dollars for advanced propulsion systems and the commencement of work on the Littoral Combat Ship (considered in the section on technology).[23] Despite its straitened circumstances and almost punitive operational tempo, the US Navy will remain the world's premier navy for the foreseeable future.

Growth is the keyword when it comes to Asia Pacific navies. According to Kerr, Asian Pacific governments are likely to be spending US$ 14 billion annually by 2009 on new naval vessels, while Europe will be cutting its US$ 13 billion naval construction expenditure by up to 25 percent during the same period.[24] Bateman is less than sanguine about these developments. "Prior to 11 September 2001", he writes, "the maritime security outlook in the [Indo-Pacific] region was reasonably positive but since then it has turned largely negative".[25] He ascribes the "general atmosphere of maritime insecurity" to "higher levels of naval activity, increased naval spending and responses to the threat of maritime terrorism". Further, he suggests that "increased naval activity... could initiate a naval arms race".[26] At least two major trends underlie the growth in regional naval power. The first is the increase in the number of submarines. The second is the increasing size of surface combatants. Everywhere one looks, one finds Indo-Pacific nations adding to their stock of conventional and nuclear submarines; a process fostered by aggressive European and Russian arms sales. In February 2004, the Indian Navy and the French shipbuilder DCN concluded negotiations whereby the former will acquire six Scorpene conventional submarines for US$ 3 billion.[27] At the same time, the Republic of Singapore was taking delivery of the last two ex-Royal Swedish Navy Sjoormen-class submarines (RSS *Challenger* and RSS *Centurion*).[28] The Chinese are reported to be acquiring a further eight Kilo-class submarines from Russia, while the Collins-class have now become fully operational in Australia and the Malaysians and even the Bangladeshis are looking to add submarine capability. According to Bateman, "the number of submarines in East Asia has increased from about 100 to approximately 140 over the past seven years or so ... Over the next decade", he concludes, "as many as 50 additional submarines may enter service in the region".[29]

The second area of growth is big surface ships. The jewel in the crown, in this regard, is the 44,500-ton Russian aircraft carrier (more precisely, Kiev-class aviation cruiser), which the Indian Navy has just acquired for US$ 652 million after nearly a decade of negotiations. As Admiral Madhvendva Singh, the head of India's Navy, observed, "Once we get [the *Admiral*] *Gorshkov* with the MiG-29s we will be in a totally different league".[30] While New Delhi is waiting for *Gorshkov*'s refit to be completed in 2008, it is pressing ahead with the construction of two Air Defence Ships, the first of which is scheduled to enter service in 2011 and the second in 2016–2017.[31] These ships, at 37,500 tons, are second only to the new carriers that the Royal Navy is hoping to construct. The carrier club is an elite one. Even the Americans have reduced the number of their carriers from 14 in 1987 to 12 in 1998. The French and a handful of other nations have carriers but the cost of operating these major weapons systems with their embarked airwings suggests that they are a class of ship facing extinction in the mid-term save for three or four navies.

Elsewhere in Asia, regional navies are going upmarket, building or acquiring more powerful naval vessels. The Royal Australian Navy is looking at Air Warfare Destroyers displacing "at least 6000 tons"[32] and two 20,000-ton amphibious warfare ships.[33] The Republic of Singapore Navy is moving from missile corvettes to 3200-ton frigates based on the French Lafayette design.[34] The Japanese have ordered two large helicopter "destroyers" that will reportedly displace nearly 20,000 tons when fully loaded. These warships will be the largest vessels in the Japanese Maritime Self-Defence Force (JMSDF). Across the Pacific, the Canadian Department of National Defence has announced that the Canadian Navy will be getting three major Joint Support Ships to replace two aging AORs and even tiny Brunei has trading up with its three Nakhoda Ragam-class, 1940-ton frigates.[35] Malaysia has done the same thing with its MEKO A 100-class building programme, while the Taiwanese are still bent on acquiring four 9000-ton Kidd-class destroyers (albeit with reduced missile suites) and the South Koreans are committed to building three, 7000-ton, Aegis-equipped KDX III destroyers.

Maritime Theatres of Operation

A central feature of the maritime outlook is the shift of naval operations from the deep seas to the shore. A corollary of this transition from blue water to coastal or littoral theatres of operation is the way in which the distinction between the sea and the land has become blurred as naval power is projected farther inland than ever before and land-based weapons systems are being directed against warships offshore.

Littoral operations are particularly demanding and dangerous. Shallow water approaches constitute complex and confusing anti-submarine warfare environments at the very time when more and more conventional submarines (many of them equipped with anti-ship cruise missiles, or ASCMs) are putting to sea in the Indo-pacific region. Asian coastal waters are extremely crowded by global standards, with a multitude of small craft plying back and forth, fishing, carrying passengers, transporting cargoes or undertaking other forms of commerce. In essence, these craft amount to an enormous shell game in an age of maritime terrorism. Which of the hundreds of vessels that cross the Straits of Hormuz every day, for example, are carrying Al Qaeda terrorists or are functioning as suicide vessels?

Coastal operations also imply jurisdictional and navigational constraints. Royal Australian Navy vessels undertaking Maritime Interdiction Operations (MIO) on behalf of the United Nations at the northern end of the Arabian Gulf constantly had to be aware of the possibility that they would lose their quarry when small tankers, loaded with illicit Iraqi oil, made a dash for the safety of Iranian territorial waters. In other instances, the application of the UN Convention of the Law of the Sea baselines gave rise to operational uncertainties. Was a vessel standing into territorial waters or not? All this at a time when mines, fast patrol boats fitted out innovatively with multiple rocket launchers and shore-based weapons (ranging from tanks to conventional missiles) make littoral operations particularly dangerous.

The shift landward implies other things as well. Should navies look more closely at utilising purpose-built vessels like the fast, light Littoral Combat Ship, or LCS, much discussed in the US Navy? Should navies alter their weapons mix to include more amphibious capability? If warfare in the approaches to Asia or Africa is likely to be the wave of the future, do navies have to develop new techniques like boarding compliant and non-compliant vessels or undertaking work akin to traditional Coast Guard activities?

There is yet another set of circumstances, a countervailing force if you will, working at odds with the expeditionary deployments that have taken many of the world's navies to distant theatres of operation. Little did the authors of the United States Navy's seminal doctrines, "From the Sea" (September 1992) and "Forward From the Sea" (November 1994) realize how profoundly the events of 11 September would affect their vision of the US Navy operating in foreign littorals.[36] Homeland defence is the order of the day in the United States now and, to a lesser degree, in a variety of "Western" nations ranging from Canada to Singapore. Homeland defence, by its various names, raises a series of vexing questions. Foremost amongst them is what should the balance be between overseas deployments and coastal/port defence in domestic waters. Paradoxically, "From the Sea" has come to mean, in practice, pressure on navies to focus, not on remote coasts, but on their own maritime approaches.

Maritime Roles

An equally challenging question in this new domestic security environment is who should do what? The answer is comparatively straightforward in the American case (although the Byzantine complexities of inter- and intra-agency orchestrations should not be underestimated for a moment). The US Coast Guard is a full-blown maritime force operating armed vessels at home and, occasionally, abroad. Clearly, it is the first line of defence in terms of ensuring the maritime integrity of the United States. The Canadian Coast Guard, by way of comparison, is a unionised merchant service that eschews the use of weapons and contents itself with monitoring and reporting. For the moment, at least, the Australians have no coast guard at all. Anecdotal evidence suggests that a number of navies are concerned that they may be drawn more deeply into coastal defence at the expense of their traditional naval warfighting capabilities. As Admiral Gregory Johnson, the Commander of US Naval Forces in Europe, observed recently, "we have to develop a much more robust security regime in the maritime dimension". Further, he noted that "maritime security is a weak link in the United States-led War on Terror that extremists will exploit if action is not taken".[37] In view of the absence or perceived inadequacy of coast guards, the suggestion seems certain to be raised, "why not let the Navy do it".

In some respects this suggestion is not as wide of the mark as it may appear. Increasingly, navies appear to be moving towards the constabulary side of Booth's famous triangle of naval power. That triangle captured the traditional roles of navies: warfighting, diplomatic and constabulary. It could be argued that the boardings associated with MIO operations in the Arabian Gulf and Leadership Interdiction Operations (LIO) in the Arabian Sea (intended to ferret out Al Qaeda and Taliban personnel fleeing westward from the Pakistani or Irani coasts) were essentially constabulary operations. The utilisation of eight warships in the Mediterranean (Operation Active Endeavour) to track cargo flows and stem illegal migration falls into the same category.[38] Similar arguments could be made with respect to Singaporean, Malaysian and Indonesian anti-piracy patrols in the Straits of Malacca, long-range fishery patrols in the Southern Ocean by the Royal Australian Navy and anti-poaching operations against Portuguese fishermen off the Grand Banks of Newfoundland by the Canadian Navy.

These activities should not obscure the fact that more and more Indo-Pacific states are setting up coast guards. Indeed, as Bateman has suggested, "coast guards are a growth industry" in the region.[39] Coast guards are cheaper and less provocative than navies. Thus, the Japanese Coast Guard is a much more acceptable force in the war on piracy in Southeast Asia than the Japanese Maritime Self Defence Force, freighted as the latter is with history. Coast guards perform a wide array of tasks, like monitoring maritime pollution, conducting search and rescue, and providing aids to navigation. While these are essential tasks, coast guards often lack the power or the legal authority to address major threats to national security; hence, the blurring of distinctions between naval and coast guard roles in an increasing number of instances.

Information

It is conventional wisdom that we live in a knowledge age; that the management of information is the key to power and success. In many ways the oceans of the world are an informational *Arabia deserta*. But this is less and less the case as a consequence of two interlocking phenomena — the evolution of netcentric warfare and the demands of post-9/11 security. Netcentric warfare is predicated on the concept of a system of systems. At first glance this may seem tautological, but, in fact, it means orchestrating systems to maximise their power and effectiveness through synergy. Thus, spy satellite systems need to be linked to fleets of unmanned aerial vehicles and the results of the two coordinated and relayed to warships operating below. They, in turn, should be able to share all or part of their findings with other ships in the task force and elements ashore right down, in theory, to the laptop-equipped private.[40] The totality of the information flows should generate sophisticated, comprehensive and precise domain awareness. In short, netcentric warfare should enable commanders to resolve the age-old battlefield conundrum, namely, what is happening on the other side of the hill? Few better examples exist than the domain awareness that prevailed during naval operations against the Taliban and Al Qaeda in the Arabian Sea and Straits of Hormuz. The naval "plot" or regional picture was densely populated with "contacts". These ranged from very large container ships plying between Mumbai and the Red Sea, small tankers outbound from Kuwait, Arab dhows, tramp steamers and hundreds of so-called "go-fasts". Go-fasts were usually small aluminum boats powered by three or four 90-horse-power outboard motors. They swarmed across the ocean between the Pakistani and Iranian coasts and the coastal states of the Arabian peninsula carrying migrant labourers, television sets, cigarettes, liquor, drugs, passengers and, occasionally, terrorists. Coalition warships were obliged to track upwards of 6000 contacts per day. But which of the vessels in this puzzle palace should they go after? And which might be loaded with explosives seeking to replicate the attack on the USS *Cole*.[41]

Interoperability lies at the heart of netcentric operations. At its simplest, the communications systems on warships must be congruent; they must be able to talk to one another. This is easier said than done and one of the biggest financial and technological challenges facing second and third tier navies round the world is remaining interoperable with the United States Navy. Conventional wisdom suggests that if your communications systems are not kept up to date for 6 months you will be severely hampered. If they are not kept up to date for a year you will be out of the game. For the moment, at least, the US Navy has displayed no interest in stopping short on technological innovation. Instead, they seem quite prepared to face the consequences of disenfranchising many of their coalition partners who have not had the foresight or capability to sustain the requisite levels of interoperability.

Interoperability, of course, is not merely a matter of compatible hardware. Rather, it encompasses congruent procedures and a willingness to share information. This can be a challenge for navies working with the US Navy since the latter embraces rigorous protocols that limit the sharing of intelligence. Certain navies enjoy privileged access to most if not all of the vast reservoir of US intelligence and find themselves cast in middleman roles forwarding elements of that intelligence through less sophisticated communications links to "junior" coalition warships.

Post-9/11 security has given rise to a vast number of initiatives aimed at enhancing awareness of maritime activities in coastal approaches. The Americans, for example, want to know what ships are approaching their shores, what those vessels are carrying, what ports they are destined for, which vessels need particular scrutiny, which vessels are engaged in operations that defy logic in commercial terms and so forth. With a certain amount of hyperbole and journalistic flourish, William Langewiesche described the high seas as a "domain increasingly beyond government control, vast and wild, where laws of nations mean little and where the resilient pathogens of piracy and terrorism flourish".[42] How to make sense out of all this? How to achieve what is known as the "recognised maritime picture"? Whereas an elaborate global air traffic system keeps track of the tens of thousands of air movements that take place every day around the world, no comparable comprehensive tracking and intelligence system prevails at sea. But the trend is in that direction; to "wire" ships so that their location, course, speed, cargo, registration, port of departure and port and time of arrival can be tracked with precision. The same approach is being applied to individual containers. On the one hand, containers have greatly facilitated maritime commerce, ensuring, to a large degree, the integrity of cargoes and standardising port procedures worldwide. By the same token, however, containers have rendered the process less transparent. What weapons of mass destruction or related components, for example, have made their way out of North Korea bound for Pakistan and the Middle East, their passage rendered invisible by lowly containers? And even if that were not a sufficient problem, in and of itself, how are the authorities to know what is in each of the 5.7 million containers that arrive in 301 US ports each year? As it is, only 5 percent of the containers are subject to reasonably close surveillance as they enter the continental distribution network.

In many cases the information is readily available but it is locked away on what the business school culture calls silos or stovepipes, institutional frameworks that distribute critical information vertically but not horizontally. What is happening, in fact, in the aftermath of 9/11 is the globalisation of information flows. Efforts are being made to breakdown institutional barriers, to share information germane to maritime and riverine security, and to harmonise activities across agency or ministerial boundaries. Thus, domain awareness is being achieved in domestic waters that rivals the recognised maritime picture in the Arabian Gulf and Arabian Sea during the War on Terror. Information from coast guard sources, customs, immigration, coastal radar systems, intelligence services, long range naval surveillance flights, the shipping industry, port authorities and law enforcement agencies is being "fused" to provide a basis for timely and informed action.[43] Or at least that is the theory. Some ships change their registries or travel in silence so that they leave no electronic intelligence spoor. Others have dubious or misleading manifests. Whatever the case, a new war is being waged at sea, the informational war; a war destined to become more and more intrusive and comprehensive.

Technology

Rear-Admiral Radon Gates, the Australian Maritime Commander, summed it all up when he said that he was "constantly looking for bandwidth".[44] Bandwidth is the key to netcentric warfare. Commanders are constantly in search of "pipes" big enough to handle all the information flowing in and out of the command and control centres on their warships. But bandwidth is only part of the realm of maritime technological innovation. The IMO has made it mandatory for all ocean-going vessels of 300 gross tons or more to be equipped with an automatic identification system, or AIS, by the end of 2004. "This device forms part of a ship-and-shore-based broadcast network operating in the VHF (very high-frequency) maritime band. The AIS automatically sends and receives ship information such as identity, position, course, speed, ship particulars and cargo information to and from other ships, suitably-equipped aircraft and the shore. Precise time and positional information is integrated via satellite".[45] Furthermore, the IMO is looking to develop, in conjunction with INMARSAT C's global positioning system, "a plan for long-range identification and tracking of ships"; an initiative that it hopes participating states will endorse by December 2004.[46]

One of the more eye-catching applications of technology is the proposed LCS or Littoral Combat Ship. The LCS has been the subject of a variety of iterations — DD(X), CG(X) and Streetfighter — as the US Navy inches hesitantly towards a decision to build. As envisioned, the LCS is intended to be "small, fast, and agile . . . optimised to operate in the complex geography of coastal warfare".[47] Expected to be less than 3000 tons, the LCS will possibly be a catamaran design made of composite materials and capable of being modularised with "plug and play" components. A particularly important feature of this 40 to 50 knot craft is the fact that it will have a core crew of 50 (although planners are contemplating 15), down more than 100 percent from contemporary warships of her displacement. Indeed, a worldwide trend is to abandon many traditional naval building specifications and move towards the less demanding expectations "of the trade" while exploiting automation, redundancy and information systems to achieve significant cost savings by reducing crew sizes dramatically.

Air Independent Propulsion for conventional submarines, railguns, new electric propulsion systems, electronic charting, double hulls, advanced missile systems, container tagging, biometric identification cards for seafarers, UAVs, miniature robotic minehunters, radiation monitors in ports and a host of other technological achievements are transforming the maritime environment for merchant vessels and warships.

Regulatory Regimes

There are some curious paradoxes associated with the addition (or perhaps more precisely the greatly enhanced prominence) of maritime terrorism to the conventional roster of threats and criminal activities at sea — piracy, armed robbery, hijacking, drug trafficking, illegal migration and fisheries violations. Whereas during the twentieth century huge efforts were devoted to protecting merchant ships from attack, we are faced with the challenge of protecting ourselves from ships. In an age now of maritime terrorism vessels and/or their crews have become potential weapons although some would argue that the real threat does not derive from the detonation of explosives-filled freighters in crowded waterways but from relatively primitive attacks on the computer ganglia that animate the world's megaports.

The second paradox is that while piracy captures the public imagination (currently the incidence of piratical/armed robbery attacks in Southeast Asian waters, the "ground zero" of global piracy, and the level of personal violence associated with those attacks is rising)[48] and is a major source of concern to ship owners, crews and shippers, it is maritime terrorism that constitutes the greatest source of threat and concern to the maritime community. Why is this a paradox? For the simple reason that while maritime terrorism has only effected a handful of vessels like the USS *Cole* and the M.V. *Limburg* its impact has been infinitely greater in terms of counterterrorist measures than piracy that effects upwards of 100 to 200 hundred times as many vessels every year.

Recently, the maritime community has been the subject of a spate of regulatory initiatives designed to fill gaps in the law, strengthen relevant national and international legal instruments, and encourage cooperation by like-minded states in the War on Terrorism. Many of these initiatives have originated out of and been driven by the United States. In broad terms the Americans have been subject to a good deal of criticism on the grounds that their initiatives endanger the sovereignty of participating nations and that the initiatives them-selves are predicated on weak or inadequate legal precedents. While these criticisms have some validity they are, all too frequently, the product of a fashionable and triumphalist anti-Americanism. Many have maintained that the Americans are moving too quickly and that the initiatives are the product of Washington's penchant for unilateralism. However, as Naim has pointed out, speed (and the speed of implementation is, in fact, pretty slow) is of the essence; that the West, with its dinosaurian bureaucratic responses, will never win against the terrorists and the drug traffickers who are quicker, more innovative and more audacious.[49] As for unilateralism, the methods of initi-ation were unilateralist but the audience is distinctly multilateralist. In many instances, the Americans are trying to prod, badger or cajole nations round the world to be more active in combating maritime terrorism and crime by drawing upon existing legal vehicles. Unfortunately, only Singapore amongst the ASEAN states is a signatory to the SUA (Convention for the Suppression of Unlawful Acts Against the Safety of Maritime Navigation). Even if they all were, the real problem is not ratification but enforcement.[50] Inadequate enforcement capability, cultures of denial and a paucity of political will will fatally compromise the vitality of many maritime conventions.

Compounding these phenomena is the woeful — not to say — crimi-nal inadequacy of the Flags of Convenience system that sees countries like Liberia and Panama being joined by Bolivia and Tuvalu in the provision of ship registrations. Stephen Flynn, the security advisor of the Council on For-eign Relations and a former US Coast Guard commander, has described the system as "managed anarchy".[51] The International Transport Workers Feder-ation (ITF) is equally strong in its scathing indictment of FOCs and the FOC culture, which, quite apart from condoning poor safety, pay and training stan-dards, frequently permits hijackers to escape detection by re-registering ships at sea for a nominal fee and serving as a layer of obfuscation in the search for the culpable.[52]

Three initiatives stand out: the Container Security Initiative (CSI), the Proliferation Security Initiative (PSI) and the Regional Maritime Security Ini-tiative (RMSI). The first of these, the CSI, is intended to strike the maritime terrorist threat at its point of origin; that is to say, in those ports where con-tainers are being filled and embarked on their way to US ports like Long Beach or Baltimore. The object was twofold: to shift much of the inspection burden onto port personnel (frequently supplemented by US Customs officials) in designated foreign countries and to keep potential threats at arms length. The CSI requires detailed manifests, crew lists (and individual documentation) and navigational intentions 24 hours before the US-destined vessel is leaving its Asian port.

The proximate origins of the PSI are the subject of some debate. Conventional wisdom has it that the PSI grew out of the inability of the Americans to seize 15 Scud missiles being carried clandestinely to Yemen on a North Korean freighter, the *So San*, in December 2002. Whatever the case, the PSI reflects Washington's growing concern about the way in which global non-proliferation regimes are unravelling. North Korea's failure to honour the 1994 Agreed Framework (which would have seen Pyongyang freeze and terminate its weapons of mass destruction [nuclear weapons] programme in return for two light water reactors for power generation) and revelations that Iran deceived the International Atomic Energy Agency (IAEA) for 18 years about Tehran's nuclear programme contributed significantly to the argument in favour of the ability to interdict vessels on the high seas suspected of carrying WMDs or related components and materials. The challenge, of course, was how to find some legal justification for boarding ships on the high seas, the last untrammeled zone for seagoing commerce. The American solution, leaving other legal arguments (self-defence through pre-emption, etc.) aside was to broker deals with FOCs like Liberia (February 2004) and Panama (May 2004) whereby Washington acquired prior authorisation to board, inspect and detain. These two deals together mean that almost 50 percent of global commercial shipping is subject to search and seizure by the US Navy.[53] While such an arrangement gives access to a significant proportion of the world's merchant fleets, it leaves thousands of vessels (save those that are proceeding in a "stateless" condition without any national flag on display, like the *So San*) largely beyond the reach of the law.[54]

The latest security initiative originates out of the US Pacific Command. The Regional Maritime Security Initiative (RMSI), according to Admiral Thomas Fargo, the Regional Combatant Commander for US forces in the Indo-Pacific region, is intended to "forge a partnership of nations willing to identify and intercept 'transnational maritime threats under existing international and domestic laws'".[55] What Fargo envisages is participating states forwarding maritime data to PACOM so that a recognised maritime picture can be obtained; a picture that would greatly enhance response options. Unfortunately, while he was quick to emphasise that RMSI would not interfere with national sovereignty and would, instead, "empower each nation to take action it deems necessary to protect itself on its own waters, thereby enhancing our collective security",[56] it has been widely criticised on sovereignty grounds.

Conclusion

The title of this chapter was derived from the first sentence in Charles Dickens' *Tale of Two Cities*. It draws the reader's attention to a paradoxical state of affairs, that it is the best of times and the worst of times. The same could, no doubt, be said for the global maritime outlook in 2004. On the one hand, we have burgeoning regional trade. The number of tankers and container ships is up. Container traffic is booming. Shipbuilding order books are full. Naval budgets are rising. A sense of maritime self-confidence, not to say assertiveness, prevails. On the other hand, the spectre of maritime terrorism haunts the maritime community. When and where will the maritime 9/11 take place? Why has it not taken place already. Billions are being spent in an effort to forestall such a calamity. Meanwhile, a proto arms race, buttressed by the latest marine technology, appears in the eyes of some to be taking shape in the Indo-Pacific region. Central to the conduct of affairs in the maritime domain is the collection and management of information and a variety of initiatives designed to stiffen international resolve in the campaign against maritime terrorism and crime and to address the shortcomings of the oceanic legal regime. Thus, the outlook is decidedly mixed. Slowly but surely a new order is being forged in the last great open space — the world's oceans. The interlocking phenomena of global maritime trade and oceanic insecurity are finally addressing the anarchy of which Flynn spoke.

Notes

1. US Department of Transportation, "Maritime Trade and Transportation 2002", Washington, DC, 2002. Also available online at http:///www.aapa-ports.org/pdf/rankworld_01.pdf; http://www.bts.gov/publications/maritime_trade_and_transportation/2002/pdf/entire.pdf; http://www.unctad.org/en/docs/rmt_2003_annexes_en.pdf.
2. Available online at http://www.trans-inst.org/irid_ Profile.html.
3. Peter Swift, "Structural Transformation and Changes in the Tanker Trade", Paper presented at the Second Asia Maritime and Logistics Conference, 2003, p. 2.
4. Peter Rimmer, "Commercial Shipping Patterns in the Asia Pacific Region: The Rise and Rise of China", in Andrew Forbes (ed.), *The Strategic Importance of Seaborne Trade and Shipping* (Australia: RAN Sea Power Centre, 2003), p. 35.
5. James Boutilier, "Reflections on the New Indo-Pacific Maritime and Naval Environment", unpublished manuscript held by the author, 2004, p. 2.
6. Swift, p. 3.
7. Seo Hang Lee, "Security of East Asian SLOCs and the Role of Navies", in *Forbes*, p. 176.

8. Anon., "US Warns Against Attacks on Commercial Vessels", *Reuters*, 31 March 2004.

9. Andy Mukherjee, "China: Gold Mine or Minefield", *International Herald Tribune*, 28 January 2004, p. B2.

10. Tan-Hwee Ann, "Shippers Raise Forecast for Cargo", *International Herald Tribune*, 28 January 2004, p. B3.

11. Bruce Constantineau, "China Trade Boosts Shipping," *Vancouver Sun*, 21 November 2003, p. G1.

12. Boutilier, p. 2.

13. Anon., "A Buoyant Time for Shipbuilders", *Asahi Shimbun*, 3 March 2004.

14. United Nations Conference on Trade and Development (UNCTAD), *Review of Maritime Transport, 2003* (New York: United Nations Publications, 2003), p. 3.

15. Ibid.

16. Ibid, p. 2.

17. Andrew Forbes, "Maritime Security in East Asia", Paper presented at the 14th International SLOC Conference, Honolulu, 18–20 January 2004.

18. Anon., "Foreign Capital Welcomed in Port Construction Project", *China Daily*, 26 February 2004.

19. H.R. Vitasa and Nararya Soeprapto, "Maritime Sector Developments in ASEAN", Paper presented in the Maritime Policy Seminar organized by UNCTAD, Jakarta, 11–13 October 1999, p. 7.

20. Sam Bateman, "More Spending on Regional Sea Power", *Asia Pacific Defence Reporter*, vol. 29, no. 9, December 2003, p. 20.

21. Ibid.

22. Haze Gray and Underway: World Navies by Andres Toppan. Also available online at http://www.hazegray.org/worldnav; Federation of American Scientists, available online at http://fas.org/man/dod-101/sys/ship/row; Defence Daily Network, available online at http://www.defencedaily.com/reports/gonavy.htm.

23. Available online at http://www.defenselink.mil/news/Feb2004/040202-D-65TDS-001.pdf.

24. Julian Kerr, "IMDEX — Details Emerge of New Singapore Frigates", *Asia-Pacific Defence Reporter*, December 2003, p. 28.

25. Bateman, p. 18.

26. Ibid, p. 18.

27. Held by the author.

28. Richard Scott, "Submarines Depart for Singapore", *Jane's Defence Weekly*, 28 January 2004, p. 8. The RSN had already taken delivery of RSS *Conqueror* and RSS *Chieftain*. A fifth boat was shipped from Sweden to be used as a source of spares.

29. Bateman, p. 22.

30. Julian Kerr, "Indian Carrier Deal", *Asia-Pacific Defence Reporter*, January 2004, p. 6.

31. Ibid, p. 6.

32. Peter La Franchi, "AAW Destroyer to be 'Jewel in RAN's Crown'", *Jane's Navy International*, January/February 2004, p. 34.
33. Peter La Franchi, "Rebuilding the RAN for High-Tempo Ops", *Jane's Navy International*, January/February 2004, p. 26.
34. Kerr, "IMDEX", p. 28.
35. Bateman, p. 20.
36. Boutilier, p. 7.
37. *Straits Times*, 10 March 2004. Available online at http://straitstimes.asia1.com.sg.
38. Ibid.
39. Sam Bateman, "Coast Guards: New Forces for Regional Order and Security", *Asia Pacific Issues*, East-West Centre (report), No. 65, January 2003, p. 1.
40. As Rear-Admiral Raydon Gates, Australia's Maritime Commander, has noted, "I need to start getting the [Australian] Army particularly involved in amphibious operations in this network-centric mentality of constant information, immediate information". La Franchi, "Rebuilding the RAN", p. 31.
41. In April 2004, Lockheed Martin inaugurated a new, 46,000 square-foot US$ 9.4 million, Maritime Domain Awareness Centre in Moorestown, New Jersey. The Centre has a 16,000 square-foot laboratory "to support work on systems that electronically link ships, aircraft and shore stations and create a common "picture" of large operational areas". Anon., "Lockheed Martin to Inaugurate Deepwater Center", *Homeland Security and Defence*, 21 April 2004, p. 2.
42. William Langewiesche, "Anarchy at Sea", *The Atlantic Monthly*, September 2003, p. 50.
43. It was announced in March 2004 that Mr Peter Ho, the Singaporean Permanent Secretary of Defence, would head an interagency team, including Foreign Affairs, Home Affairs, Transport, the Republic of Singapore Navy, the Police Coast Guard and the Maritime and Port Authority, to address the question of maritime security. Goh Chin Lian, "High-level Task Force to Boost Maritime Security", *The Straits Times*, 3 May 2004. Also available online at http://straitstimes.asia1.com.sg.
44. La Franchi, "Rebuilding the RAN", p. 31.
45. Michael Richardson, "Maritime Plan Aims to Make the Region's Waters Secure", *The Straits Times*, 26 April 2004, p. 2.
46. Ibid.
47. John Dikkenberg, "The LCS: No Shortage of Challenges", *Asia Pacific Defence Reporter*, March/April 2004, p. 22.
48. International Maritime Bureau, "Piracy and Armed Robbery Against Ships 2003", p. 16. Indonesia recorded the highest number of attacks, 121 out of a worldwide total of 445 (up from 370 in 2002). Twenty-one seafarers were killed in 2003 compared with ten the year before.
49. Moises Naim, "The Five Wars of Globalization", *Foreign Policy*, January 2003, p. 5.

50. J. N. Mak, "Piracy in Southeast Asia: Priorities: Perspectives and the Hierarchy of Interests", Paper presented at a Conference on Maritime Security in East Asia, Honolulu, January 2004, p. 3. One of Mak's conclusions was that "securing national ocean space against pirates is not a priority for all the ASEAN members" despite the disturbingly high levels of piracy in the ASEAN region.

51. Anon., "Brassed Off", *The Economist*, 16 May 2002.

52. ITF, "A Brief Guide to Flags of Convenience", *Global Policy Forum* (ca. 2004), p. 1.

53. Anon., "Panama to allow U.S. to search vessels", *Kansas City Star*, 12 May 2004.

54. Calvin Lederer, "The Role of Maritime Law Enforcement in the War on Terrorism", Paper presented at the Military Law Conference, Victoria, Canada, May 2004, p. 5. See also Kerry Lynn Nankivell, "The Container and Proliferation Security Initiatives: A First Look", and Michael Byers, "Policing the High Seas: The Proliferation Security Initiative". Papers held by the author.

55. Richard Halloran, "Navy Launches Vast Maritime Security Plan", *The Washington Post*, 10 May 2004.

56. Ibid.

Chapter 2

Regional Maritime Security Outlook: Northeast Asia

VADM (Ret) Hideaki Kaneda

Introduction

Maritime security is undoubtedly the most significant factor in the highly dynamic Asia-Pacific region. The global economy with its increasing interdependence has made it more critical than ever to ensure the safety of the SLOCs (sea lines of communication) and ports of the world for international shipping and trade, as they are becoming more vulnerable to new, unconventional threats — from international terrorism to the proliferation of weapons of mass destruction or ballistic missile attacks.

Recently, the regional nations have sought to improve maritime security through combined efforts, ranging from Container Security Initiative (CSI) and Proliferation Security Initiative (PSI), to joint maritime patrols under many bilateral and multilateral arrangements. Such efforts will not only provide substantial implications to international maritime law, regional cooperation and overall development and stability, but also require continued dialogue and coordination among them during a period of transition.

In this chapter, I would like to present my assessment on the challenges to, and the solutions for, maritime security in this region from the viewpoint of Northeast Asia. This involves an overview of major themes and contemporary challenges associated with maritime threats, competition over resources, points of potential conflicts and ways of dealing with these current and future challenges in order to maintain maritime security in this region.

Instability Factors in Asia-Pacific Region at the Beginning of the 21st Century

At the beginning of the 21st century, there are several major factors of security instability in the Asia-Pacific region. The first factor is the proliferation of weapons of mass destruction and ballistic missiles from North East Asia to other regions. The second factor is international terrorism, arising after the 9/11 terrorist attacks. International terrorist groups are gaining strength through their alliances in and out of the Asia-Pacific region, and escalating attacks with bombs and other weapons targeting mainly countries with weaker governments.

The third factor is the rapid build-up of Chinese military power, mainly naval and air power, the continuation of which may tip the balance of regional military powers. The fourth factor is the confrontational military structure, which originated during the Cold War and still remains in the Korean Peninsula and Taiwan Strait, bringing instability, uncertainty and insecurity to the region.

The fifth factor is the historical disputes and confrontations over territories, religions and ethnicities. Disputes over the possession of islands in particular are likely to affect the stability of the whole region significantly, while obstructing maritime security. The sixth factor is the confrontational structures surrounding oceanic interests, which are closely related to the disputes over island possession. The last factor involves the increase in internationalised and organised illegal activities, such as piracy, drug trafficking or slave trades, throughout the oceans of the Asia-Pacific region.

Proliferation of weapons of mass destruction and ballistic missiles

The United States, Russia and China are the countries that possess nuclear weapons in the Asia-Pacific region. North Korea is currently under fire over its nuclear programme, and is said to possess several nuclear weapons. However, its actual status is unclear due to its unique brinkmanship diplomacy. They are suspicions of close information exchanges on the development and manufacturing of nuclear weapons and of the actual transport of relevant materials between North Korea and Pakistan[1] or others.

Biological and chemical weapons are thought to be manufactured and possessed by several countries in the Asia-Pacific region, such as the United States, Russia, North Korea and China. The Ohm cult's sarin attacks in Tokyo's subways in 1995 and the mailing of anthrax in the United States following the 9/11 terrorist attacks in 2001 forced the international community to realise how easy it is to make chemical and biological weapons and how they can be used outside of state-to-state military confrontations.

Regarding ballistic missiles, the Soviet Union and other countries exported Scud B missiles in mid-1980s to many countries and regions, including Iraq, North Korea and Afghanistan, while China exported Dong Feng 3 (CSS-2) and North Korea exported Scud series missiles.[2] Through these exports, the total number of nations currently possessing these missiles has risen to nearly 50.[3] Furthermore, some countries are developing and manufacturing longer-range missiles. Even today, we find further proliferation of ballistic missiles to Pakistan, the Middle East and East Africa by North Korea, and the continued efforts of China to modernise and strengthen its ballistic missile arsenals.[4]

The transfers of weapons of mass destruction and ballistic missiles by exporting countries is continuing and even flourishing despite the risks that such exports pose to international security. Among those countries seeking weapons of mass destruction, there are some that possess governments with feeble governing capabilities and lack sensitivity to the danger they are placing over their own people and territories. There are also some countries seeking weapons of mass destruction and which are home to the increasingly vigorous activities of international terrorist organisations. It could also be argued that such countries are more likely to have less hesitation in using their weapons of mass destruction. Unfortunately, there has not been any effective regime or system that can put the brakes on the proliferation of weapons of mass destruction and ballistic missiles in the region.

However, a more favourable trend can be seen to be emerging recently. Since the proliferation of weapons of mass destruction and ballistic missiles in the Asia-Pacific region is likely to be through the SLOC, and the movement of relevant personnel will go via sea and air, measures introduced since September 2003 as a part of the effort to develop stronger inspection systems for international land, maritime and air routes[5] will go some way to curbing the proliferation of weapons of mass destruction. These measures include joint maritime inspection exercises conducted between navies and coast guards and interception training between air forces, based on the PSI (Proliferation Security Initiative),[6] which is participated by 11 countries, including the United States, the United Kingdom, Japan and Australia.

The PSI participants have already been involved in planned drills in the Coral Sea, the Mediterranean Sea and the Arabian Sea. Recently, four more countries including Singapore and Russia joined the participating countries. Japan — with a number of countries such as Singapore — is now creating initiatives to monitor and stop an illegal "detour" trade of weapons of mass destruction related parts[7] and is inviting both members and non-members of ASEAN countries, as well as China and Korea, to participate in a multinational joint drill off the coast of the Tokyo Bay, which Japan plans to host at the end of October 2004. For this joint drill, the Maritime Self-Defence Force of Japan, which used to participate only with observer status, is to send its destroyers and P-3C patrol aircrafts for the first time.[8]

Expansion of indiscriminate terrorism by international
terrorist groups

Since the 9/11 terrorist attacks, various countries led by the United States formed an international coalition against terrorism, and have been fighting a long and difficult war against terrorism with the goal of destroying every international terrorist organisation. Despite extensive effort, however, the risk of terrorist attacks has not diminished and is even said to be mounting, as international terrorist organisations seem to be continuing to expand their networks throughout the world. In 2003, terrorism incidents including inter-national terrorist attacks reached their worst with over 3200 cases reported in the world.[9]

The risks of such incidents are also rising in the Asia-Pacific region. The suicide bomb attack in Bali, Indonesia, in December 2002 was attributed to Jemaah Islamiah (JI), which is an Islamic radical group with a network covering the entire South East Asia region and is said to have connections with Al Qaeda.[10] After the Bali attacks, JI repeatedly attacked targets across Indonesia, and is believed to be extending its influence throughout the entire South East Asia region, especially strengthening its connection with the MILF (Moro Islamic Liberation Front) in the Philippines.[11]

International terrorist groups are becoming more active, not only on land but even at sea, in the neighbouring Asia-Pacific region, in particular in the horn of Africa and the Middle East. As indicated by the seizing of a Moscow theatre in 2002 and this month's school siege in North Ossetia by a Chechen military group, or the explosion of a packed commuter train in Madrid by an Al Qaeda related terrorist group, the risk of attacks by international terrorist groups can occur in any country and anywhere in the world.[12]

The efforts to coordinate the fight against international terrorism being sought all over the world centre around the United States. In the Arabian Sea, coalition forces including Japan still continue their maritime blockade operations as a part of the effort to destroy international terrorist organisations. In the Asia-Pacific region, the United States and Philippines are to conduct a joint exercise named "Balikatan 2004"[13] as they did in previous years, in order to wipe out Abu Sayyaf, an international terrorist group in the Philippines. The United States and Indian naval forces conducted joint patrols to protect US naval ships passing through the Straits of Malacca in April 2002 to September 2002.[14] In 2002, ASEAN and the United States signed a declaration denouncing international terrorism,[15] and ASEAN countries have demonstrated better cooperation in the fight against international terrorism in various fields both inter-regionally and with countries world wide, such as Japan, China and India.[16]

At the International Sea-power Symposium (ISS)[17] held in 2004 at the US Naval War College, the leaders of world's navies and coast guards gathered for the first time and discussed the fight against international terrorism at sea. The subjects discussed at this symposium included the need for further national and international collaboration among navies and coast guards, and the adaptation of international laws and regulations to make the response against international terrorism more effective.

Military power build-up in China that may tip the regional military balance

From the beginning of the 1990s, the national defence budgets of countries in the Asia-Pacific region, which had risen during their unprecedented economic growth, started to decrease in many countries due to the fall of their currencies and the deterioration of the fiscal situation, in what is now known as the Asian Currency Crisis of 1997. This significantly affected their ability to procure military equipment and conduct exercises. By the beginning of 1999, the countries of the Asia-Pacific region seemed to feel that the worst of the crisis was almost over. However, the future direction of their national defence budgets and military build-up would now defer significantly, depending on how each was affected by the economic crisis.

In view of the Asia-Pacific region as a whole, the gap between the military power of the regional countries may continue to expand further, as the different effects of the economic crisis sink in on top of the original differences in their economic powers. Particularly outstanding in the region in terms of their military build-up will be some South-East Asian countries such as Singapore, Malaysia and Indonesia, which are increasing and modernising the military power of their navy and air force.[18] Neighbouring nations have not yet considered such moves as immediate threats; however, no one can deny the possibility that the threat of rapid changes in regional military balance will develop into political problems in the future. This is particularly true given the already existing political discord within the region, following the currency crisis.

There is one country in particular in the Asia-Pacific region whose rapid military build-up is raising anxiety among neighbouring countries; and that country is China. China considers its People's Liberation Army as a fundamental power for building its unique socialism, and providing important security assurances for the development of its economy and the longer-term stability of the regime.[19] China has clearly stated its intention to focus on missions that defend its sovereign rights over its land, air and sea (and space) territories, secure its maritime interests and protect the unification and security of the nation. This will be done by advancing its efforts to improve the quality of its military forces, and by strengthening its combat forces, so that they can respond to the needs of modern warfare.[20]

These missions will require the reorganisation and reform of obsolete military forces to build up a capable combat force, and the modernisation of equipment through scientific and technological advancement. For this purpose, China has been expanding its national defence budget by more than 10 percent each year since 1989, and has not slackened its rate of increase of 9.6–17.6 percent each year even in the 2000s.[21]

As seen in the 11.6 percent increase over the previous year in the Chinese national defence budget of 2004 disclosed on March 6, China continues to build up its military power mostly in its naval and air forces as well as in its ballistic missile capability. The acceleration of China's military build-up continues to be the greatest concern of countries in South East Asia.[22]

There are two distinct views on the prospect of future military build-up in China, including military modernisation.[23] One view finds that the recent increases in their national defence budget, the rapid modernisation of military forces, mainly naval and air forces, the transfer and proliferation of Chinese-made weapons, the purchases of the advanced weapons systems mainly from Russia and the aggressive advancement into neighbouring waters such as the South China Sea or East China Sea will clearly impose threats on other countries of the Asia-Pacific region, and such trends will accelerate further in the future.

Another view considers that their defence budget increase is modest compared with their inflation rate, and, in view of their backwardness in military equipment, it will be extremely difficult for China to achieve true modernisation, so the current trend does not necessarily constitute a true build-up of military power, and will not pose a real threat to neighbouring countries for the moment.

Yet, despite the various excuses by China and the justification of its efforts, most of the regional countries recognise the trend as unquestionably an extensive military force build-up. Nonetheless, the consensus of the Asia Pacific region is that, for today and in the immediate future, the military power of China does not present a serious and significant threat to the region, except to Taiwan. However, as China continues its economic development, its active investment in the modernization of its military forces, especially in its naval and air forces, and the improvement of its capability to project its power over neighbouring waters, will make China a serious threat to the region in the near future. Moreover, there is regional concern over the obscurity of China's intentions and the uncertainty of the future direction of its military forces.[24]

The concerns of the countries of the Asia-Pacific region over China's potential military movements in the near future include: military advances to Taiwan even with the risk of confronting the United States; direct military action to solve disputes with neighbouring countries other than Taiwan or neighbouring regions; military action taken to reduce domestic or regional instability; and general intimidation backed by military power, which may pose a significant threat to regional countries.[25]

Continuing confrontation in the Korean Peninsula and the Taiwan Strait

Regarding the Korean Peninsula issue, leaders of South and North Korea signed a South–North Joint Declaration as a result of a South–North Summit, which took place in June 2000, in which the South and North agreed to self-resolve the unification issue. It was agreed that the solution would take the form of a "federation" (or "united regime"), thus settling the issue of separated families. It would also involve economic cooperation and cultural exchanges.[26]

The dialogue between the Southern and Northern authorities on the implementation of this declaration was expected to further deepen their contacts, and direct them towards a détente in the Korean Peninsula. Yet, there were strong concerns over the obscurity of the declaration, including how progress in the South–North dialogue would lead to the mitigation of military confrontation in the Korean Peninsula, and how it would link to the solving of issues such as North Korea's nuclear programme and its ballistic missile development.[27]

To this day, North Korea not only maintains massive military power deployment along the Demilitarised Zone (DMZ), but also engages in military exercises, and demonstrates unilateral brinkmanship diplomacy, by continuing the development, production and export of ballistic missiles and weapons of mass destruction. Furthermore, the dialogue between the Northern and Southern authorities has shown no substantial progress since the Summit.[28]

The United States has taken every opportunity to express its concern over the issue of North Korea's ballistic missiles and weapons of mass destruction. When Deputy Secretary of State, James Kelly, visited North Korea in October 2002, the North Korean government admitted they had planned to make enriched weapons-grade uranium.[29]

When the United States requested that North Korea completely abolish its nuclear weapon programme in an irrevocable and verifiable manner, North Korea did not respond and instead demanded that the United States enter into a non-aggression pact with North Korea, while again re-declaring its withdrawal from the Non-Proliferation Treaty (NPT). The United States, in turn, indicated that it had no intention to attack North Korea, while expressing unwillingness to offer any compensation through negotiation. The United States managed to hold six-party meetings by drawing in China and Russia in addition to Japan, the United States, and South Korea, and claimed that the North Korean nuclear issue would not be a bilateral problem between the United States and North Korea but an international issue.[30]

However, the outcome of the six-party talks is still unclear at this point. The third round of the six-party talks on the nuclear development programme of North Korea was held in Beijing in June 2004, but the discussion remained at a standstill with parties failing to reach any concrete agreement. In preparation for the next meeting, the six parties agreed to continue the discussion by forming a working group.[31]

Due to the uncompromising stance of North Korea on the abduction issue,[32] over which the United States strongly supports Japan's claim, Japan has completed a revision of its domestic legislation, including the revision of the Tariff Law, in order to allow phase-by-phase economic sanctions if necessary, and the creation of a law to prohibit the traffic of certain suspicious ships including the Man Gyong Bong-92, in order to fulfil its strategy of "dialogue and pressure" against North Korea.[33]

Concerning the Taiwan Strait issue, the Chinese Government was strongly offended in July 1999 by a statement from Li Denghui, the then president of Taiwan, which proclaimed that: "Taiwan and China are in a unique state-to-state relationship". In their effort to influence Taiwan's presidential election scheduled for March 2000, the Chinese Government, published a White Paper on Taiwan titled "The principle of one China and Taiwan issue" immediately before the election, indicating that it would exercise military power in cases when: (1) Taiwan declared independence; (2) a foreign power invaded or occupied Taiwan; and (3) if Taiwan refused to negotiate unification infinitely. In this way, China attempted to exert political pressure on Taiwan.[34]

When President Li Denghui visited the United States in July 1995, and when the direct election of the Taiwanese president was held in March 1996, China test-launched ballistic missiles off the coast of the water near Taiwan, and gravely affected the safety of the SLOCs in the adjacent region. As enumerated here, China has used every opportunity to exert military and political pressures on Taiwan, and despite the progress of the China–Taiwan relationship in economic cooperation, the basic stance of China towards Taiwan in political and military terms is not likely change in the near future.[35]

Against this aggressive Chinese posture, President Chen, who was first elected in February 2000, stated repeatedly that Taiwan would not resort to a one nation two systems regime, while trying at the same time to avoid irritating China as much as possible. However, some people in Taiwan have shown their dissatisfaction at Chen's stance in relation to China.

On the other hand, Taiwan's domestic economy sector is putting pressure or President Chen, claiming that his careless statements and actions have adversely affected Taiwan–China trade relations. So the focus is on whether President Chen will make any decisions, such as the revision of the constitution or a change of country name.[36]

The victory of current President Chen, following Taiwan's presidential election on March 20 2004, is predicted to heighten the political tension in the China–Taiwan relationship. China is raising its guard against Taiwan in the fear that opportunities for the democratisation of Taiwan will increase while the Chen administration accelerates the move towards independence. Therefore, China is likely to take every opportunity to press political tensions in the future.[37]

In terms of economic cooperation, the China–Taiwan issue has seen certain reinforcement in their relationship, even though significant confrontation remains in the political and military arenas. They are likely to find difficulty in responding to the requests of various countries, led by the United States, who are asking for a maintenance of the "status quo". The Bush Administration has taken a clear stance to adhere to the "Taiwan Relations Act"[38] and based on this proposal, in 2001, a list of weapons that can be sold to Taiwan include modernised naval and air force equipment such as four Kydd-class destroyers (and it is thought, aged AEGIS cruisers in the future), eight diesel engine submarines and 12 patrol planes (P-3C).[39]

The military power balance between China and Taiwan should be assessed not only in terms of a simple comparison of quantities, but also in terms of operation preparedness, skill of necessary personnel and logistic support systems. Their general characteristics are stated below. There is no doubt that in the future, the success or failure of naval and air force development by the two countries will determine the superiority or inferiority of their overall military forces:[40]

1. In terms of ground military force, China has overwhelming power, but their capability to land and invade the main island of Taiwan is limited.
2. In terms of naval and air forces, China has overwhelming power in quantity but Taiwan dominates in quality.
3. Regarding ballistic missile forces, China possesses many short and medium range ballistic missiles, which cover Taiwan in their range. Taiwan's offensive or defensive missile capability is extremely limited. However, they will have the Patriot PAC-3 BMD capability from 2005.

China's domestic production, and purchases from Russia, of ballistic missiles, naval vessels including submarines and high performance fighter jets, reached their highest level in 2003, indicating that China will continue to strive for the modernisation of its armed forces in order to improve its capability to execute modern wars.[41] As a result, it is believed that there would be the reversal of the military power balance between China and Taiwan in the near future.[42]

Territorial, regional and ethnic conflicts with historical roots

In the Asia-Pacific region, there are many factors that have the potential to cause conflict, which are based on territorial, religious and ethnic disputes and are intertwined in very complex ways, with deep historical roots that are unique to this region. Several of these issues surfaced after the Cold War ended. Among them, the territorial disputes over islands are deeply related to the oceanic interests of the regional countries, and present problems that may lead to direct military confrontation between the relevant countries in the future. It is vital that the issues are addressed, as they are likely to have a profound affect on regional stability.

Well known are Japan's territorial disputes over the Northern Islands (with Russia), Takeshima (with Korea) and the Senkaku Islands (with China and Taiwan).[43] However, the most noted territorial dispute over islands in this region is the one regarding the territorial rights to the Spratley Islands.

The origin of this issue goes back to the time of the San Francisco Peace Conference in 1951, when Japan, which used to essentially govern these islands, renounced its territorial right and no country was subsequently named to have the title over these islands. As the islands are reported to offer rich fishery resources, China, Taiwan, Philippines and Vietnam claimed their territorial rights at first. In the 1980s, when the presence of rich sea bottom mineral deposits became known, Malaysia and Brunei also claimed their territorial rights. At present, China, Taiwan and Vietnam are claiming territorial rights over the whole archipelago, while Malaysia, Philippines and Brunei claim their territorial rights over some of these islands.[44]

From the late 1980s, China became increasingly active in its territorial claim, and had a military confrontation with Vietnam in 1988. After the end of the Cold War, and in response to the shrinking presence of the United States and the Soviet Union (later Russia) in the region, China intensified its attempts to expand its maritime activity range, and reinforced its activity bases mainly in the Spratley and Paracel Islands where territorial rights are disputed with ASEAN countries.[45]

In 1992, China proclaimed its territorial rights over the Spratley and Paracel Islands, as well as the Senkaku Islands, which is also claimed by Japan,[46] by citing its Territorial Water Law. In 1995, the dangers of military confrontation with Philippines were heightened over Mischief Atoll.[47]

Following these incidents, the possibility of a military confrontation subsided. However, in 1997 China enacted the National Defence Law that clearly stated the protection of their ocean interests along with the defence of security in territorial land, sea and airspace.[48] What were the implications for the dispute? In 1999, regional nations accelerated their moves to gain practical control of the disputed islands, and the possibility of conflict was brought back. Faced by such a situation, the relevant countries, the ARF and others addressed the issues in bilateral and multilateral talks. Even during these talks, some countries proceeded with their efforts to establish practical control of the islands.[49]

However, in November 2002, China signed the "Declaration on the Actions of Interested Parties in the South China Sea" with ASEAN, and moreover, in October 2003, China became a member of TAC (Treaty of Amity and Cooperation in Southeast Asia), thus raising the hope of a peaceful solution to this territorial issue. In reality, however, when a sightseeing group from Vietnam visited the Spratley Islands in April 2004, the Chinese government protested and claimed that the act was a "violation of territory". The incident demonstrates that, in the South China Sea area, the conflicts of interests over the Spratley Islands still remain among surrounding nations, thus it should come as no surprise that initiatives to establish a "Regional Action Standard in South China Sea" between ASEAN and China, which started in 1999, are making little progress.[50]

Confrontational structure regarding oceanic interests

The common characteristic feature of the military power restructuring conducted by the countries of this region after the Cold War was their focus on the modernisation of naval and air power, which seemed to lag behind the capabilities of their ground forces. After the currency crisis, their efforts to reorganise military power share the common factors of protecting ocean interests over the waters, such as archipelagic waters of the South China Sea, and East China Sea, and of attempting to improve their maritime operation capability, with an intention to secure the SLOCs, which passes through the region as the shared lifeline for their economic development. China in particular is advancing its development and reinforcement of its naval and air power, and exerts every effort to develop its military strength and to improve its operational capability in order to secure their oceanic interests in the South China Sea and the East China Sea.[51]

As the rapid economic growth in this region is likely to enable these countries to realise their intentions in the future, the potential for confrontation over oceanic interests will increase further. We must not overlook such possibilities. Due to their geo-political importance, any future instability regarding these oceans will undoubtedly seriously affect the survival and prosperity of the countries involved as well as the region as a whole.

In other words, the confrontational structure of oceanic interests, which developed after the Cold War, has become the largest destabilising factor for the security of the Asia-Pacific region. There are already indications of a manifestation of these instability factors in the South China Sea and East China Sea.

However, an effective framework to discuss this matter is largely non-existent in this region, and for now, methods of addressing the issue depend on bilateral or multilateral talks among the countries involved, thus casting a dark shadow over regional security.

In recent years, China has been conducting various exercises in the waters of the exclusive economic zone of Japan using its ocean survey ships.[52] For this matter, both Japan and China established "the Framework for Mutual Advanced Notification of Ocean Survey Activities", in February 2001. This applied in particular to the scientific survey activities of oceans near the water of the counterpart in the East China Sea (except territorial waters of each). However, there were still some exercises conducted by China's ocean survey ships, which were in violation of the obligation of mutual advanced notification set out in the Framework.[53]

Moreover, Chinese naval units have been active in the waters near Japan. Japan noted the presence of 27 Chinese ships in 1999, 15 in 2000 and 8 in 2001 and 2002.[54] Japan also observed the activities of Chinese naval units, which were thought to be conducting intelligence collection and ocean survey activities. Indeed, China is aiming for a true "Ocean-going Navy".[55] These ships are likely to have been conducting survey and intelligence collecting activities in order to gather the data required for future naval operations in that water. China continues to practice such activities occasionally, and despite Japan's protests and requests to halt such activities, China has not made any moves to address this issue.[56]

Recently, it was confirmed that China conducted an ocean survey within the territorial waters of Japan, and their submarine (Ming class) made surface navigation on the neighbouring waters.[57] It is clear that the "Mutual Advanced Notification System", agreed between Japan and China, has been ignored by the Chinese side, and Japan's constant objections have had no sufficient effect on China. In 2003, China violated the agreement in nine separate cases; however, in 2004, the number of incidents rose significantly, reaching 26 violations in just 7 months.[58]

Globalised and organised piracy

According to the statistics of International Maritime Bureau (IMB) of the International Chamber of Commerce, cases of piracy have increased drastically worldwide since the late 1990s, and the waters of South-East Asia have the largest number of pirate incidents, with almost half of global piracy occurring in the Malacca and Singapore Straits, the surrounding waters of Malaysia, Indonesian archipelagic waters and the waters surrounding the Philippines.[59] Piracy in these waters is characteristically organised with sufficient weapons and criminal skill.[60]

The increase in the volume of maritime traffic and the widening of the gap between the "haves" and the "have-nots", due to regional economic development, are major factors contributing to the recent rise in Asian piracy. The poor started piracy with ties to organised crimes, and escalated their activities by taking advantage of undermanned maritime guards because of economic crisis and deterioration in domestic security. In recent years, local authorities even tolerate such activities,[61] and sometimes the piracies are the works of anti-government organisations or international terrorist groups.[62]

The Malacca and Singapore Straits, and the Indonesian Archipelagic waters are strategically important locations in maritime transport, yet coast guard and naval force presence in these areas is significantly low, which allows piracy to flourish.[63]

In order to counter piracy in these waters, Singapore, Malaysia and Indonesia started to reinforce their patrols of the straits on a bilateral bases, in their own territories in the 1990s. They set up an informational exchange hot line, conducted joint patrols between Indonesia and Singapore, and organised a team for planning maritime operations in order to conduct joint patrol of the Malaccan Straits between Indonesia and Malaysia.[64] The coast guards of some ASEAN members also conducted informational exchanges or joint exercises, and in July 2004, the three countries started their trilateral joint patrols of the Malacca and Singapore straits.[65]

As a result, piracy incidents in Malacca and Singapore Straits have begun to decrease. However, the number of incidents in Indonesian Archipelagic waters have not reduced but have multiplied.[66] These organised pirates will simply move to wherever the patrol is weaker, thus the effective patrolling of these waters cannot be done by the military forces of these three countries alone. At present, the regional Anti-Piracy Centre of the IMB in Malaysia is recommending that a multilateral cooperative operation take place, which is participated in by regional countries. However, the prospect of such a cooperative operation being implemented is bleak due to boundary disputes over territorial waters.[67] Moreover, these pirates are said to be active in other illegal activities such as drug and human trafficking. So like the piracy issue, patrolling for such activities has become a common concern of this region.[68]

Since the "International Conference on Piracy Measures" held in Tokyo in April 2001 under the proposal by the Late Prime Minister Obuchi, Japan has taken initiatives to solve this problem (and also throughout the years of former Mori Administration and current Koizumi Administration). Japan has held several international conferences and implemented the dispatch of its coast guard patrol ships to the region.[69]

The RMSI (Regional Maritime Security Initiative), introduced by ADM Doran, Commander, US Pacific Fleet, and seconded by ADM Fargo, Commander US Pacific Command, at a speech in Singapore, is to cover a wide range of issues such as piracy, drug trafficking, illegal human trafficking, etc. with a focus on Southeast Asia, including the Straits of Malacca, and the archipelagic waters of Indonesia and Philippines.[70] The goal of RMSI is to develop a partnership among willing regional nations with varying capabilities and capacities to identify, monitor and intercept transnational maritime threats within existing international and domestic laws and regulations.

Creating A Maritime Coalition for Regional Security

The aforementioned factors undoubtedly have the potential to destabilise regional security. There is an increasing need to create, sooner or later, a multilateral regional organisation that covers the entire region, which can provide a framework to discuss these issues regularly, work continuously towards a peaceful solution, and given the authority to impose enforcement measures, if necessary.

It is also important to share common values with regard to the regions' waters and SLOCs, this is particularly important given that they are a potential source of benefit to the development of each nation and the region as a whole. It is perhaps more appropriate then to create a "Maritime Coalition" in the form of a multilateral entity, in order to build a consensus among regional countries, which would aid in the harnessing of the common benefits of the oceans. Also, as shall be discussed below, a "maritime coalition" would be the most appropriate forum for securing the regions SLOCs.

"Maritime" as the common keyword for regional security and safety

Surveying the aforementioned factors, which contribute to the instability of the region, it is clear that there is a common theme running through these various security concerns — which is the maritime environment. Regarding the first factor of instability, many paths used for the proliferation of weapons of mass destruction and ballistic missiles rely heavily on SLOC routes, and the threat of ballistic missiles in the Asia-Pacific region is structurally and geographically extended through aerial routes over oceans (in space) except in the case of threats between terrestrial neighbours.

Similarly, the second factor — of the increasing threat from international terrorism — relies heavily on SLOC for the proliferation of weapons and the transport of terrorists themselves. In addition, terrorist attacks have occurred within the maritime environment, as was the case in the suicide bomb attack against the *USS Cole* at Port Aden in 2000, and the attack against the French tanker *Limburg* off the coast of Yemen in 2002.[71] Also, in 2004, there was a suicide bomb attack against a tanker berthed at an oil terminal near Basra in Iraq.[72]

The third factor of China's military build-up also has a maritime component. It is clear that not only China but also many other regional countries are focusing on the build-up and modernisation of their naval and air power in their military reorganisation efforts. The problem is how such efforts affect regional security; in other words, what implications will they have on maritime safety and security of SLOCs.

Similarly, the fourth factor of the confrontational military structure, present in both the Korean Peninsula and Taiwan Strait, has serious implications for regional maritime safety and the security of the SLOCs. Should the situation deteriorate between the various parties concerned, their proximity to strategic SLOC means that there is added cause for concern. The factors of the archipelagic territorial disputes, of oceanic interests, and of illegal maritime activities such as piracy are all issues that have direct implications for regional maritime safety and the security of SLOC.

Creating regional frameworks for a "maritime coalition"

The Asia-Pacific region continues to show strong economic growth except for a brief period during the currency crisis in late 1990s. Although the effects of the currency crisis still linger in some countries of South-East Asia, even these countries will undoubtedly continue their steady growth in the future. Therefore, the future problems and issues faced by the countries in this region will be those that face every country undergoing rapid economic growth.

These issues include: how to secure the necessary energy and resources to maintain economic growth; a rapid population increase resulting from economic affluence earned through economic growth, the securing of food to feed this larger population; and the development of measures to address the adverse global environmental effects that have arisen in the process of, and as a result of, economic development. Even in developed countries, which have already addressed these issues, such as maritime pollution, over fishing, habitat destruction or global warming, there will be a need to adopt new and effective measures to allow for the participation of additional countries.

If countries could unite and adopt the necessary measures to address these issues, then their problems would be solved, but, in reality, addressing these issues is not easy, whether politically or technologically. Rather, each country is likely to consider their national interests first, and try to develop and adopt the measures necessary to protect them. This may lead to the rise of new conflicts between neighbouring countries or in the region as a whole, generating an unstable situation in regional security.

As mentioned before, many countries have high expectations regarding the oceans, and anticipate that they will be the source of energy, resources and food. On the other hand, the oceans can also become a stage for tangled national intentions and interests. This is the very reason why there is an urgent need to build a regional consensus, through the creation of a "Maritime Coalition", for maritime safety and the security of the region's SLOCs.

Security framework in the Asia-Pacific region

As the places of multilateral dialogue to discuss political and security issues covering the Asia-Pacific region, there are such organisations as the ASEAN Regional Forum (ARF). However, ASEAN has been extremely cautious to get involved in issues concerning security beyond the framework of voluntary multilateral cooperation, whether in or out of ARF. This is due to their principle of not interfering in other countries' domestic matters.

Today, the ARF has grown into a forum that includes 24 countries. Ministerial Meetings have been held every year since 1994, and North Korea started to participate in the Ministerial Meetings from 2000. In 2003, there were some attempts at strengthening ARF activities; these included advancing the ARF process to a higher "preventive diplomacy" level, and the Chinese proposal to host an "ARF Security Policy Meeting". The ARF also started to cooperate in the prevention of piracy and other threats to maritime security.[73]

Moreover, the 9th ASEAN summit meeting in October 2003 adopted the second Bali Statement, which promised to establish an ASEAN community, composed of ASC (ASEAN Security Community), AEC (ASEAN Economic Community) and ASCC (ASEAN Socio-Cultural Community) by 2020.[74] Nevertheless, the need for a new multilateral security framework is an issue to be addressed in the future. So far, several maritime security conferences were held in this area, but there is currently no multilateral security framework to cover this region.

The need for a multilateral security framework is especially apparent in North East Asia, which has a particularly unstable and uncertain security environment. The region is still plagued by legacies of the Cold War, where it was the frontline of the East–West confrontation. This is particularly evident in the South–North Korea relationship and the China–Taiwan relationship, as discussed earlier.

How to proceed with the security framework for the Asia-Pacific region in the future is the topic of many debates, but there seems to be two distinct thoughts that incorporate the unique features of this region. One is to further develop the ARF, and to create a "cooperative" multilateral security framework covering North East Asia and South West Asia, with some enforcement authority, but without presuming any exercise of military power; this framework could coexist with bilateral military alliances that centre around the United States.

Another thought is that now that the Cold War regime has ended, the regional countries should resolve bilateral alliances phase by phase or mitigate alliance relationships and then create a "binding" security structure with a certain degree of enforcement authority to cover the multilateral region, including the United States.

The latter thought presents an ideal security structure but has less chance of being created. Practically, the region is likely to pursue the former idea through various approaches. In this respect, the major issue of the future will be how the ARF can depart from the current policy prioritising "coordination" mandate and adopt, to a certain extent, a "mandatory" enforcement system. How the region's bilateral military alliances, which centre on the United States, would be distributed in this new security framework is also an important consideration.

Nonetheless, the importance of the "Maritime Coalition" for maritime safety and security in the Asia-Pacific region will be evident in many different ways in the future, as described before, and the issues will undoubtedly present the potential to destabilise regional security. Therefore, there is likely to be a need, sooner or later, to create a multilateral regional organisation, which covers the entire region, provides the framework to discuss these issues regularly and continuously, and has the authority to impose enforcement measures, if necessary.

A "Maritime Coalition" for "Maritime Safety in Peacetime"

"Maritime Safety and Security" cannot be achieved through the efforts of a single country. Only the mutual understanding and cooperation of regional countries can fulfil it. For this, regional countries need to start by sharing views on the benefits that regional maritime safety and security can provide. Undoubtedly, this is not an easy task for any country, but if regional countries look into the future of the region as a whole and of each nation, it will not be impossible to build a consensus on the needs of such views.

In the end, what is necessary is to recognise these issues as part of regional security issues, and to let individual nations adopt responsive measures. As stated before, however, it will be difficult to create a so-called "binding" style of framework in this region, at least for the foreseeable feature. Therefore, the following process may be the only way forward for the moment: firstly, the creation of a "Maritime Coalition" by willing countries in order to coordinate efforts within a structure unique to this region; secondly, the initial "Maritime Coalition" could then gradually develop into a more effective framework participated in by every relevant county in the region.

Initially, the coordinating structure or framework may require a means of building consensus on regional issues concerning maritime safety and security, such as economic or environmental problems, international terrorism, and piracy controls, while staying away from any political problems. The next stage will be to consider which method enables regional countries to comply with the consensus building efforts. Lastly, it will be important to address the ways in which to impose certain "obligations" on regional countries.

Viewed from another angle, the pathway to a "Maritime Coalition" may be to first set up a framework limited to the "Maritime Safety in Peacetime" only, while shelving the sensitive issue of "Maritime Security at Wartime". Measures to address problems like humanitarian aid distribution, such as in the case of maritime disaster rescue and relief for a large-scale natural disaster, or the evacuation of foreigners at a time of domestic security deterioration, in addition to the control of piracy and international terrorism, could be implemented phase by phase.

Once such a framework becomes a reality, it would help to build common values in the region which would secure "Maritime Safety in Peacetime". This could be done through various training opportunities and meetings. It would also promote a better understanding of the significance of a "Maritime Coalition", from which it may then be possible to develop to the stage of a "Maritime Coalition", which addresses the issues of "Maritime Security at Wartime" or "Various Maritime Activities".

The realisation of this initial framework could take one of the following two routes. The first option would be to build a consensus among the member parties under existing regional frameworks such as CSCAP (Council for Security Cooperation in the Asia-Pacific)[75] or the ARF on the need to maintain maritime safety and security, and address humanitarian issues in the entire Asia-Pacific region. The "Maritime Coalition" would be gradually created in the region step by step, and would eventually expand to include the entire region.

The second approach is a process in which willing countries start to implement concrete measures in advance on issues that are relatively easy for these countries to reach a consensus on. Then, the ring of participating countries could expand step by step. The initial participating countries could start bilateral or multilateral talks, implement concrete measures, establish a standing council for the "Maritime Coalition" among them and undertake concrete actions over the open sea to avoid any conflict or instability. Once the coalition gradually expanded to include other countries, it could begin to address the issues of humanitarian aid, as described earlier, and develop into a "more" multilateral forum that includes other regional countries, and involved the regimes of both PSI and RMSI.

There are several options for the ultimate structure and scope of the regime. For example, it could be a multilateral voluntary alliance led by the United States and possibly backed-up by the United Nations, or it could follow from the development of existing regional frameworks such as CSCAP and the ARF. It could also be based on the expansion of existing military consultation organisations such as WPNS (Western Pacific Naval Symposium),[76] or a joint patrol based on an entirely new voluntary agreement in the region.

A "Maritime Coalition" for "Maritime Security at Wartime"

A "Maritime Coalition" for maritime security at wartime would be more difficult to implement than a coalition for maritime safety in peacetime. However, a "Maritime Coalition" that is concerned with defence would be of great importance to the security of the whole region. There are two reasons for this.

Firstly, a framework of this sort could play an important role in the "prevention of war" and "confidence building for mutual trust". Developing a framework that incorporated a security aspect would, firstly, enable regional countries to resolve misunderstandings and clear any doubts through the efforts of creating "Maritime Coalition" on the basis of consensus building for peacetime, with the eventual aim of using the same mechanism for wartime;

and secondly, increase the transparency in the intention of each country. This would lead to the development of trustful relationships between the region's countries, which would in turn prevent any occurrence of conflicts, and would increase the chances of success of efforts to enhance maritime security.

Secondly, there is the importance of "joint responses" to the region's security. If, for example, there is an actual war or conflict in the region over the ocean due to resource competition or territorial boundary disputes, then military and economic SLOC may be interrupted, with serious consequences to the relevant parties. In addition, when regional maritime security is disrupted, countries other than those directly involved will also suffer, not only in terms of economic impact, but also to the extent that the very existence of that nation itself could be in jeopardy, if such disruption persists for a long time. Therefore, it is particularly important to secure SLOCs during conflicts. However, if large-scale conflicts occur simultaneously in a number of regions, then individual nations, including the United States, may not be able to respond to every conflict at the same time. It would be necessary in this case to adopt joint response efforts among regional countries not directly involved in the conflicts in order to secure the security of the SLOCs. Moreover, these countries may also need to maintain maritime transportation with one or all parties involved, depending on the situation. In such a case, the adoption of a joint response approach is essential.

In light of the evidence above, the building of a framework for a regional "Maritime Coalition" at wartime should be promoted, however difficult. There are several possible approaches for the building of such a framework, including: the extension and development of subsidiary organisations under a security forum such as ARF, which would already be part of a peacetime framework for a "Maritime Coalition" as discussed above; or the elevation of a navy-to-navy forum such as WPNS to a higher level and to include a wider region. During the building of such a framework, a key point of discussion would be in what way regional countries could accept the presence of the US Navy, which has committed itself to the whole region. Building a consensus for such a framework will depend on how regional countries will address this issue.

Needless to say, SLOCs link not only regional countries but extend to other regions of the world through neighbouring waters. It may be necessary to consider association with neighbouring regional waterways such as the Indian Ocean and Oceania.

A "Maritime Coalition" for "Various Maritime Activities"

As mentioned before, regional counties are likely to rely on the oceans as the future source of various resource supplies, which are essential for the future development of each nation. The greater the expectation of each country regarding oceanic resources, the greater the chance are for a conflict of interests to occur. Moreover, such conflicts of interests will certainly have serious effects on regional security. In the past, this type of issue has been addressed at bilateral talks, but as the regional countries rapidly expand their range of economic activities, the talks may need to involve many other countries. Bilateral talks seem to have reached the limit of their effectiveness, and sooner or later, it may become difficult to hold such talks by themselves.

Therefore, what is important now is to focus on shared common values that regard the regions waters as a source of resources that can benefit the development of each nation and the region as a whole. That is why it is appropriate to create a "Maritime Coalition" in the form of a multilateral framework, i.e. a coalition for regional maritime use. It will facilitate the process of building a consensus between the regional countries for obtaining the common benefits from the oceans. The process can begin through the adoption of regional responses to multilateral issues, which the region's countries are likely to face in the future, such as maritime environmental issues, including maritime pollution, over fishing, habitat destruction or global warming, whilst continuing the conventional bilateral talks, and then gradually incorporating them into the forum so that every problem is discussed in the future.

As a framework for this purpose, the ARF model may cause difficulties because the issue must be based on UNCLOS (United Nations Convention on the Law of the Sea). In such a case, it may become necessary to establish the framework as a sub-regional or sub-functional organisation under the United Nations.

Conclusion

Many countries have high expectations regarding the world's oceans. They see them as a solution to such problems as the securing of energy, resources and food, and because of this, the oceans can become a stage of tangled national intentions and interests. In the Asia-Pacific region, there are several major factors that have the potential to cause the destabilisation of regional security, all of which are related to the oceans.

Therefore, regional countries need to share their common values and views on the potential benefits of maritime safety and security, within a framework provided by a regional coalition. Undoubtedly, this is not an easy task for any country, but, if regional countries look into the future of the region, as a whole and as individual nations, it should not be impossible to reach a consensus on the needs of the region.

How can we begin this difficult process? Firstly, the sensitive issue of "Maritime Security at Wartime", should be shelved for the time being. A framework for a regional "Maritime Coalition", limited to "Maritime Safety in Peacetime" should be set up. Then it would it be possible to pursue concrete plans that address the various issues comprehensively, and implement any measures and solutions step by step.

Once such a framework becomes a reality, it would be helpful to develop common values in the region in order to secure the "Maritime Safety in Peacetime". This could be done through various training opportunities and meetings that would help to promote an understanding of the significance of a "Maritime Coalition". Ultimately, a way should be found to develop such a framework into a "Maritime Coalition" for addressing the issues of "Maritime Security at Wartime" and/or even "Various Maritime Activities".

As Singapore's Deputy Prime Minister Tony Tan said in his opening keynote speech at the recent conference on Maritime Security: "The region could not just wish the problem away or wait until an attack occurred before acting. If an accident happens, or should I say when it happens, everyone will wake up and scramble for a solution. But it will be too late. The time to act is now!"

Notes

1. Testimony by former Pakistani Prime Minister Bhutto to *Asahi* Newspaper, 18 July, 2004.
2. Defense of Japan 2003, "Proliferation of WMD and Ballistic Missiles", *Japan Defense Agency (JDA)*, 2003, p. 7.
3. Defense of Japan 2003, "What is the Ballistic Missile?" *JDA*, 2003, p. 311.
4. Defense of Japan 2003, "Proliferation of WMD and Ballistic Missiles", *JDA*, 2003, p. 7.
5. Defense of Japan 2004, "Proliferation Security Initiative", *JDA*, 2004, pp. 252–255.
6. US Department of State website; http://www.state.gov/t/np/rls/fs/23764pf.htm.

7. East Asian Strategic Review, "Prevention of Proliferation of WMD and Ballistic Missiles", *National Institute of Defense Study (NIDS)*, 2004, p. 219.
8. *Yomiuri* Newspaper, 4 August 2004.
9. *Yomiuri* Newspaper, 29 April 2004.
10. East Asian Strategic Review 2004, "Terrorist Network", *NIDS*, 2004, p. 113.
11. Ibid, p. 116.
12. Defense of Japan 2003, "Fight with global proliferation of Terrorists", *JDA*, 2003, p. 6.
13. Ibid.
14. Defense of Japan 2003, "Military Situation of India", p. 77.
15. East Asian Strategic Review, 2003, "ASEAN and the U.S.", *NIDS*, 2003, p. 38.
16. East Asian Strategic Review, 2004, "Closer relationship between ASEAN with China & India", *NIDS*, 2004, p. 133.
17. US CNO website; http://www.nwc.navy.mil/pao/CNO remarks.htm.
18. East Asian Strategic Review 2003, "Expansion of military power in ASEAN countries", *NIDS*, 2003, pp. 184–186.
19. Defense of Japan 2004, "Regional military situation, China", *JDA*, 2004, p. 50.
20. Shigeo Hiramatsu, "China's strategic maritime advancement", *Keiso Books*, 2002, pp. 15–18.
21. Defense of Japan 2004, "Regional military situation, China", *JDA*, 2004, p. 54.
22. Ibid., pp. 55–57.
23. Ibid., p. 58.
24. Defense of Japan 2004, "Regional military situation, China", *JDA*, 2004, p. 55.
25. Defense of Japan 2004, "Overview of regional military situation", *JDA*, 2004, p. 36.
26. East Asian Strategic Review 2001, "Historic summit meeting between South and North", *NIDS*, 2001, p. 18.
27. Defense of Japan 2004, "Regional military situation, North Korea", *JDA*, 2004, p. 43.
28. Ibid.
29. East Asian Strategic Review 2003, "Enriched uranium plan", *NIDS*, 2003, p. 19.
30. East Asian Strategic Review 2004, "New approach, 6 parties talk", *NIDS*, 2004, p. 23.
31. Ibid., p. 24.
32. During the 1970s and the 1980s, there were a number of Japanese people reported missing under very unnatural circumstances. The subsequent investigation by Japanese authorities and the testimony of defected North Korean spies aroused strong suspicions that these were cases of abduction by North Korean agents. Since 1991, the Government of Japan has taken every opportunity to submit such suspicions to North Korea, but the North Korean government obstinately and persistently denied the charges. During the Japan–North Korea Summit held in Pyongyang on 17 September 2002, the North Korean side finally admitted to the

abduction of Japanese nationals for the first time after a long period of denial, expressed regrets and promised to prevent a recurrence. Presently, the Government of Japan has acknowledged 15 Japanese people as North Korean abductees, and five of them were able to return to their homeland on 15 October 2002, after about 24 years of captivity. However, North Korea has not presented sufficient information on the remaining 10 people, and their safety is still unknown.

33. East Asian Strategic Review 2004, "New approach, 6 parties talk", *NIDS*, 2004, pp. 24–25.
34. Defense of Japan 2004, "Regional military situation, China", *JDA*, 2004, p. 51.
35. Ibid.
36. Ibid.
37. Ibid.
38. The Taiwan Relations Act states that the United States shall supply defensive weapons to Taiwan in order for Taiwan to maintain sufficient self-defence capability. Although the United States traditionally presented the list of saleable weapons every year in April, since 2002 it was decided that they would discuss on weapons sales whenever necessary.
39. Defense of Japan 2004, "Regional military situation, Taiwan", *JDA*, 2004, p. 60.
40. Ibid.
41. East Asian Strategic Review 2004, "Military confrontation between China and Taiwan", *NIDS*, 2004, p. 105.
42. Defense of Japan 2004, "Regional military situation, China", *JDA*, 2004, p. 60.
43. Ibid., p. 59.
44. Shigeo Hiramatsu, "China's maritime advancement", *Keiso Books*, 1997, p. 39.
45. Defense of Japan 2004, "Regional military situation, South-East Asia", *JDA*, 2004, p. 67.
46. "Regional military situation, China," p. 58.
47. "Regional military situation, South-East Asia," p. 67.
48. "Regional military situation, China," p. 58.
49. "Regional military situation, South-East Asia," p. 67.
50. Ibid.
51. "Regional military situation, China," p. 58.
52. Ibid.
53. Ibid.
54. Ibid., p. 59.
55. Ibid.
56. Ibid.
57. Ibid.
58. *Yomiuri* Newspaper, 22 July 2004.
59. *Yomiuri* Newspaper, 27 July 2004.
60. *Yomiuri* Newspaper, 4 July 2004.
61. *Sankei* Newspaper, 16 August 2004.

62. *Yomiuri* Newspaper, 26 June 2004.
63. *Yomiuri* Newspaper, 4 July 2004.
64. *Sankei* Newspaper, 16 August 2004.
65. Ibid.
66. Ibid.
67. Ibid.
68. East Asian Strategic Review 2002, "Counter nontraditional threat", *NIDS,* 2004, p. 80.
69. Maritime White Paper 2004, "Movement of Asia", Ship and Ocean Foundation, Tokyo, 2004, p. 112.
70. US PACOM website; http://www.pacom.mil/rmsi.
71. Michael Richardson, *A Time Bombs for Global Trade* (Singapore: Institute of Southeast Asian Studies, 2004), p. 18.
72. *Yomiuri* Newspaper, 22 April 2004.
73. East Asian Strategic Review 2003, "Strengthening ARF Function," *NIDS,* 2003, pp. 179–182.
74. East Asian Strategic Review 2004, "2nd Bali Declaration", *NIDS,* 2004, pp. 129–133.
75. CSCAP website; http://www.cscap.org/maritime.htm.
76. US PACOM website; http//www.pacom.mil/ops/exerlist.shtml.

Chapter 3

Maritime Security Outlook for Southeast Asia

Rommel C. Banlaoi

Introduction

It is not easy to come to grips with the issue of maritime security in Southeast Asia because the term maritime security encompasses such a broad concept that a panoply of notions like maritime safety, port security, freedom of navigation, security of the sea lines of communication (SLOCs), security from piracy attacks, including armed robberies against ships, and security from maritime terrorism can be included as part of the concept of maritime security. In fact, although many experts have spoken on the topic of maritime security, there is still an absence of a commonly accepted definition that will form the basis for regional cooperation.

Despite the lack of a workable definition, the growing concern on maritime security have led participants to issue the *Statement on Cooperation Against Piracy and other Threats to Maritime Security* at the 36th ASEAN Ministerial Meeting and the 10th ARF Post Ministerial Conferences held in Cambodia on 16–20 June 2003. The Statement does not have a clear definition of maritime security and only regards maritime security as "an indispensable and fundamental condition for the welfare and economic security of the ARF region".[1]

The Statement goes on to say that ensuring maritime security "is in direct interests of all countries"[2] and even attempts to limit the issue of maritime security to "piracy and armed robbery against ships and the potential for terrorist attacks on vulnerable sea shipping"[3] as a form of quasi-definition.

The lack of a workable definition has also not deterred ASEAN from issuing its own Communiqué at the conclusion of the 37th Ministerial Meeting held on 29–30 June 2004 in Jakarta, where members reaffirmed their commitment to the establishment of an ASEAN Security Community. In the Communiqué, ASEAN ministers stressed the importance of maritime cooperation to the evolution of a security community in the region and urged each other to "explore the possibility of establishing a maritime forum" in Southeast Asia. The Communiqué thus hints at the increasing awareness of Southeast Asian countries to the importance of regional security cooperation, particularly in the areas of piracy and maritime terrorism. However, despite the issuance of the Communiqué, regional cooperation to promote maritime security in Southeast Asia still remains limited. There is even a view that maritime security in Southeast Asia is "inconsistent and largely ineffective"[4] and as a result encourages intervention by extra-regional powers to improve regional maritime security.

Having said that, as a maritime region, maritime security is inevitably one of Southeast Asia's most vital security concerns and enhancing the maritime security in Southeast Asia is an integral component of the regional security agenda. Therefore, discussion of maritime security in the region should be broad and not deal only with piracy, sea robbery and maritime terrorism, as the ARF document suggests. This is because the issue of maritime security in Southeast Asia has always been comprehensive and multifaceted and includes traditional security issues like territorial disputes in the South China Sea (and to a certain extent the territorial issues in the Taiwan Straits and the Korean Peninsula), and the security impact of major power rivalries.[5] It also includes non-traditional security issues like environmental degradation, weapons proliferation, as well as arms, drugs and human smuggling.[6]

Hence, although maritime security must be viewed in its various dimensions and nuances in order to have a holistic understanding of maritime security in Southeast Asia, this chapter will not take the comprehensive approach in dealing with the issue of maritime security in Southeast Asia. Instead, the central aspect of this chapter is to describe the maritime security outlook for Southeast Asia in the areas of piracy and maritime terrorism and analyses both issues in the context of shipping and force modernisation trends in the region. This chapter contends that piracy and maritime terrorism in Southeast Asia have root causes and addressing these root causes is crucial to promoting regional maritime security. This chapter concludes with the advocacy that defence development is imperative to increase the capacity of Southeast Asian countries to surmount the gargantuan challenges of maritime security in the region.

Southeast Asia: Still a Piracy Hotspot

Despite the constant denial of Southeast Asian countries to the existence of piracy,[7] Southeast Asia has the long-standing reputation of being the piracy hotspot of the world. It remains the most prone region to acts of piracy, and has accounted for around 50 percent of all attacks worldwide. Indonesian waters continue to be the world's most dangerous in terms of the frequency of pirate attacks. According to the 2003 report of the International Maritime Bureau, of the 445 actual and attempted piracy attacks on merchant ships worldwide, 189 attacks occurred in Southeast Asian waters. Of these 189 attacks, 121 attacks occurred in Indonesian waters, with 35 occurring in the waterways around Malaysia and Singapore, particularly in the congested Straits of Malacca. The data represent an increase of 18 attacks over those recorded in 2002 for Indonesian waters alone, with an increase of 33 attacks for the whole region. Thus, piracy attacks in Southeast Asian waters are high when compared with the incidences of piracy attacks in other regions of the world like Africa and Latin America.

A study has shown that acts of piracy in Southeast Asia occur mostly in ports or anchorages and pirates range from opportunistic fishermen and the common criminal to members of sophisticated Asian crime syndicates.[8] In 2002, it was reported that 95 of the 123 reported attacks occurred in ports, representing 77 percent of all attacks in Southeast Asia.[9] Although the proportion of attacks in ports dropped to 50 percent of all attacks in Southeast Asia in 2003, ports remained vulnerable as ports that were not targets in 2002 became hot targets in 2003.[10] In 2003 alone, acts of piracy were reported in 10 anchorages in Southeast Asia as compared to the 27 anchorages worldwide.[11] Acts of piracy also range from the classic boarding and hijacking of a merchant vessel on the high seas to the more common act of stealing from the ship while it is anchored.[12] Thus, three types of piracy have been identified: harbor/anchorage attacks, attacks against vessels on high seas or territorial waters and hijacking of commercial vessels on high seas.[13]

Cost of Piracy

Besides the high number of incidents of piracy in Southeast Asia, the cost attributed to acts of piracy is also alarming. James Warren of the Asia Research Institute at the National University of Singapore has claimed that piracy in the region has cost the world economy a staggering US$ 25 billion a year.[14] Alan Chan, a vocal anti-piracy advocate and owner of Petroships in Singapore, has also said that piracy has cost the region around US$ 500 million a year.[15] But despite the high number of incidents and the cost resulting from attacks, ship owners have not taken much action due to the high cost of preventive measures. The Organisation for Economic Cooperation and Development, for example, has stated that new security measures to counter the threat of attacks will require an initial investment by ship operators of at least US$ 1.3 billion, and will increase annual operating costs by US$ 730 million.[16] Despite the high cost of piracy now, the cost of piracy is projected to increase in the future, as the incidents become more bloody, ruthless and sophisticated.

Causes of Piracy

The problem of piracy in the region remains unabated despite serious efforts to combat piracy in Southeast Asia, because of the failure of concerned states in addressing the root causes of piracy. Pervasive poverty, the low level of economic development and the poor quality of governance has helped make piracy an alternative means of livelihood for a large number of people in Southeast Asia. On top of this, the huge coastline of the affected countries, lax port security measures, weak maritime security forces and limited anti-piracy cooperation also makes the region highly vulnerable to piracy. In particular, countries in Southeast Asia do not have adequate funds and strong political will to fight piracy.[17] Adding insult to injury is the fact that despite the mouthful of rhetoric, there is very limited regional maritime security cooperation in Southeast Asia. As a result of the myriad of factors that has resulted in the high piracy rates, resolving the issue is both difficult and complex. Each issue will now be examined in turn to unearth the root causes of piracy.

The first cause of piracy is pervasive poverty. Pervasive poverty in the region is one cause of piracy. Poverty incidences in the region range from 16 to 55 percent[18] and it is this poverty in Southeast Asia that has prompted people to resort to piracy as an alternative means of livelihood. The harsh economic and development impact of the 1997 Asian financial crisis aggravated the poverty situation in Southeast Asia as many people lost their jobs. The deteriorated situation encouraged people in Southeast Asia, particularly those from the coastal areas, to return to "old ways" of finding a living, one of which is the resort to piracy to supplement income. Resorting to piracy acts as a source of livelihood in Southeast Asia is not very difficult since piracy in the region "was thought to be an acceptable part of the local culture, a normal but illegal means of making money".[19]

The second cause of piracy is weak governance. For example, the high incidences of piracy in Indonesian and Philippine waters could be attributed to political instabilities and weak institutions of governance in these two countries. Weak institutions of governance make these countries unable to effectively protect and control their huge territorial waters. Although Singapore has relatively strong governance among countries in Southeast Asia, weak governance of its neighbours also makes Singapore's waters highly vulnerable to piracy attacks. A compounding factor is the sad reality that countries in Southeast Asia just do not have adequate funds and strong political will to fight piracy.[20]

The third cause of piracy in Southeast Asia is the huge coastline and weak port security in the countries of concern. Southeast Asian countries have a combined coastline length of 92,451 km, which is 15.8 percent of the world's total. The archipelagos of Indonesia and the Philippines (the two largest in the world with more than 20,000 islands combined) alone contribute 59 and 24 percent, respectively, to the region's coastlines.[21] Such a coastline makes ensuring port security in Southeast Asia highly difficult and very expensive. Kenneth Button, an American academic, said that Britain and the United States alone spent billions to protect their coastline. If this were the case, then most Asian countries will not have the money to protect their coastlines as their coastlines are longer than those in the United States and Britain and their countries poorer. The long coastline in Southeast Asia provides ample hideouts for pirates and is a source of vulnerability for many coastal states in the region.

The fourth cause of piracy in Southeast Asia is the relatively weak maritime forces of Southeast Asian countries. Weak maritime security forces attract pirates to operate in Southeast Asia because the existing maritime armed forces in the region do not have the effective wherewithal to deter, prevent and pre-empt pirates in their acts. Cindy Vallar argues that "Once pirates meet little or no resistance from their victims and aren't pursued by law enforcement authorities, they are more likely to strike again".[22] Indonesia, the largest archipelago in the world, has a weak maritime force and Indonesia's defence budget is the lowest in Southeast Asia.[23] With the scourge of the Asian financial crisis, the value of the Indonesian defence budget has also declined by 65 percent from 1997 to 1998. This worsened the already tight fiscal problems and prevented the country from allocating more to its maritime security force.[24] The Philippines, the world's second largest archipelago, has one of the most ill-equipped maritime forces in Asia. The American military withdrawal in 1991 aggravated the already poor state of Philippine maritime forces. Though the Philippine military ventured into a force modernisation programme in 1995, the 1997 Asian financial crisis prevented its implementation and prompted even one of its own naval officer to lament that the Philippine Navy "lags both in quality and quantity among the other navies in the region".[25]

Underpaid members of the maritime security forces in Southeast Asia (coast guards, port guards, naval guards) also encourage officers and rank and file to seek other sources to supplement their income. One of these sources is piracy. An analyst observed that most of the personnel employed in Southeast Asia's maritime security forces "are grossly underpaid".[26] With a very limited budget allocated for defence, the military forces in Southeast Asia often cannot afford "to provide sufficient pay to officers and lower ranking members, who then resort to off budget sources of income".[27]

The fifth cause of piracy in Southeast Asia is the limited instances of maritime security cooperation in the region. As an attempt at gathering more information on regional piracy, a Piracy Reporting Centre was established in Kuala Lumpur under the auspices of the International Chamber of Commerce's International Maritime Bureau. However, one shortfall is that the Centre is non-governmental and acts only as a central information reporting and warning centre. It does not coordinate regional maritime patrols and operations to combat regional piracy.

Regional cooperation against piracy in Southeast Asia is predominantly bilateral in nature rather than multilateral. Indonesia, Malaysia, the Philippines and Singapore have entered into bilateral agreements to coordinate naval patrols and anti-piracy exercises. For example, the Philippines and Malaysia have a border crossing agreement to protect their maritime borders. Indonesia and Singapore also have an agreement to coordinate their maritime patrols and a regime for hot pursuit to combat piracy. Indonesia and Malaysia also have similar arrangement to deal with maritime issues arising out of a common border.[28] Singapore and Malaysia have their own bilateral cooperative mechanisms to discuss common maritime issues.

Besides bilateral arrangements, Southeast Asia has also adopted multilateral responses in the campaign against piracy, an example is the adoption by ARF members during 16–20 June 2003 of the Statement on Cooperation against

Piracy and other Threats to Maritime Security. The Statement recognises that maritime security "is an indispensable and fundamental condition for the welfare and economic security of the ARF region". Despite the adoption of the Statement, actual regional efforts continue to be limited. Singapore Deputy Prime Minister and Defence Minister Tony Tan observed that "Southeast Asian states have taken action to combat piracy, with some success, but more can be done". Although ASEAN has taken a lot of initiatives to suppress regional piracy, one of which is the adoption of the work programme to implement the Plan of Action to Combat Transnational Crimes signed in Malaysia on 17 May 2002, regional cooperation remains limited due to various domestic considerations.

Why then is cooperation amongst ASEAN countries to combat the piracy threat so poor? In response, some analysts contend that the ASEAN principle of "non-interference" in internal affairs is a major obstacle in the regional efforts to combat piracy and other threats to regional maritime security. And because the principle of "non-interference" is so central to the existence of ASEAN, deeper levels of cooperation is difficult.[29] So central is the principle of "non-interference" to the existence of ASEAN that signing of Bali Concord II in 2003, which declared the development of an ASEAN Security Community, again re-affirms the principle of non-interference.

Despite this, it is noteworthy that Indonesia, Malaysia and Singapore have decided to come together to promote maritime security in the Straits of Malacca through coordinated patrols that observes the territorial sovereignty of each country. The port authorities of the Philippines and Indonesia have also decided to establish a coordination system that would advance maritime security interests of both countries.[30] These initiatives are important developments to promote maritime security cooperation in Southeast Asia.

Piracy, Maritime Terrorism and Shipping Trends

A concomitant security issue of piracy problems in Southeast Asia is the spectre of maritime terrorism. It is possible for terrorists to use piracy as a cover to conduct acts of maritime terrorism because of the high incidences of piracy in Southeast Asian waters. Although the different motives of the pirate and the terrorist will make them strange bedfellows, with the former pursuing economic gain and the latter pursuing political gain,[31] terrorists still have the ability to either adopt pirate tactics or "piggyback" on pirate raids.[32] Maritime terrorists, rather than simply stealing, "could either blow up the ship or use it to ram into another vessel or a port facility".[33] As such, security experts have observed the blurring of the line between piracy and terrorism. These experts stress that "not only do pirates terrorise ships' crews, but terror groups like Al Qaeda could also use pirates' methods either to attack ships, or to seize ships to use in terror attacks at megaports, much like the September 11 hijackers used planes".[34]

A more sinister scenario is the threat that a small but lethal biological weapon could be smuggled into a harbor aboard a ship and released into the port.[35] In fact, terrorist groups regard seaports and international cruise lines as very attractive targets because they "reside in the nexus of terrorist intent, capability and opportunity".[36] It may be even asked: "if pirates can act with such impunity, what is stopping terrorists?"[37]

The increasing trends of commercial shipping in Southeast Asia make the challenges of piracy and maritime terrorism in the region even more acute. As early as 1999, the US Coast Guard Intelligence Coordinating Center has forecasted that the world commercial shipping activities will enormously increase by 2020 and this will also trigger the proliferation of transnational crimes at sea.[38] It also forecasted that the tremendous growth in the cruise line industry and the emergence of high-speed ferries would be the key developments in the maritime passenger transport business through 2020.[39]

Shipping has long been the major form of transport and communication connecting Southeast Asia and the rest of the world.[40] Some of the busiest international commercial shipping routes are in Southeast Asia, namely: the Malacca, Sunda, Lombok and Makassar straits.[41] More than 50 percent of the world's annual merchant fleet tonnage passes through these straits while more than 15 percent of the value of world trade passes through Southeast Asia yearly.[42] As a result of rapid expansion of global trade, this trend has been projected to grow in the years to come unless major disasters occur in the region. The Malacca Strait alone is carrying more than a quarter of the world's maritime trade each year. More than 50,000 large ships pass through the strait annually, not to mention that 40–50 oil tankers sail in the said strait daily.[43] Because the strait is the region's maritime gateway between the Indian Ocean and the Pacific Ocean, its present status as the world's centre of maritime activities will inevitably persist in the future. If terrorists hijack one of the ships passing through the Malacca Strait and turn it to a floating bomb to destroy ports or oil refineries, the effects will be undoubtedly catastrophic. This kind of incident will not only cripple world trade and slowdown international shipping, it will also sow awesome fear — greater than what happened on 9/11.

Though an analyst argues that it is difficult for terrorists to disrupt shipping in the strait by sinking a ship in a precise spot,[44] the possibility of these kinds of maritime incidents is not very remote. Container shipping is very vulnerable and its possibility of being used as weapon of mass destruction by maritime terrorists has already been properly documented.[45] Thus, maritime terrorism in Southeast Asia is no longer the question of if, but rather of when and where.[46] A maritime security expert even asserts that maritime terrorism, regionally speaking, is not a question of when, but how often and what are we going to do about it.[47]

Al Qaeda and its operatives in Southeast Asia have a keen awareness of maritime trade and have a deep understanding of its significance to global economy.[48] Al Qaeda also knows the impact of maritime terrorist attacks on maritime commerce. Al Qaeda has therefore planned to conduct sea-borne attacks to wage maritime terrorism.[49] Al Qaeda's maritime terrorist capability has already been demonstrated by suicide attacks on the destroyer *USS Cole* in 2000 and the French Oil tanker *Limburg* in 2002. Intelligence community has, in fact, identified 15 cargo ships believed to be owned by Al Qaeda and these ships could be used for future maritime terrorist attacks.[50] Al Qaeda operatives are also learning about diving with a view to attacking ships from below.[51]

What is more bothering is the fact that Southeast Asia, as a maritime region, is home to some indigenously based terrorist groups with maritime traditions.[52] The Abu Sayyaf Group (ASG), the Moro Islamic Liberation Front (MILF), the Gerakan Aceh Merdeka (GAM) and the Jemaah Islamiyah (JI) have been identified as terrorist groups with tremendous intention and capability to wage maritime terrorism. In the Strait of Malacca, for example, the Aegis Defence Services, a London-based security organisation, said that the robbery of a chemical tanker, *Dewi Madrim*, appeared to be the work of terrorists "who were learning how to steer a ship, in preparation for a future attack at sea".[53] In Singapore, intelligence and law enforcement forces have uncovered the JI plot planning to bomb US Naval Facility in the Island State. In the Philippines, the ASG claimed responsibility for the explosion and fire on the ship *Superferry 14* carrying 899 passengers on 27 February 2004. Although the Philippine government belittled the capability of ASG to wage such kind of maritime attacks, ASG spokesperson Abu Soliman said the attack on *Superferry 14* was a sample of things to come and treated the *Superferry 14* incident as a revenge for the on-going violence in Mindanao.[54] A reliable source from the Philippine intelligence office said that the Marine Board Inquiry in charge of investigating the incident confirmed that the ASG masterminded the *Superferry 14* explosion.[55]

With the sinister linking of terrorists and pirates, Southeast Asia has become the focal point of maritime fear.[56] This led Singapore Home Affairs Minister

Wong Kan Seng to declare that pirates roaming the waters of Southeast Asia should be regarded as terrorists.[57] In an interview, the Home Minister argued, "Although we talk about piracy or anti-piracy, if there's a crime conducted at sea sometimes we do not know whether it's pirates or terrorists who occupy the ship so we have to treat them all alike".[58]

However, exact definitions for piracy and terrorism are problematic because many experts and policy makers are unsure at which point piracy becomes terrorism.[59] A maritime security analyst even stressed that the distinction between piracy and terrorism is becoming blurred because "pirates collude with terrorists, terrorists adopt pirate tactics and policymakers eager for public support start labeling every crime as maritime terrorism".[60]

The Regional Maritime Security Initiative

As a result of the growing incidences of piracy and the possibility of the conduct of maritime terrorism in Southeast Asia, Admiral Thomas Fargo, Commander-in-Chief, US Pacific Command, spoke of the concept of a Regional Maritime Security Initiative (RMSI) during his testimony before the US House of Representatives Armed Services Committee on 31 March 2004.[61] Fargo introduced the concept of RMSI as a means to combat transnational threats in Southeast Asia, and based on the principle of a coalition of the willing. Fargo mentioned that the RMSI was meant to operationalise both the Proliferation Security Initiative and the Malacca Straits Initiative in order to promote regional security in the midst of the growing threats to maritime security.

The RMSI specifically aims to promote cooperation among navies of the region in order "to assess and then provide detailed plans to build and synchronize interagency and international capacity to fight threats that use the maritime space to facilitate their illicit activity".[62] It was widely reported in the media that the RMSI intended to combat transnational crimes in the Straits of Malacca through the mobilisation of US Marines.[63] Although Fargo testified that he found this concept "well received by our friends and allies in the region", Malaysia and Indonesia — the two main littoral states in the Straits of Malacca — expressed objections to the RMSI arguing that the concept could violate their national sovereignty. Marty Natalegawa, spokesman of the Indonesian foreign ministry, stressed that the security of the Malacca Straits was the joint responsibility of Indonesia and Malaysia. Deputy Prime Minister of Malaysia, Najib Razak, supported this view when he told the Bernama news agency that Malaysia and Indonesia were responsible for ensuring security in the Straits.[64] Razak underscored that Indonesia and Malaysia "do not propose to invite the US to join the security operations we have mounted there (Malacca Strait)" and "even if they wish to act, they should get our permission as this touches on the question of our national sovereignty".

Given the strong sentiments expressed by both Indonesia and Malaysia, Fargo provided further clarification of the RMSI during the Military Law and Operations Conference on 3 May 2004 in Vancouver, British Columbia.[65] Mindful of the national sensitivities of concerned states in Southeast Asia, Fargo explained that the goal of RMSI was "to develop a partnership of willing regional nations with varying capabilities and capacities to identify, monitor, and intercept transnational maritime threats under existing international and domestic laws".[66] US Naval Pacific Fleet Commander Adm. Walter F. Doran further explained that the RMSI would focus predominantly on intelligence sharing rather than on the deployment of troops. The US Assistant Secretary of State for East Asia and Pacific Affairs even recognised the capability of Malaysia and Indonesia to safeguard the Malacca Straits and stressed that the United States would not deploy troops without the approval of the littoral states.[67]

Building National Capacities to Combat Piracy and Maritime Terrorism: Force Modernisation through Defence Development

Apparently, one major challenge to regional cooperation against piracy and maritime terrorism in Southeast Asia is the issue of national sovereignty. Strong sentiments of nationalism and sensitivity to sovereignty issues make cooperation in maritime security even amongst countries in Southeast Asia utterly difficult. In addition, most countries in Southeast Asia are also reluctant to deeply involve extra-regional powers in the security affairs of their respective countries. Indonesia and Malaysia, particularly, are not willing "to grant an extra-regional power the freedom to conduct patrols and law enforcement at will in their backyard" even in the name of regional maritime security.[68] Therefore, the only way to combat piracy and other transnational maritime security threats in Southeast Asia is to build the national capacities of the respective littoral states through force modernisation to confront these threats[69] since territorial integrity is paramount and the principle of non-interference so sacred.

But how do we go about building up national capacities? As highlighted earlier, piracy abounds in Southeast Asia because the national capacity to combat the threat is limited. The Philippines and Indonesia, the two archipelagic states in the region, "have not merely very limited resources in policing their coastlines, but the maritime area and length of coastlines they have to keep under surveillance are extremely large".[70] Indonesia alone needs enormous resources to protect its very long maritime zones. This is in stark contrast with tiny states of Singapore and Brunei with enough economic resources to ably police their short coastlines.

Although Southeast Asian countries have ventured into force modernisation programmes to varying degrees in the mid-1990s, this does not equate, however, with military effectiveness to address various threats, including maritime, to their national security.[71] The 1997 Asian financial crisis aborted most of these force modernisation efforts, particularly in Indonesia, the Philippines and Thailand. Although Singapore, Brunei, Myanmar and to a certain extent Malaysia are pushing ahead with their force modernisation programmes in the aftermath of the financial crisis,[72] present capabilities of littoral states in Southeast Asian remain limited to address the growing maritime security problems in the region. These limitations will be reflected in the present quality and quantity of their maritime forces.[73]

To build the capacities of armed forces in the region to combat threats to maritime security, it may be better for extra-regional powers like the United States, Japan and Australia to intensify their assistance to Southeast Asian countries and build up their capacities through force modernisation to address the maritime security threats that confront them.

An excellent example in capacity building is the cooperation between the United States and the Philippines. The United States is assisting the Philippines in the area of counter-terrorism[74] through the Philippine Defence Reform initiative to enhance the capacity of the Armed Forces of the Philippines and other security sectors to address various threats to the country's internal security, which includes among others, the ASG, the MILF and the New People's Army. The US assistance is broad based and extends beyond the conduct of joint military exercises. The US assistance includes defence strategic planning, defence programming and budgeting, human resource development, defence acquisition and military capability building.[75] With the help of Australia, the United States also plans to assist the Philippines in building its national capability to address its maritime security problems. In fact, Australia is broadening its defence ties with the Philippines because of the convergence of their mutual interests in maritime security given that both countries are maritime nations.[76]

Besides the Philippines, the United States also provides assistance to Malaysia in the area of counter-terrorism. Despite Malaysia's criticisms of US actions against Afghanistan and Iraq, the United States continues to intensify its bilateral security relationship after 9/11. Malaysia's consent to the setting up of the Regional Counter-Terrorism Centre in Kuala Lumpur with US assistance has been regarded as a clear manifestation of closer security ties between the two countries.[77] These evolving security ties may yet spillover to the area of maritime security.

Indonesia also receives assistance from the United States in the building up of its national capacity to confront both land-based and maritime terrorism. The United States is rebuilding its defence ties with Indonesia and has openly pursued the restoration of full military-to-military relations with Jakarta[78] as a result of the US global campaign against terrorism.[79] In the campaign against piracy and maritime terrorism in Southeast Asia, the United States and Indonesia can forge greater cooperation to promote maritime security in the region, especially in the pirate-infested Straits of Malacca.

Regional Responses

Aside from the United States, other regional powers can also help in building the capacities of Southeast Asian countries to address their maritime security problems. Japan has long been involved in maritime security cooperation in Southeast Asia by hosting various workshops on piracy and conducting maritime security training.[80] Japan has even introduced the idea of "ocean governance" to strengthen maritime security management in the Asia-Pacific.[81]

China, on the other hand, is broadening its cooperation with ASEAN countries to include maritime security. A Chinese military official even proposed joint maritime military exercises between China and ASEAN countries.[82] Although ASEAN countries are concerned about China's expanding maritime ambitions,[83] they, however, see the role of China as an opportunity, with concomitant security challenges, rather than a threat.[84] China's accession to the 1976 Treaty of Amity and Cooperation in Southeast Asia is a positive indication of China's peaceful rise in the region. The signing of China–ASEAN strategic partnership agreement in October 2003 also provides several opportunities for China and Southeast Asia to promote their common maritime security interests.

Australia is presently strengthening its ties with Southeast Asian countries to advance its maritime security interests in the region[85] as Australia regards Southeast Asia as an integral part of its strategic space. Thus, it is in the interest of Australia to assist Southeast Asian countries in the promotion of maritime security in the region. In its recent white paper, Australia has enumerated its efforts in promoting maritime security in Southeast Asia by providing financial assistance to countries that are presently strengthening their capabilities in port security. For example, Australia has provided $1.3 million to the port security capacity-building project in the Philippines to help the Philippine government strengthen its port security arrangements and comply with the security requirements of the International Maritime Organization.[86] Australia has to sustain these efforts to build the capacities of Southeast Asian countries in the fight against piracy and maritime terrorism.

India's look east policy also provides opportunities for maritime security cooperation with Southeast Asian countries. Individual ASEAN countries have enhanced their bilateral ties with India.[87] With the signing of the Framework Agreement on Comprehensive Economic Cooperation between the Association of Southeast Asian Nations and the Republic of India on 8 October 2003, hopes are high that their scope of cooperation will spill over to maritime security.

Assistance of major powers, however, shall not be limited to training of law enforcement agencies like Coast Guard or Marine Police. Assistance must also be comprehensive to address the root causes of piracy and maritime terrorism in Southeast Asia. Assistance therefore must be extended to other reform initiatives like security sector reforms, governance reforms and socio-economic reforms to produce a virtuous cycle. Without a comprehensive reform package, the region will continue to face the vicious cycle of maritime security threats.

An interesting component of a comprehensive reform package to address maritime security threats is national defence development — a new approach that aims to reform the national defence sectors in the developing world.[88] Developing national defence sectors increases the capacity of states to address security threats. Otherwise known as defence sector reform, the defence development approach claims that underdeveloped defence sectors "endanger neighboring states, contaminate domestic politics and markets, engage in transnational crimes, such as piracy and maritime terrorism, and even fail in their assigned mission: to provide adequate national security".[89] In this context, defence development is inextricably linked with economic and political development. Successful reform in the national defence sector in the developing world can facilitate economic growth and good governance as well as promote regional and international security. Thus, international donor agencies and development organisations are urged to make defence an integral part of their overall development agenda. Defence development can enhance national capacities of Southeast Asian states to address not only maritime threats but also other threats to their security.

Conclusion

Piracy and maritime terrorism will continue to plague Southeast Asian waters if the root causes of their conduct are not effectively addressed. If national capacities to combat piracy and maritime terrorism are not built in the littoral states of Southeast Asia, these maritime security threats may escalate as the recent increase in piracy attacks in Southeast Asia shows. However, piracy and maritime terrorism are just two of the many maritime security concerns in Southeast Asia. The comprehensiveness and complexity of maritime security concerns in the region are gargantuan challenges that Southeast Asia countries have to face in the years to come. Thus, assistance of major powers is needed to increase the capacity of littoral states to address their maritime security concerns and the development of the defence sectors, which includes force modernisation, of the affected Southeast Asian countries is one way to enhance the national capacity to combat the transnational security challenges that have already risen and may yet arise in the future. The development of the defence sectors also has the secondary effect of boosting national confidence and stronger national confidence can open the gate for greater regional and international security cooperation without the anxiety of sacrificing national sovereignty.

Notes

1. ARF Statement on "Cooperation against Piracy and other Threats to Maritime Security", Phnom Penh, Cambodia, 16–20 June 2003.
2. Ibid.
3. Ibid.
4. Tamara Renee Shie, *Ports in a Storm? The Nexus Between Counterterrorism, Counterproliferation, and Maritime Security in Southeast Asia* (Honolulu: Pacific Forum CSIS, July 2004), p. 1.
5. See S. Enders Wimbush, "Maritime Security in East Asia in 2025: Critical Uncertainties" and Joshua Ho, "Prospective Maritime Challenges in East Asia: A Singaporean Perspective" (papers prepared for presentation for the Conference on Maritime Security in East Asia organized by the Center for Strategic and International Studies and American-Pacific Sealanes Security Institute, Inc., held at Hilton Hawaiian Village, Honolulu, Hawaii, 19–20 January 2004).
6. See Andrew T.H. Tan and J.D. Kenneth Boutin eds., *Non-Traditional Security Issues in Southeast Asia* (Singapore: Select Publshing Pte Ltd., 2001), and Ralf Emmers, *Non-Traditional Security in the Asia Pacific: The Dynamics of Securitization* (Singapore: Eastern Universities Press, 2004).

7. Shie, p. 33.
8. Mark Valencia, "International Cooperation in Anti-Piracy Efforts in Asia: Some Considerations", available at http://www.apan-info.net/maritime/key_piracy_view.asp (accessed 27 April 2004).
9. Shie, p. 13.
10. Ibid.
11. Ibid.
12. Dana Robert Dillon, "Piracy in Asia: A Growing Barrier to Maritime Trade", *The Heritage Foundation Backgrounder*, No. 1379 (22 June 2000), p. 2. Also available online at http://www.heritage.org/Research/AsiaandthePacific/BG1379.cfm (accessed 5 August 2004).
13. See Peter Chalk, "Threats to the Maritime Environment: Piracy and Terrorism" (Presented at the RAND Stakeholder Consultation at Ispra, Italy, 28–30 October 2002). Available online at http://www.rand.org/randeurope/news/seacurity/piracyterrorism.chalk.pdf (accessed 16 August 2004).
14. "Asia Piracy Costs $25 bln a year, says experts", *Reuters News Service*, Singapore, 11 December 2002. Also available online at http://www.planetark.com/dailynewsstory.cfm/newsid/18987/newsDate/11-Dec-2002/story.htm (accessed 27 April 2004).
15. Bintan Eric Ellis, "Piracy on the High Seas is on the Rise in Southeast Asia", *Fortune* (29 September 2003). Also avaliable at http://www.singapore-window.org/sw03/030919fo.htm (accessed 27 April 2004).
16. See report of the Organisation for Economic Cooperation and Development, "Price of Increased Maritime Security is Much Lower than Potential Cost of a Major Terror Attack", avaliable at http://www.oecd.org/document/30/0,2340,en_2649_201185_4390494_1_1_1_1,00.html (accessed 27 April 2004).
17. "Asia Lacks Fund and Will to Fight Piracy: US Academic", *Business Times*, 10 March 2004.
18. "Globalization and Poverty in Southeast Asia: NGO Response", available at www.asiacaucus.net.ph/resources/poverty_research.doc (accessed 6 May 2004).
19. For more discussions on this topic, see Stuart W. Smead "A Thesis on Modern Day Piracy", available at http://www.angelfire.com/ga3/tropicalguy/piracymodernday.html (accessed 4 May 2004).
20. "Asia Lacks Fund and Will to Fight Piracy: US Academic", *Business Times*, 10 March 2004.
21. For more discussions, see "Southeast Asia as the Global Center of Marine Biodiversity", available at http://www.pemsea.org/info%20center/articles/tropcsts0797_globlcntrmrnbiodiversity.htm" (accessed 4 May 2004).
22. Cindy Vallar, "The Cost of Modern Piracy", availble at http://www.cindyvallar.com/modern3.html (accessed 4 May 2004).
23. Dillon, p. 1.
24. Ibid.

25. Cdr Jose Renan C. Suarez, "Towards a Navy of Substance: A Modernization Program", *Navy Digest*, Vol. 3, No. 1, January–June 2003, p. 32. Also see Lt. Antonio F. Trillanes, "An Implementation Analysis of the Philippine Navy Modernization Program", *Navy Digest*, Vol. 3, No. 1, January–June 2003, pp. 21–28. Trillanes is one of the principal actors in the July 2003 Oakwood Mutiny. He is presently in military custody awaiting court martial.

26. Dillon, p. 2.

27. Ibid.

28. Hasjim Djalal, "Piracy in Southeast Asia: Indonesian and Regional Responses" (paper prepared for presentation for the Conference on Maritime Security in East Asia organized by the Center for Strategic and International Studies and American–Pacific Sealanes Security Institute, Inc., held at Hilton Hawaiian Village, Honolulu, Hawaii, 19–20 January 2004), p. 6.

29. For more discussions on the author's view on this issue, see Rommel C. Banlaoi, "Security Cooperation and Conflict in Southeast Asia After 9/11" (paper presented at the First Congress of the Asian Political and International Studies Association, 27–30 November 2003, Oriental Hotel, Singapore).

30. Allen V. Estabillo, "RP, Indonesia Want Strong Maritime Security System", *MindaNews*, 16 January 2004.

31. Shie, p. 13.

32. Patrick Goodenough, "Maritime Security Takes Center Stage in SE Asia", *CNSNews.com*, 29 June 2004. Available online at http://www.cnsnews.com/ (accessed 27 July 2004).

33. Ibid.

34. Ibid.

35. Richard Halloran, "Link Between Terrorists, Pirates in SE Asia a Growing Concern", *HonoluluAdvertiser.com*, 7 March 2004. Available online at http://the.honoluluadvertiser.com/article/2004/Mar/07 (accessed on 28 July 2004).

36. Tanner Campbell and Rohan Gunaratna, "Maritime Terrorism, Piracy and Crime", in Rohan Gunaratna, ed., *Terrorism in the Asia Pacific: Threat and Response* (Singapore: Eastern University Press, 2003), p. 72.

37. Zachary Abuza, "Terrorism in Southeast Asia: Keeping al-Qaeda at Bay", *Terrorism Monitor*, Vol. II, No. 9, 6 May 2004, p. 4.

38. Office of Naval Intelligence, *Threats and Challenges to Maritime Security 2020* (US Coast Guard Intelligence Coordination Center, 1 March 1999), Chapter III. Also see electronic version of the report at http://www.fas.org/irp/threat/maritime2020/CHAPTER3.htm.

39. Ibid.

40. H.R. Vitasa and Nararya Soeprapto, "Maritime Sector Developments in ASEAN" (paper presented in the Maritime Policy Seminar organized by the United Nations

Conference on Trade and Development and the Ministry of Communications of Indonesia, Jakarta, 11–13 October 1999).

41. For a good reference on this topic, see John Noer and David Gregory, *Choke-points: Maritime Economic Concerns in Southeast Asia* (Washington DC: National Defence University, 1996).

42. US Pacific Command, "Shipping and Commerce", available at www.pacom. mil/publications/apeu02/s04ship7.pdf (accessed 6 August 2004).

43. Abuza, p. 5.

44. Joshua Ho of the Singapore-based Institute of Defence and Strategic Studies gave this analysis in an interview with the *Economist*. See "Shipping in Southeast: Going for the Jugular", *The Economist* (10 June 2004). Also available at http://www.economist.com/World/asia/displayStory.cfm?story_id=2752802 (accessed 6 August 2004).

45. Michael Richardson, *A Time Bomb for Global Trade: Maritime-Related Terrorism in the Age of Weapons of Mass Destruction* (Singapore: Institute of Southeast Asian Studies, 2004).

46. This is the main theme of the session "The Terrorist Threat to the Maritime Sector in Southeast Asia and the Straits of Malacca", at the International Maritime and Port Security Conference held in Singapore, 4–5 August 2004.

47. John F. Bradford, "Maritime Terror in Southeast Asia: Will the Fire Spread in a Region Already Ablaze?" (paper presented at the International Maritime and Port Security Conference held in Singapore, 4–5 August 2004).

48. "First Sea Lord Warns of Al-Qaeda Plot to Target Merchant Ships", *Lloyd's List Daily News Bulletin*, 5 August 2004. Available at http://www.lloydslist.com/ bulletin (accessed 6 August 2004).

49. Associated Press, "Expert: Al Qaeda Planning Seaborne Attack", *Fox News Channel*, 17 March 2004. Also see "Al Qaeda Planning Seaborne Attack", *Fox News Channel*, 17 March 2004. Available online at http://www.foxnews.com (accessed 6 August 2004).

50. Abuza, p. 5.

51. See "Al-Qaida Plans High-Sea Terror", *WorldNetDaily*, 13 October 2003. Available at http://www.worldnetdaily.com/news/printer-friendly.asp?ARTICLE_ID=35047 (accessed 6 August 2004).

52. Watkins, p. 7.

53. Goodenough, p. 2.

54. See Rommel C. Banlaoi, "Maritime Terrorism in Southeast Asia: The Abu Sayyaf Threat" (unpublished manuscript, 27 May 2004).

55. As of this writing, however, the Philippine government continues to deny the involvement of ASG in the *Superferry 14* explosion.

56. Halloran, p. 1.

57. "Piracy Equals Terrorism on Troubled Waters: Minister", *Agence France Presse*, 21 December 2003.

58. Ibid.

59. Bantarto Bandoro, "When Piracy Becomes Terrorism in the Strait", *The Jakarta Post*, 29 July 2004.

60. Rubert Herbert-Burns and Lauren Zucker, *Malevolent Tide: Fusion and Overlaps in Piracy and Maritime Terrorism* (Washington DC: Maritime Intelligence Group, 30 July 2004), p. 1.

61. For an excellent commentary on the RMSI, see Joshua Ho, "Operationalising the Regional Maritime Security Initiative", *IDSS Commentaries*, 27 May 2004.

62. Testimony of Admiral Thomas B. Fargo, United States Navy Commander US Pacific Command Before the House Armed Services Committee, United States House of Representatives regarding US Pacific Command Posture March 31, 2004. Also available at http://www.pacom.mil/speeches/sst2004/040331housearmedsvcscomm.shtml (accessed 27 July 2004).

63. Shie, p. 23.

64. Goodenough, p. 2.

65. "Regional Maritime Security Initiative (RMSI): The Idea, The Fact", avaliable at http://www.pacom.mil/rmsi/ (accessed 28 July 2004).

66. Ibid.

67. Shie, p. 23.

68. Ho, p. 1.

69. Rommel C. Banlaoi, "Regional Cooperation Against Maritime Terrorism and Proliferation in Southeast Asia" (discussion paper presented at the Conference on Maritime Security in East Asia organized by the Center for Strategic and International Studies and American-Pacific Sealanes Security Institute, Inc., held at Hilton Hawaiian Village, Honolulu, Hawaii, 19–20 January 2004).

70. Joon Nam Mak, "Piracy in Southeast Asia: Priorities, Perspectives and the Hierarchy of Interests" (paper prepared for presentation for the Conference on Maritime Security in East Asia organized by the Center for Strategic and International Studies and American-Pacific Sealanes Security Institute, Inc., held at Hilton Hawaiian Village, Honolulu, Hawaii, 19–20 January 2004), p. 1.

71. Andrew Tan, "Force Modernization Trends in Southeast Asia", IDSS Working Paper, No. 59, January 2004, p. 1.

72. Ibid. p. 37.

73. For an excellent analysis of conventional military balance in Southeast Asia, see Anthony H. Cordesman, *The Conventional Military Balance in Southeast Asia: An Analytic Overview: A Comparative Summary of Military Expenditure; Manpower; Land, Air, and Naval, Forces; and Arms Sales* (Washington DC: Center for Strategic and International Studies, 27 February 2000). Also see Sheldon Simon, "Asian Armed Forces: Internal and External Tasks and Capabilities", *NBR Analysis*, Vol. 11, No. 1, 2000, pp. 1–19, and Derek Da Cunha, "ASEAN Naval Power in the New Millennium" in Jack McCaffire and Alan Hinge, eds., *Sea Power in*

the New Century: Maritime Operations in the Asia Pacific Beyond 2000 (Canberra: Australian Defence Studies Centre, 1998), pp. 73–83.

74. See Rommel C. Banlaoi, "The Role of Philippine–American Relations in the Global Campaign Against Terrorism: Implications for Regional Security", *Contemporary Southeast Asia*, Vol. 24, No. 2, August 2002, pp. 294–312. Also see Larry Niksch, "Abu Sayyaf: Target of Philippine–US Anti-Terrorism Cooperation", CRS Report for Congress, 25 January 2002.

75. The Philippine Department of National Defence (DND) and United States Army in the Asia Pacific (USARPAC) co-hosted a strategic planning workshop at Oakwood Premier Ayala Center on 5–7 March 2002. As a followthrough, the DND, USARPAC and the Australian Department of Defence conducted another workshop at Oakwood Premier Ayala Center on 6–8 August 2002. The purpose of this workshop was to learn the best practices in defence planning, programming and budgeting of the US, Australia and the Philippines. To make defence procurement as an integral part of the annual DND planning, programming and budgeting, the three countries held another workshop on defence acquisition system at Oakwood on 3–5 December 2002. The workshop identified some constraints in defence procurement system in the Philippines. The three countries held another workshop on 9–11 December 2003 at Oakwood to exchange ideas on career management system. On 13–15 July 2004, the three countries held the trilateral strategic defence capability planning symposium.

76. Rommel C. Banlaoi, "Broadening Philippine–Australia Defence Relations in the Post 9/11 Era: Issues and Prospects", *Contemporary Southeast Asia*, Vol. 25, No. 3, December 2003, pp. 482–483.

77. Pamela Sodhy, "US–Malaysian Relations During the Bush Administration: The Political, Economic, and Security Aspects", *Contemporary Southeast Asia*, Vol. 25, No. 3, December 2003, pp. 363–386.

78. International Crisis Group, "Resuming US–Indonesia Military Ties", *Indonesia Briefing*, 21 May 2002. Also see Reyko Huang, "Priority Dilemmas: US–Indonesia Military Relations in the Anti-Terror War", Center for Defence Information Terrorism Project, 23 May 2002.

79. Anthony L. Smith, "A Glass Half Full: Indonesia–US Relations in the Age of Terror", *Contemporary Southeast Asia*, Vol. 25, No. 3, December 2003, pp. 449–472.

80. Shie, p. 31.

81. Masahiro Akiyama, "Prospect for Change in the Maritime Security Situation in Asia and the Role of Japan" (paper read at the IIPS International Conference on Maritime Security in Southeast and Southwest Asia, 11–13 December 2001, Ana Hotel, Tokyo, Japan), available at http://www.iips.org/Akiyama_paper.pdf (accessed on 29 July 2004).

82. Lee Kim Chew, "China Could Play Part in ASEAN's Maritime Security", *Strait Times*, 24 June 2004.

83. See Lee Jae-Hyung, "China's Expanding Maritime Ambitions in the Western Pacific and Indian Ocean", *Contemporary Southeast Asia*, Vol. 24, No. 3, December 2002, pp. 549–568.

84. Rommel C. Banlaoi, "Southeast Asian Perspectives on the Rise of China: Regional Security After 9/11", *Parameters: US Army War College Quarterly*, Vol. 33, No. 2, Summer 2003, pp. 98–107.

85. Commonwealth of Australia, *Australian Maritime Doctrine* (Canberra: Commonwealth of Australia, 2000).

86. Commonwealth of Australia, *Transnational Terrorism: The Threat to Australia* (Canberra: Commonwealth of Australia, 2004), p. 94.

87. Satu Limaye, "India's Relations with Southeast Asia Take a Wing", *Southeast Asian Affairs 2003* (Singapore: Institute of Southeast Asian Studies, 2003), p. 50.

88. Rand Corporation, "Defence Development: A New Approach to Reforming Defence Sectors in the Developing World", *Research Brief*, 2004. Available online at http://www.rand.org (accessed on 5 August 2004).

89. David C. Gompert, Olga Oliker, and Anga Timilsina, "Clean, Lean and Able: A Strategy for Defence Development", RAND Occasional Paper, No. 101, January 2004, p. 2.

Chapter 4

Regional Maritime Dynamics in Southern Asia in the 21st Century

W. Lawrence S. Prabhakar

Introduction

Southern Asia and the Indian Ocean region constitutes a pivotal geo-strategic space of competitive and cooperative maritime security that features the contending factors and forces in a regional naval buildup and extra-regional naval forces posture.

The inter-regional maritime dynamics are governed by the evolution of maritime forces as a significant arm of the armed forces of the South Asian states. The strategic significance of the region is evident from the emergent missions, new doctrines and technologies that are being evolved by the regional navies and the growing capabilities of the extra-regional naval forces. The extra-regional maritime dynamics are premised on the competitive force postures of the extra-regional navies deployed for the tasks of regional power projection; securing of geo-energy reserves and the associated sea lines of communication (SLOCs) security related to energy supplies; and sea-based nuclear deterrence. The last task is evident in the nuclear navies of the extra-regional naval powers that optimally exploit the salience of nuclear-powered and nuclear-armed naval assets for power projection in the region and the emergence of missile defences.

The Southern Asian region in its interface with Indian Ocean region has a strategic significance and contiguity with West Asia, East Africa and South East Asia.

The colonial and the postcolonial perceptions of maritime power have influenced the evolving architecture and doctrine relating to maritime security. Significantly, the Cold War and the post-Cold War regional dynamics evident in the bilateral alliances and the regional tensions has been catalytic in the evolution of naval power in the region.

The entry of the extra-regional navies into the region began with the second Cold War in the 1970s. The India–Pakistan War in 1971 was a watershed event in this regard. It witnessed significant naval engagements of the two navies with the sinking of the Pakistani submarine *PNS Ghazi* in an encounter in the Bay of Bengal. It also witnessed the dispatch of the US Carrier Task Force with the US nuclear carrier *USS Enterprise* in an apparent measure of US support to Pakistan. The *USS Enterprise* mission has been regarded by India as a measure of nuclear intimidation and has often been quoted as one of the secondary factors for its nuclear options. The post-Cold War era and the regional events following the 9/11 incidents and the Second Gulf War have transformed the maritime space of the Indian Ocean and the heartland of Afghanistan into the theatre of US-led coalition operations.

The regional maritime dynamics of Southern Asia can be defined in terms of five factors:

1. The geo-strategic significance of the Southern Asian region emerging as a zone of conflict as well as a zone of resources astride the Indian Ocean region. The South Asian region has regional contiguities with West Asia, and Central Asia; China through the land interface; and South East Asia through the maritime interface.
2. The maritime strategic significance of the Southern Asian region is due to its contiguity with the Indian Ocean region and the SLOCs that lie astride the region with its huge volume of oceanic trade of energy and other merchandise transacted through the region.
3. The Indian Ocean region and the Southern Asian region with its expansive littoral space provides substantial scope for maritime access and basing in the region. Maritime access and anti-access are vital issues in the case of extra-regional navies vying for access and influence.
4. The region's nuclear developments and the penchant to evolve sea-based nuclear deterrence in the long term is evident in the naval modernisation

plans of India, Pakistan and China. Nuclear and missile deployments by India and Pakistan has propelled the region into a competitive template between the regional nuclear/missile powers and have enhanced the risks of crisis escalation prompting extra-regional diplomatic and military intervention. Nuclear and missile deployments of the regional powers have also heightened initiatives by the extra-regional powers to counter proliferation and this is evident in the evolution of missile defences in the region.

5. The stakes of the extra-regional naval presence are premised on the missions of regional power projection through littoral dominance strategies; securing of hydrocarbon energy reserves; SLOC security; sea-based nuclear deterrence evident in the deployment of nuclear-powered and nuclear-armed naval assets by extra-regional powers in the region; and the emergent missile defence capabilities.

Trends in Southern Asian Regional Maritime Balance

Southern Asia has been a pivotal region since the beginning of the 20th century. The Southern Asian region and the Indian Ocean were variously regarded at different points in time: as an imperial territory and as a colonial lake; as an area for colonial basing and expansion during the pre-1945 period; in the 1950s and 1960s it was a region for colonial domination and of interest to the United States. The 1970s was a period of emergent superpower interest, with the British naval forces exiting from the East of Suez region resulting in the dominance of the United States and the Soviet Union until the late 1970s and 1980. The Indian Ocean as a Zone of Peace and Regional Cooperation was vigorously promoted in the late 1980s and 1990s by several littoral states with a predominant South Asian endorsement.

With the end of the Cold War, Southern Asia and the Indian Ocean have emerged as areas of geo-economic and geo-strategic significance, given the enormous energy and natural resources of the region. The impact of globalisation in the post-Cold War era has the promise and potential for further regional economic development. In the 21st century, the Southern Asia–Indian Ocean region would be a critical strategic geographic hub for emergent power rivalries, power transitions, emergent asymmetric conflicts and significant geo-economic and geo-energy stakes in the adjoining West Asian and Central Asian Regions.

In the geo-economic sense, the United Nations Convention on the Law of the Sea (UNCLOS) treaty endowed a new significance to resource-based interests with an enhanced sense of competition for resources for the countries of the region. The premium on exploitation of oil, gas and offshore minerals, fishing, harnessing of thermal, wave and tidal energy are some spheres of new interests. Resources in the Exclusive Economic Zone (EEZ) are considered as an extension to those on land. India has a huge 2.2 million square kilometers of EEZ as its maritime resources enclave and thus it has a dominant position in the region.

There are varying levels of competitive bilateral and multilateral rivalries and relationships that are evident in the first decade of the 21st century and the persistence of this phenomenon is likely to continue. Four points are worth considering:

1. Extra-regional powers with their alliances and coalitions in the Indian Ocean region are in the quest for access and basing facilities with the strategic objectives of gaining littoral access and regional access to the geo-energy and geo-resource points. South Asia offers littoral access to the Central Asian region. The maritime strategic dimension of littoral dominance is pivoted on a neo-Mahan paradigm of gaining access to the rim land with a view of access to the heartland in the region.

    The alliances have been substantive in scope with long-term interests in economic and strategic matters. The United States, the United Kingdom, France and China have been prominent in their endeavour to nurture regional alliances and coalitions, and establishing a substantial forward presence to stake their strategic and geo-economic interests. The systemic implications of these alliances have been evident in the exacerbated regional tensions in the Indian Ocean region amongst the regional and littoral states as they engage in high-intensity competition.

2. The power rivalries in the region have given the regional powers immense strategic significance by virtue of their geo-strategic location. Regional countries like India, Pakistan and Iran straddle the Indian Ocean rim and thus enjoy strategic spatial significance. Regional powers do exert leverage in terms of their potential to offer basing and access facilities. The regional states of Southern Asia — India, Pakistan, Sri Lanka, Bangladesh and the Maldives — enjoy substantial maritime access facilities and basing facilities and hence are potential hosts to extra-regional naval presence.

3. There has been significant bilateral and multilateral economic and security exchanges between the regional and the extra-regional powers in the nurture of their enclaves of interest in order to sustain their access and stakes in the region. The primary concern of all the extra-regional powers has been their interest in protecting and securing their SLOCs, as they constitute the predominant slice of their trade, aiding their growth and development and regarded as the umbilical cord of their existence.

4. Extra-regional powers like the United States have developed strategies of littoral dominance premised on maritime–air power projection capabilities. The evolution of these capabilities are in tune with counter-proliferation objectives, the securing of geo-energy interests and the tackling of the asymmetric threat of terrorism that has emerged in the region. Extra-regional naval presence and intervention capabilities go along with an evolving system of strategic alliances and coalitions.

These trends predominate, influence and drive the regional maritime dynamics, and the force structures and trends of modernisation in the region. The significance of the extra-regional naval presence and the operational capabilities are balanced by the developments in the inter-regional maritime dynamics that have witnessed constant efforts in modernisation.

Inter-regional Maritime Forces: Balance and Order

The nature and dynamics of the inter-regional arms race and the balance of forces constitutes a significant dimension. The Indian Navy dominates the inter-regional maritime forces order. Its evolving capabilities and operational doctrines are in terms of sea-control and sea-denial capabilities along with limited power projection capabilities. The analysis of the inter-regional maritime order of battle (ORBAT) would be based on capabilities and likely strategies to be adopted.

The Indian naval ORBAT in the 21st century would be a dominant regional navy with a carrier task force centred around a light aircraft carrier/Air Defence Ship along with the assortment of seven to eight destroyers, 17 frigates, 18 submarines, 23 corvettes of various sizes and capabilities, and assorted naval-air arm of *MiG-29ks*, *Jaguar* Maritime strike aircraft, *MiG-27s*, *Sea Harriers*, *Sea Kings* ASW strike rotor craft, *Ka-27/28* and the *Ka-31* AEW.[1]

In the hierarchy of the inter-regional naval ORBAT, the second rung would be the Pakistani Navy premised on largely sea denial roles with anti-shipping missile inventories. The Pakistan Navy has missions to keep its sea lanes open from the Gulf of Oman to the Persian Gulf and other global destinations. Pakistan's access in this regard is limited and hence its interests are driven in nurturing a cooperative security partnership with regional powers in the region, excluding India. Pakistan has its EEZ in the Northern Arabian Sea for its exploitation of sea-based resources.

The Pakistani Naval ORBAT in the 21st century would be about six conventional submarines of the *Agosta* class and the newer *Scorpene* Air Independent Propulsion submarines for its outer perimeter of maritime defence, three midget submarines for littoral defence, nine destroyers, six frigates (Type-21 ex-UK), plus the new acquisitions of the ex-Chinese *Jiangwei II* frigates along with its naval-air arm of 12 *Mirage IIIs*, two to three *Atlantic* LRMP/strike, two *Orion P3C*, five *Fokker 27*s, six *Sea Kings* and three *Lynx* ASW.[2]

The Pakistani naval strategy would be to avoid the Indian blockade and entanglement of naval assets in Karachi that it had encountered in previous wars with India and most recently during the 1999 Kargil War. It would prefer the dispersal of its naval assets to new bases or locations to avoid the Indian naval blockade. In its efforts to develop new ports and bases, Pakistan has been developing the Gwadar port with Chinese technical assistance. The extensive naval infrastructure numbering 23 piers in the Gwadar port would be a site of alternate naval deployments for Pakistan.[3] In terms of its nuclear deterrent options at sea, there have been Pakistani attempts to equip its submarines with cruise missiles and to deploy submarine versions of its Medium Range Ballistic Missiles *Shaheen I and II*, which are deployed on board their surface vessels.[4] How effective this deployment would be is questionable. There have been attempts to miniaturise Pakistan's nuclear warheads to fit into the Harpoon missiles, but the results of these attempts have been inconclusive.

Indian and Pakistani navies apart, the other navies of Southern Asia are those of Sri Lanka, Bangladesh and the Maldives. They represent the typical coastal brown water capable units and are mainly focused on the primary duties of coast guard, customs and EEZ protection.

The Bangladesh Navy has not been affected by the post-Cold War restructuring and its traditional maritime roles have persisted. Its missions have been the protection of its national territorial sovereignty and integrity, the protection of its maritime and riverine trade, the protection of its EEZ and its continental shelf, and deterring the growing naval power of Myanmar to its east. In terms of its operational strategy, the Bangladesh Navy pursues a sea-denial strategy of about four missile-armed frigates, ten fast attack craft-missile, eight fast attack craft-torpedo, four large offshore patrol craft and a coast guard of ten light force craft, and about five minesweepers. Bangladesh is also seeking *Jiangwei* class frigates from China.

The Bangladesh Navy has been in joint naval manoeuvres with Pakistani and Myanmarese naval units in the adjoining waters of the North Andaman Sea in 2001.[5] There has been close Bangladesh–China collaboration resulting in Chinese naval arms transfers and new endeavours in joint naval manoeuvres with China. China's nurturing of Bangladesh has been with a view to securing its access into the Bay of Bengal. To China, Bangladesh would be a vital access and basing location for its listening posts to eavesdrop on Indian naval developments and would provide access facilities should China require to surge across the Straits of Malacca into the Indian Ocean.

The Sri Lankan navy sits astride the major sea routes of the north-central Indian Ocean. Given its limited resources and its internal war with its focused land operations, the maritime dimension of the war has been the prosecution of the maritime low intensity conflict with the Liberation Tigers of Tamil Eelam (LTTE), a violent non-state actor with substantial naval capabilities.

Sri Lanka pursues a strategy of sea-denial and littoral defence and has been engaged in limited amphibious operations in its east coast. It has also been engaging in the limited naval interdiction of the LTTE's convoys, with no decisive results. The Sri Lankan Navy battle order consists of ten fast attack craft, two LCU/infantry large *Shanghai* class, three LCU/infantry *Yunnan* class, and *Wuhu-A class* medium from China, four FAC from France, 12 *Super Dvora-MK II* from Israel, three *Sheldog* class LCU medium from Singapore and four *Killer* class from South Korea. It has also decided to acquire two *Sukanya* class Indian Offshore Patrol Vessels along with three *Chetak* light helicopters. The Sri Lankan navy lacks the naval-air arm that would be a requisite in low-intensity maritime operations.

The Maldives Navy has a micro-naval establishment with the primary duties of patrolling its EEZ and containing possible outbreaks of low-intensity maritime conflict. The Maldives Navy has six patrol craft — one FPB *Fairey Marine* class, one *Daggar* FPB, one *Cheverton* FPB and three *Tracker II* FPBs. Given its small size and economy, the Maldives cannot afford a substantial defence capability and has to solicit assistance from India.

Given the wide disparities in the inter-regional naval ORBAT, the inter-regional competition and rivalry is between the dominant powers of Southern Asia: India and Pakistan, with its extension to the naval domain.

Southern Asia is also the convergent market for substantial arms sales from the extra-regional powers. The extra-regional powers seek access and basing facilities in the region on a reciprocal basis. Pakistan has been known to be the hub of transfers of weapons of mass destruction (WMD) in the region, with much of the trade through the maritime space in the region.[6]

The nature of the inter-regional arms race has been asymmetric. The regional littoral powers have been engaged in the buildup of forces and capabilities that has produced a cascade effect in the destabilisation of the region.

The India–Pakistan arms buildup is the most comprehensive arms buildup that has led to wars and triggered periodic crisis escalations. The nature of arms buildup and racing is across the spectrum of forces and capabilities: conventional, chemical, biological, nuclear and missile sectors. The India–Pakistan arms dynamic would be a critical and destabilising factor in the Indian Ocean region and the implications are quite evident even as they have been competing in submarine acquisition and building programmes.

In pursuit of its sea-denial capabilities, Pakistan is interested in acquiring French *Scorpene* and the newer *Agosta 90B* Class submarines.[7] The prospect of India and Pakistan engaging in naval arms racing and equipping themselves with platforms like the French *Scorpeone* class, the *Agosta* class and the Russian EKM 877 *Kilo* class platforms is quite high.[8] The Indian deployment of its nuclear-powered submarine has been on the cards, with either cruise or ballistic missile capabilities. The prospect of such deployment would further spurn the naval arms race with China's deployment of the Type 093 nuclear-powered attack submarines, with cruise missile capabilities.[9]

The India–Pakistan naval arms race would feature the continual technological modernisation of their respective capabilities and operational parameters. The Pakistani buildup has already been substantially aided by Chinese technical and economic support, which has ranged from the transfer of military hardware, missiles, and naval equipment to infrastructure development.

In assessment, the Pakistani naval-based threat to India will be modest though substantial progress in acquiring the new *Agosta* class submarines has been made. The deployment of submarines with Air Independent Propulsion (AIP) technologies would provide longer submerged endurance, providing Pakistan with longer sea presence.

The prospective Chinese naval ORBAT in the Southern Asian–Indian Ocean region would be to deploy a Carrier Battle Group (CVBG) by late 2020 with its flotilla having access to Myanmar. The likelihood of the PLA-Navy CVBG being able to transit the Straits of Malacca into the Andaman Sea is a real possibility.

It is also possible for China to have an air cover for the PLA-Navy CVBG by forward basing some of its land-based SU-MKK 30s in Myanmar. However, there are no signs that this has happened. The CVBG, if deployed, would have the naval versions of the SU-27s deployed on board the PLA-Navy carrier along with its complement of fixed wing attack and anti-submarine rotary aircraft of the Ka-50 class.

China's access in the region would be through Pakistan and Myanmar, who are its dependable regional allies. While there are inherent limitations for an independent Chinese carrier group operating in the Indian Ocean, there is the prospect of Chinese nuclear attack/ballistic submarines operating from Gwadar and Ormara in the Pakistani coast. The prospect of Chinese nuclear submarines in the Northern Arabian Sea heightens Indian apprehensions. There is the prospect of Chinese nuclear submarines operating in the North Andaman Sea in the vicinity of the Myanmarese waters, with its repercussions for India. These developments and possibilities would lead to Indian responses, fueling the regional arms race. Thus, the India–Pakistan–China security complex and arms race is a triangular inter-regional arms buildup that would have a significant destabilising impact on the region.[10]

Having analysed the inter-regional maritime forces and balance, the analysis will now focus on the roles and postures of the extra-regional navies and their specific missions.

Extra-regional Maritime Forces: Missions and Roles

The prospective patterns of maritime balance in the 21st century in the Southern Asian–Indian Ocean region would be highly competitive in nature. The extra-regional navies would be engaged in alliance formations with regional navies in the quest to seek cooperative security in the region.[11] Cooperative security could have a significant role tailored to the region's uniqueness that vary from conventional perceptions. The following patterns of cooperative security roles are evident.

1. *Strategic Partnerships.* Strategic partnerships are formed by extra-regional navies and their regional naval partners. An example is the India–US naval interest in the region that is no longer viewed as threatening but as having evolved through maritime cooperation.
2. *Inter-dependent Maritime Relationships.* Extra-regional navies in independent deployment of their naval assets endeavour for bilateral maritime partnerships that are premised on the quest to establish a regional power profile. These navies seek partnerships with regional navies for access, and reciprocate in terms of infrastructure projects and the transfer of conventional arms. Examples are the Sino–Pakistan alliance and the Sino–Myanmarese naval alliance.
3. *Quest for Maritime Autonomy.* Regional navies in their maritime domains that would like to zealously preserve their *maritime autonomy* and would resist extra-regional maritime hegemony of the region. An example is Iran.
4. *Quest for Maritime Countervailing Capabilities.* Regional navies are developing modest yet optimal second-strike nuclear strategic capabilities to deter hostile powers with the emphasis on nuclear-tipped cruise missiles.

Examples are India's *Sagarika* on board the ATV and Israel's *Popeye Turbo* cruise missiles on board its Dolphins.

5. *Emergent Maritime Reconnaissance Surveillance ASW Capabilities.* Maritime reconnaissance, surveillance and anti-submarine warfare capabilities are bound to increase with the introduction of the extra-regional aerial and missile platforms, viz: the Harpoon Block III anti-ship missiles, SS-N-22 *Sunburns/Moskits* on Chinese naval platforms such as the *Soveremenyys* and the Indian *Brahmos* anti-ship cruise missiles. Maritime reconnaissance capabilities and anti-submarine warfare capabilities of the inter-regional and extra-regional forces are likely to grow with the new Maritime Reconnaissance and Anti-Submarine Warfare aircraft, which could be in the form of *P3C Orions* or the updated *TU-142s* that are being deployed in the region.

6. *Submarine Order of Battle.* The submarine ORBAT of the Indian Ocean region powers would be in the order of *EKM 636/877* class, and *Kilo* class in the Indian, Iranian and Chinese PLA-Navy, the *Agosta* 90B class submarines with the Pakistani navy and the *Dolphin* class with the Israeli navy constituting the conventional submarine forces. In the nuclear realm the Indian ATV would have been deployed by 2008. The PLA Navy would have deployed its Type 093 nuclear attack and Cruise missile platforms in the Indian Ocean that would be joined by its Fleet Ballistic Missile Submarine of the Type 094 class SSBN with JL-2 submarine-launched ballistic missiles (SLBMs) in regular patrol station in the Indian Ocean.

The extra-regional nuclear submarine forces of the United States would be dominant with their *SSN-688 Los Angeles* class, *SSN-774 Virginia* class and the *SSN-21 Sea Wolf* class. Extra-regional submarines like the French *Scorpene* class submarines would also be in service with the Indian and Pakistan navies with AIP technologies, with enhanced endurance, and equipped with Land Attack Cruise Missiles (LACM).

Naval Access and Naval Basing

The second context would be the trends of naval basing and access facilities in the post-Cold War era. While there has been the complete receding of Russian naval power, it has been matched with the gradual ascendancy of new players in the region, significantly India and China, who have emerged with new autonomous roles in their respective maritime domains. The 21st century would witness the contending and competing roles of the Indian and Chinese PLA-Navy forces from maritime areas contiguous to Australia and the Straits of Malacca to the entire swath of the Indian Ocean all the way to the Straits of Hormuz along the Arabian Sea to East Africa.

India had envisioned its maritime domain from the Straits of Hormuz to the Straits of Malacca and the South China Sea in its policy declarations. The competitive maritime balance in the region would envisage the deployment of the PLA-Navy ships in the Bay of Bengal–Indian Ocean–Arabian Sea contiguous areas. India's capabilities is with its surface and sub-surface platforms and its access points in the Andaman and Nicobar Islands, where its Far-Eastern Naval Command is located. The Western and South Western Naval facilities in Mumbai, Karwar, Cochin, Trivandrum and the Lakshwadeep Islands also provide for its offshore reach and basing for its regional power projection.[12]

China's zest to expand into the Indian Ocean with sustained and dedicated platforms may be far fetched at the moment but its growing capabilities in new platforms are evident in the numbers and quality that are evolving to be a formidable force posture. China has been nurturing viable maritime naval alliances with Myanmar, Bangladesh and Pakistan in the form of collaborative maritime infrastructure development through the building of naval air stations, upgraded SIGINT/ELINT facilities and piers for the large container ships of COSCO (China Overseas Shipping Corporation), which is the logistics arm of the PLA-Navy.

In December 2001, Premier Zhu Rongji visited the Maldives with a view to expand Chinese ties and negotiate agreements to build new ports and access facilities in the Maldives for visitation and access rights for the PLA-Navy ships and China's Ocean Merchant Marine. This access would have provided China with a vital foothold in the Indian Ocean space and could have enabled it to network with its access in Karachi in Pakistan. However, the bid to secure the facilities has not been successful. China has been engaged in naval diplomacy of port calls and naval exercises with the navies of South Asia for a long time with a view to nurture relations and ensure access to facilities for the PLA-Navy should it want to deploy into the Indian Ocean region.

The US Fifth Fleet is firmly nested in Diego Garcia in the Chagos archipelago/British Indian Ocean Territory that is the hub of its Central Command. Their access to Trincomalee in Sri Lanka provides the vantage position into the Bay of Bengal and the Straits of Malacca region. The United States has been expanding its naval access facilities in the region for its operations in the post 9/11 period in Djibouti, Yemen, Oman, Pakistan, India and Sri Lanka. The French have basing rights in Djibouti with their standing naval force. The British have their own operational arrangements and the deployments of their nuclear attack submarines and surface warships have been in conjunction with the US Fifth Fleet. The US–UK naval deployments in the Afghan theatre of operations signify the symbiotic and synergistic arrangements with the United States in Diego Garcia.

The Australians have also shown interest in the region and their naval deployments and access coordinates operate within the overall US-led Western naval armada in the region in the contexts of Operation Enduring Freedom and the Second Gulf War. The Japanese are the new players in the region with their entry in the context of Operation Enduring Freedom and in the post-conflict stabilisation process in Iraq. Units of the Japanese Maritime Self Defence Force and the engineer corps of the Japanese Self Defence Forces have been engaged in reconstruction work in Iraq. The Japanese sensitivity to the vulnerabilities of their oil-SLOCs and their commitments to the US-led coalition are factors for their new naval activism east of the Straits of Malacca.

Sea-based Nuclear Missile Arsenals in the Region

The third context of the Southern Asian–Indian Ocean maritime balance is the roles of the extra-regional nuclear navies in terms of their postures and influence in the Indian Ocean littoral. The range of nuclear weapons deployed in the region include an assortment of SLBMs of the D-5 Trident class that form part of the US Fifth Fleet, which is under the aegis of the US CENTCOM, the French and the British Fleet Ballistic missile submarine forces (SSBNs) and the nuclear-powered and cruise missile attack submarines.

The PLA-Navy has also been deploying its nuclear fleet ballistic submarines. In the 1990s, China had occasionally deployed its *Xia* class SSBN in the Arabian Sea region equipped with the JL-1 SLBM. Its improved Type 094 SSBN and JL-2 SLBMs are now being readied for deployment.[13] The nuclearisation of the Indian Ocean region is a reality with the regular presence of these platforms deployed with the primary intents and goals of establishing forward presence and peacetime engagement. The objective of the extra-regional powers would therefore be for the sustenance of a forward presence and posture to dissuade hostile acts and deter potential and actual WMD threats from emerging in the region against their interests.

For example, the US Navy has its new SIOP-4 War Plan (Single Integrated Operations Plan-4), which was operational since October 2003 and provides for a flexible retargeting strategy. The SIOP-4 War Plan is the product of the US Nuclear Posture Review 2002 and allows for the use of US nuclear weapons to missions other than its continental defence. This posture signals an abandoning of its earlier negative security assurances and shows that the United States is priming for contingency operations in the region.[14] The SIOP-4 would provide for the SLBM retargeting system against the hostile regional adversaries of the United States, should the escalation of the regional crisis cross the nuclear threshold.

Sea-based Nuclear Strike and Intervention Capabilities

The fourth context would be the independent intervening capabilities of littoral and hinterland states in the Indian Ocean region. Israel is one power that has been formulating strategic plans to develop a forward presence of its submarines in the Red Sea (Bab-el-Mandab) in joint operations with its Air Force in interdiction strikes against Iranian targets. Israel is also developing intervention capabilities in land battles by Special Forces with air support and advanced PGMs (Precision Guided Munitions) in the region.

Israel anticipates graphic increases in the quantum of WMD threats and proposes to devote up to 30 percent of its strategic nuclear weapons, comprising the Jericho II & III IRBM platforms, to aim at interior targets in excess of 300 km inside Iran. Israel's partner in Africa, Eritrea, has allowed Israeli naval access to Asmara at the entrance of the Red Sea, which would give Israel good vantage points from which to strike at Iranian targets.[15]

Israel has tested its Popeye Turbo Cruise Missile capabilities from its Dolphin submarines at the coast off Sri Lanka, in May 2000. This is an indication of its emergent submarine strike capability with the possibility of introducing and deploying nuclear tipped Cruise Missiles of the Tomahawk variety in land attack missions.

Iran has also been developing countervailing capabilities against Israel. The Iranian Shahab-3 missiles have been test fired in response to Israel's *Shavit* launchers. The Iranian nuclear programme is yet another source of proliferation and the possibility that Iranian nuclear payloads on the *Shahab* series of missiles are targeting Israel or even Diego Garcia, with conventional payloads on an extended Shahab series, adds to the emergent crisis escalation template in the IOR.[16]

Maritime Expeditionary Capabilities in the Region

The fifth context would be the impact of the deployed Marine Expeditionary Forces (MEFs) in the region in 2020. Their viability and operational effectiveness would be crucial for the stay of the extra-regional navies in the region. The mode of deployment would be offshore in maritime prepositioned ships and onshore in naval bases or facilities. The United States would have the largest of the offshore deployments in the form of Marine Expeditionary Brigades for power projection. The US Conventional Forces Realignment in August 2004 has envisioned such plans. The US MEFs would be based on the evolving naval doctrines of the US Navy Sea Power 21 ably supported by air logistics.

A modest Chinese deployment of expeditionary forces in the Myanmarese facilities is a possibility that cannot be ruled out in 2020. The development of Special Forces by India would have its Marine component for possible roles in its Far Eastern Naval Command, based in the Andaman and Nicobar islands, for possible deployment in the Western naval theatre also. The deployments would reinforce the rationale of forward presence and enhance intervention capabilities. The capabilities of intervention of the extra-regional forces of the United States, the United Kingdom and France would be substantial. In terms of individual forces, the US forces are formidable with comprehensive maritime capabilities in the form of standing maritime pre-positioned forces afloat on sea-lift ships, comprehensive, precision-attack platforms with net-centric warfare capabilities that would entail sea strike operations to exert direct, decisive and sustained influence in joint campaigns.[17]

The MEF will be capable of persistent intelligence, surveillance and reconnaissance; time-sensitive strike; ship-to-objective manoeuvre; information operations; and covert strike to deliver devastating power and accuracy in future campaigns. The MEF would also feature effects-based striking power, and increased precision attack and Information Warfare operations.

Sea-based Theatre Missile Defences in the Region

The sixth context would be the feasibility and operational impact of sea-based theatre missile defences (TMDs) deployed to thwart regional ballistic missiles with WMD/nuclear payloads. Such TMDs are deployed on board the Arleigh Burke class destroyers and AEGIS cruisers. The obvious implication of substantial sea-based TMD deployments in the Indian Ocean region would be to target and neutralise the regional nuclear arsenals with ballistic missile inventories in the MRBM/IRBM and extended IRBM ranges. The sea-based Navy Theatre Wide (NTW) systems would be primarily oriented against missiles launched from the states of concern that would be to intercept missiles as early as possible in flight before countermeasures are dispersed and allow time for secondary attempts.

Sea-based missile defence systems provide for mobility and flexibility, and shipboard systems enable a new dimension of power projection ability premised on an offence–defence technology template.[18] Sea-based missile defence systems offer the advantage of mobility in that it makes the defensive missile system less vulnerable to a preemptive strike and allows for adaptation on a flexible scale. It also allows for offshore basing without having to deploy in land territory that is vulnerable to preemptive ballistic missile strikes and the political consequences of deploying missile defences in allied territory. The Indian Ocean region would thus emerge as a significant region for the deployment of missile defence systems in view of the regional nuclear missile arsenals.

Evolving Patterns of Alliances and Coalitions in Southern Asia

The evolving matrices of alliances and coalitions in the Southern Asia–Indian Ocean region circa 2020 would be one of complex interdependence. The nature of interdependence would be driven by geo-economic considerations, energy-dependent profiles and the competitive dynamics of the markets of the littoral and regional countries in the region. With the failure of the IOR-ARC (Indian Ocean Region-Association for Regional Cooperation in the 1990s), the Indian Ocean region in the 21st century would be characterised by a mix of limited bilateralism and competitive strategic rivalry that would be premised on the quest and access to geo-energy sources, markets and the striving for regional hegemonic dominance.[19]

The following patterns of alliances and coalitions are likely to emerge in the period:

1. The *geo-strategic alliances* would be the US-led coalition, which would be premised on the campaign against terrorism; the coalition against belligerent states that are opposed to extra-regional influence and therefore impact on US and allied access to the Persian Gulf oil reserves. There could also be a possible coalition against a resurgent China with varied partnerships.

   The US-led coalition against terrorism would be of the Western powers — the United Kingdom, France (France would adopt its own course of action where it has its stakes), Ethiopia, Kenya, Pakistan (expediency oriented), Japan, Australia, Singapore, Thailand, Malaysia, Indonesia (Malaysia and Indonesia would have their own course of action in matters of the Islam world), Philippines and South Korea as partners complementing the US efforts.

2. The *geo-economic* idea of a US-led collective security alliance would be in place, which would include Russia and China, as part of a cooperative security alliance for the predominant Asia-Pacific bloc that would endeavour to sustain the process of globalisation and enhanced economic cooperation.

   In other words, the Asia-Pacific Economic Council (APEC) would be substantially enlarged to include the Indian Ocean littoral countries. This would be perhaps the largest free-trade area in the world in view of the inclusion of the resources of the Indian Ocean region along with the Pacific region.

3. The strategic corollary could lead to the creation of an *Asian-NATO* that would have the possible elements of a containment of the regional hegemon: a possibly "adventuristic" China. The possibility of such an alliance would emerge in the event to contend a hegemonic China. Spearheaded by the United States, Japan, Australia, India and some ASEAN countries could form the alliance. The alliance would be premised on the basis of an expanding regional theatre of ballistic missile defences initiated by the United States and with a cooperative maritime security accord in place. The areas of contention would be the South China Sea and the Straits of Malacca that would intersect with the Chinese naval presence and passage. Beijing's deployment of its nuclear missile submarines and its surface flotilla in the region would be sure to arouse hostile sentiments in the region.

4. The *China-led coalition* would be the sequel to a US-led coalition, and would have prospective partners like Pakistan, Myanmar and Tanzania, which would be based on two patterns of alliance formation:[20] (i) Chinese technical, economic and military aid along with generous infrastructure development assistance to the recipients who would establish a *quid pro quo* of alliance formation for naval and air access facilities; (ii) prevalent anti-US, anti-Western sentiments could reciprocate in the bilateralism between the regional powers and could allow China to exploit the situation to its advantage.

5. The *Russia–China–India strategic triangle* could possibly emerge as an alternate premier anti-US, anti-hegemonic alliance that would have the elements of economic–military–technological cooperation, premised on the diplomatic–political strategy to resist and oppose the United States in its economic–military hegemonic dominance of the region. The triangle would be at best dyadic with Russia acting as the balancer between India and China. The scope for bilateralism in this triangle would be

more optimal, with the Sino–Russian and Indian–Russian ties as the viable partnerships. The collaborator state in this alliance would be Iran given its good diplomatic, economic and military links with all the three powers. The substance and domains of collaboration for the triangle would be the Central Asian Region that lies next to the geo-energy reserves of the world.

The *Russia–China–India–Iran axis* would emerge as a formidable anti-western, anti-US alliance in the Middle East, Southern Asia, Indian Ocean and Far East regions. It would deter the hegemonic economic and strategic domination of the United States and the Western Coalition. The prospects of the integration of interests of the partner states in this alliance would at best be a loose alliance with expediency oriented diplomatic strategies.

6. The alliance of the *states of concern* would be the revisionist alliance in 2020 with the Teheran–Damascus–Pyongyang axis gaining credence. The alliance would be the response to the preemptive and coercive strategies of the United States. The alliance would be the club of premier proliferators in WMD and missile technologies that abet clandestine trade in WMD. The preemptive and coercive strategies of the United States could result in a backlash with penchant for an accelerated WMD and missile brinkmanship in the region.

7. In a scenario that would have hyper-nationalist ideologies in power in Iran and India deploying nuclear weapons and ballistic missiles, the possibility of Iran and India emerging as the *regional pivots* alliance in the Middle East–Persian Gulf–Southern Asia–Indian Ocean region is likely. The strategic convergence of this relationship would be premised on increasing understanding and coordination on matters relating to Afghanistan and Central Asia with the dependence on energy being an issue for India and the dependency on technology an issue for Iran. The evolution of a maritime relationship with joint exercises in the Persian Gulf–North Arabian Sea could also become feasible. The alliance would be resistant to extra-regional hegemonic attempts to dominate the region and would be supportive of each other when vital interests are at stake.

8. India and Israel could form the *strategic partners* alliance that would be convergent on issues of counter-terrorism, technology cooperation, intelligence sharing, trade and economic cooperation. The partnership would be mostly symbiotic and would be enduring despite India's relations with Iran and the other Arab powers. The India–Israel relationship would be built on the convergence of geo-political and geo-strategic factors that would facilitate an Israeli presence in the Indian Ocean.

The dynamics of alliances and coalitions would be dependent on a host of variables that would interact with the prevalent geo-strategic, geo-economic and geo-political milieu derived from the terms of economic aid, techno-logical transfers, military aid and hardware supplies, infrastructure develop-ment ventures, leverages of the extra-regional powers over littoral powers and vice-versa, patterns of intervention, posture and deployment of extra-regional forces and basing patterns.

The convergence and divergence of the alliance patterns would be dictated by geo-energy profiles and markets that would drive the geo-political and geo-strategic forces in the region.

Nuclear Proliferation and Missile Defences in Southern Asia — The Maritime Dimension

Nuclear weapons and ballistic missiles are now embedded in the security com-plex of India, Pakistan and China. The dynamics of nuclearisation in Southern Asia emerges with the following implications and impact. The pathways of India and Pakistan to nuclear weaponisation have been paved with varying objectives:

1. India has reaffirmed nuclear deterrence in the context of defensive-defence with certitudes of assured retaliation premised on Minimum Credible Deterrence. It combines the doctrine of active defence in the event of imminent threats and aggression. Pakistan's declaratory military doctrine, policy and posture rely on the imperative of securing the initiative for the offensive in view of its conventional and nuclear weakness vis-à-vis India. China relies on a military doctrine of Active Defence with regard to India, with a strategic intent to extend its deterrence to Pakistan. China's nuclear doctrines are in the process of transformation from limited deterrence to sufficient deterrence.
2. There is a penchant to deploy a survivable and assured retaliatory second-strike capability in the operational doctrines of India, Pakistan and China. The achievement of second-strike capability is possible with preference for a sea-based nuclear deterrence. Sea-based nuclear deterrence constitutes the reliable leg of the nuclear triad that would be the logical culmination for all nuclear force postures that could be survivable and credible.

China has developed and deployed its nuclear powered ballistic missile submarine *Xia* class SSBN Type 092 with the 1760 KM range *JL-1* SLBM.

It is also developing the Type 094 SSBN with a *JL-2* SLBM with a possible strike radius of 8000–10,000 km.

India reportedly is acquiring various types of ship-launched missiles, as well as submarine-launched cruise missiles, from Russia including the SS-N-21 missiles and has a programme to develop short-range, SLBMs. India had tested the *Dhanush* — the navalised version of the *Prithivi* SSM from an Offshore Patrol Vessel OPV *Subhadar.*

India has been experimenting with the Advanced Technology Vessel with SLBM/SLCM capabilities. India's SLBM programme — *Sagarika* — would have its probable operational capability by 2008–2010, enabling it to move to a meaningful survivable nuclear triad. The *Sagarika* would be deployed on probable platforms of the *Kilo 877, Scorpene* or the *Akula II,* which are primarily cruise missile platforms. Much would depend on how the missiles could be mated with the platforms.

Pakistan has been developing its submarine capabilities with the Agosta and the improved *Agosta 90 B* class and has been attempting to evolve navalised versions of its land-based MRBMs/IRBMs with no success. The possibilities are there to equip Pakistani submarines with Tactical Land Attack Cruise Missiles of Chinese origin with nuclear warheads. However, the feasibility of such cooperation with China remains doubtful.

The imperatives for a sea-based deterrence and the dynamics of theatre missile defences have assumed significance in the light of the proliferation of WMD and missile technologies. The instabilities apparent in the ballistic missile environment have prompted regional powers in the Indian Ocean region to prefer survivable nuclear forces that would be submerged and reinforce the assured retaliatory capability.

The strategic environment circa 2020 would feature the Indian Ocean region as a high-intensity theatre in terms of deployed surface and sub-surface nuclear platforms equipped with long-range cruise missiles with nuclear and conventional payloads as well as payloads in the land-attack mode. The nuclear navies of the US Fifth Fleet, the United Kingdom, France and China would be dominant extra-regional navies deploying substantial nuclear assets in the surface and sub-surface platforms.

In addition to nuclear naval platforms, the United States would be deploying its assorted NTW systems on modified *Aegis* class cruisers by 2011–2014.[21] The two theatres of sea-based missile defence deployment would be in North East Asia to deter and neutralise the North Korean missile threat and the Indian Ocean region to deter and neutralise the Iranian threat.

The US deployment of the NTW system would provide for synergistic capabilities of a 24/7 space-based tracking and surveillance of the missile forces in the Middle East–Southern Asia region with feeds into the NTW System for post-boost phase interception strikes. It would enable the United States to devise strike options of neutralising ballistic missile launches in the region while retaining its offensive strike options using nuclear tipped Air Launched Cruise Missiles (ALCMs), Submarine Launched Cruise Missiles (SLCMs), and Submarine Launched Ballistic Missiles (SLBMs).

Given this scenario, the imperatives for the nuclear powers of the region, viz. India, Pakistan and possibly Iran, would be to disperse their land-based assets to survivable modes of deployment. In this context, the emphasis of sea-based deterrence with SLBMs and nuclear tipped cruise missiles would also be on survivable modes of nuclear deployment.

The deployment of nuclear-tipped land attack cruise missiles would be in operation. There is a likelihood of deployment of modified ex-Russian cruise missiles of the *Klub* class by the Indian and Iranian navies and deployed onboard the EKM 877. There is also a possibility of the deployment of the 128 SS-N-21 missiles with ranges of 3000 km on the Type 0970/971 *Severodvinsk*.

India's efforts to build its boats based on the Type 970/971 *Akula* I & II or its acquisition would mature by 2020 to enable its effective transition to sea-based deterrence. Pakistan would also be attempting to shift some of its nuclear assets to its *Agosta* and *Scorpene* submarines and would attempt to develop naval variants of the *Shaheen II* to be deployed on the *Tariq* Type 21 frigates.[22]

China's deployment would be its cruise missiles of the C-802 type, which could have a nuclear payload. The combination of nuclear-tipped cruise missiles with land attack capabilities and its JL-2 SLBMs on board the Type 094 SSBNs (Submersible Ship Ballistic Nuclear) would provide the Chinese with good options for sea-based deterrence.

Sea-based deterrence would be the dominant technological option due to the versatility it affords to operations. The operational capabilities of survivability, endurance, deception, manoeuvre, dispersal, precision strike and connectivity with a host of VLF (Very Low Frequency) stations enable flexible deployment. The quantum of dedicated anti-submarine forces to track the nuclear-propelled submarines would have to be quite high and the reliability to track them in the warm waters of the Indian Ocean would be quite difficult given the isothermal complexities of the warm layers and high salinity.

Missile defence options among the regional powers would not be viable given the high costs and technological complexities. Indian options to deploy anti-missile defences to protect land-based missiles against formidable Chinese IRBMs or possible US Trident D-5 SLBMs would not be technologically feasible given the MIRV payloads and quick saturation that would be achieved by the massed attack that could take place using such ballistic missiles. The technological viability of interception of various kinds of ballistic missiles would still be unproven in Indian conditions to justify its deployment. Pakistan would actually invest in more offensive missiles rather than spend on missile defences.

The implications of nuclear weaponisation at sea offer several advantages for the regional powers vis-à-vis the extra-regional nuclear naval powers in any crisis escalation situation.

1. Sea-based deterrence would be the optimal policy and strategic solution for the regional powers given its feasibility. Sea-based deterrence would give credence to assured strike capability that could be based on either cruise missiles or ballistic missiles launched from submarines with the advantages of dispersal and stealth.[23]

2. The relative saturation of the ground-air defence environment with anti-missile defences would result in newer means of dispersal of land-based nuclear assets of manned attack aircraft and land-based missiles to newer locales with the high probability of being tracked and destroyed in pre-emptive strikes.[24]

   Given such a context, the options of sea-based deterrence would be viewed as credible and the assured retaliatory capability as secure. The optimal dispersal of the platforms and payloads would enable the maintenance of a credible deterrence in terms of survivability.

3. Sea-based deterrence would reinforce the delayed yet assured retaliation in the face of an omni-directional threat. It would provide for sufficient options to retaliate from different locations in the seamless medium of the oceans so as to avoid detection and maintain stealth and precision.

4. Sea-based deterrence would enhance the ability of a viable targeting strategy by India, Pakistan or China and avoid the possibility of a "defanging strike" of its nuclear arsenal by the United States in a preventive strike against the Indian and Pakistani nuclear arsenals. With the viability of anti-missile defences against a wide spectrum of missiles yet to be proved. Circa 2020 would therefore be a period where offensive missiles would be deployed in greater quantities than defensive missiles.

Regional powers would thus have more incentive for sea-based nuclear deterrence and would build enhanced conventional, littoral, defence capabilities with a view to deny access and saturate the combat environments of the littorals. The 21st century would see the high-intensity contest between access and denial strategies as regional powers and extra-regional powers develop capabilities to deter each other in the maritime realm of the region.

Cooperative Maritime Security: The Evolving Agenda

The maritime realm offers scope for cooperation even though competition remains at stake. Cooperative security requires a transnational approach and requires states to build the relevant capacities to transcend primary sources of contention and evolve a functionalist perspective in cooperation for mutual benefit.[25]

Cooperative security in the maritime space as a functionalist factor has prospects for success. The maritime domain provides for a transnational space that facilitates the common goals of cooperation, search and rescue, and disaster management. Cooperative security in the maritime realm is also quite feasible since it is the least contentious of the three armed forces. It also provides for a meaningful framework of confidence building measures. Cooperative security in the maritime realm presents the capacity to evolve institutional measures that would accrue confidence and stability. Cooperative security has advantages in the realms of economic development and the environment within regional frameworks of bilateral and multilateral arrangements.

The accents of cooperative security in the Southern Asian context lie in the bilateral and multilateral aegis that has scope to be optimised well in the maritime realm. The transnational concerns and issues of energy, SLOC, exploitation of the resources in the EEZ, combating and containing of transnational threats of piracy, maritime-based terrorism, interdiction and containment of the spread of WMD technologies can provide the basis for cooperation. In the naval realm, basis for cooperation include Search and Rescue (SAR), Prevention of Incidents in High Sea (INCSEA), combat of narcotics and interdiction, and the maritime initiatives in counter-proliferation. There are two issues that attract serious attention in the realm of Cooperative Maritime Security, viz. the interdiction of WMD technologies in maritime transit and the combat of maritime low-intensity conflicts.

The essence of the Maritime Confidence Building Measures has gained significance owing to the following factors:

1. The maritime realm offers the transnational convergence of security of all states in a region. Despite the prevalence of high-intensity tensions in the conventional and even in the nuclear realm, the naval/maritime space offers the prospect of a reduction of tensions as the maritime realm is the least contentious of the three realms of the armed forces.[26] Naval forces can engage in coercive as well as constabulary functions and the Indian Navy has optimally demonstrated the potential in terms of these roles.

2. The prospects of a multilateral framework in cooperative security and maritime confidence building measures customised to the region could be evolved among the states of the Arabian Sea littoral, involving India, Pakistan, Iran, Oman, as well as the Bay of Bengal littoral involving India, Bangladesh, Myanmar, Thailand. Issues of convergence could range from EEZ protection and energy exploitation.

3. The functionalist advantages accrued from experimentation in the multilateral aegis could be transferred to the bilateral framework. The optimisation of the bilateral framework could be initiated with the introduction of risk reduction in the maritime space. The imperative for risk reduction emerges from the fact that the Indian and Pakistani Navies have structural and strategic asymmetries and hence the incentives to competitive security are more than the imperatives of cooperative security.

The agenda of Cooperative Maritime Security in the India–Pakistan context and in the India–China context in the 21st century could emerge. The basis of initial cooperation could feature: (1) increased cooperation for the Prevention of Incidents in High Seas, (2) joint naval operations in the management and control of marine pollution and (3) interdiction and curbing of smuggling through the sea.

The second level of bilateral engagement could be focused on institutional cooperation protocols between the Coast Guard of India and the Maritime Security Agency of Pakistan. Cooperation between the countries could be facilitated with an agreement that would entail a Cooperative/Joint Activity Zone along the disputed maritime boundary of the two states and the prospect of a joint hydrographic survey of the Arabian Sea. This measure could allow the fishermen of both sides to operate free from fear of apprehension and avoid the acrimonious politicisation of the disputes. Given the resource-rich zones of Sir Creek, there is scope for bilateral scientific cooperation between the two states.[27] The possibilities of a multilateral exercise in the Southern Asian–Indian Ocean region in the areas of oceanography, marine ecology and weather pattern study are also feasible initiatives.

4. The imperatives to establish Maritime Risk Reduction Centres (MRRC) between the two countries would in the longer run constitute the viable means of risk reduction. The deployment of military communication assets and GPS systems would help facilitate the risk-reduction management process.

   The MRRC would provide for a reliable means for escalation control and a reliable means of communication at sea between the Indian Western Naval Command and Pakistan's counterpart in Karachi. It would also provide synergy of the channel of communication between the Indian Coast Guard and Pakistan's Maritime Security Agency over the issue of maritime boundary violations. The MRRC would be involved in: (1) exchanging notifications on conduct of major naval exercises as required by the agreement of 1991 and any agreements that follow in future, (2) exchanging notifications as required by the incidents at sea agreement once formalised, (3) exchanging urgent information related to a recent incident at sea, (4) exchanging information on maritime boundary violations, and (5) exchanging notification of ballistic missile firing tests at sea. The MRRC would be part of the National Nuclear Risk Reduction Center (NRRC), whenever such a centre is established.[28]

5. The accents of cooperative maritime security are also premised on the traditional instruments of naval policy and operation, that is cooperative naval security in the realm of bilateral/multilateral frameworks in the contexts of maritime low-intensity conflicts and terrorism and the clandestine transfer of WMD technologies.

Cooperative Security and the Containment of Asymmetric Threats

The 21st century Southern Asia–Indian Ocean region would be known for its volatile potential of emergent maritime asymmetric threats and the sea-based commerce of the clandestine trade of WMD. The imperatives to combat and contain these threats would be a concern in the cooperative security agenda of the states in the region. However, there would be differences in perception and varying scopes of involvement and operations in regard to these two issues given the stakes and interests of the states.

India has been engaged in the combat of maritime-based terrorism and insurgency in two previous instances.[29] In the first instance, India's navy had challenged terrorism at sea, which was well demonstrated during the capture of mercenaries who held the Maldives Minister of Education hostage in November 1988. In that incident, 150 members of the Sri Lankan Tamil extremist organisation, the People's Liberation Organisation of Tamil Eelam (PLOTE), had landed in the Maldives and quickly overpowered the Maldivian Militia using rockets and machine guns and attacked the President's residence. The Maldives government sent out calls asking for assistance and India responded with the launching of *Operation Cactus*. A large contingent of Indian paratroopers made an unopposed landing in the capital Male and the island was secured within 30 minutes after the arrival of forces. Shortly afterwards, the mercenaries, with hostages onboard, including the Maldives Minister of Education, was seen fleeing Male. An Indian Navy maritime reconnaissance aircraft detected the ship and the Indian navy vessels subsequently captured the ship.

In the second instance, the Indian Coast Guard, tasked with maintaining order at sea in the IEEZ, demonstrated its capability by capturing the M.V. *Alondra Rainbow*, a 7000 ton Panama-registered vessel belonging to Japanese owners. The M.V. *Alondra Rainbow* was hijacked by pirates in the Malacca Straits. The Piracy Reporting Centre, Kuala Lumpur, had given a worldwide alert and the interdiction was initiated by M.V. *Shuhadaa*, a merchant ship operating in the area. Upon receiving the alert, the Indian coast guard moved into action even as the pirates resisted arrest. Meanwhile, a Thai fishing boat picked up a life raft carrying 10 people some 60 nautical miles west of the Thai province of Satun. The people onboard the life raft revealed that they were the crew of the ill-fated M.V. *Alondra Rainbow*. The pirated vessel was finally captured by Special Forces. The incident highlighted the importance of using Special Forces to board vessels and apprehend culprits as well as the importance of close cooperation between the Indian Navy, the Indian Coast Guard, and between the PRC and Indian governments.

The threats of maritime-based terrorism and low-intensity conflicts have serious implications for state security in the region.[30] The geographical spread of terrorist groups in the contiguity of the Southern Asian–Indian Ocean region include the LTTE in Sri Lanka, Al Qaeda in Yemen, Somalia and Pakistan, Abu Sayef in the Philippines, and the Free Aceh Movement in Indonesia. All these groups have strong terrorism/insurgency profiles with a propensity to use the maritime space. The imperatives of cooperative security in the realms of intelligence sharing and monitoring of these groups is therefore vital. Joint naval manoeuvres among regional navies and similar multilateral initiatives are considered important in deterring these terrorist threats.

The imperative to combat the spread of WMD technologies by sea-based transfer is yet another important issue. Although the Southern Asian states are not partners of the Proliferation Security Initiative, India has a strong interest to monitor, contain and interdict the sea-based transfer of WMD technologies and products due to Pakistani complicity with North Korea and Iran in the trafficking of WMD technologies through the high seas.

In summation, the essence of the regional maritime dynamics in Southern Asia in the 21st century contain elements of the competitive and the cooperative. The asymmetry of naval assets and capabilities is an inherent feature of the inter-regional naval order and it is further complicated by the formidable intervention capabilities of the extra-regional navies in the region. The structural balance of maritime power in the region is dominated by India with a modest countervailing balance by Pakistan. The issues of SLOC security, EEZ protection, energy flows from the Persian Gulf–Middle East region are all conditioned by the nature of access and the anti-access strategies evident. Therefore, in net assessment, the prospects of the Regional Maritime Balance in Southern Asia are predicated on the twin forces of competitive and cooperative dynamics of maritime security.

Notes

1. K.R. Singh, *Navies of South Asia* (New Delhi: Institute of Defence Studies & Analysis, 2002; Rupa & Co). R.B. Suri, *Shape and Size of Indian Navy in Early Twenty-first Century* (New Delhi: United Services Institution of India, 1998).
2. *Janes Fighting Ships 2000–2001.* Also available online at http://jfs.janes.com/.
3. John Garvar, "The Future of the Sino-Pakistani Entente 'Cordiale'", in Michael R. Chambers, ed., *South Asia in 2020: Future Strategic Balances and Alliances* (Carlisle: Strategic Studies Institute, US Army War College, November 2002).
4. Ayesha Siddiqa-Agha, "South Asia Nuclear Navies?" *Bulletin of Atomic Scientists,* Vol. 56, No. 5, September–October 2000, pp. 12–14.
5. Subir Bhaumik, *Bangladesh–Pakistan Joint Naval Exercises; Musharaff's Visit to Myanmar; India's Encirclement Begins,* 28 April 2001. Also available online at http://tehelka.com.
6. Mohan Malik, "The China Factor in the India–Pakistan Conflict", *Parameters,* Spring 2003, pp. 35–50. See also Mohan Malik, "The Proliferation Axis: Beijing–Islamabad–Pyongyang", *Korean Journal of Defence Analysis,* Vol. XV, No. 1, Spring 2003; Shirley A. Kan, "China and Proliferation of Weapons of

Mass Destruction and Missiles: Policy Issues", *Report for Congress RL 31555*, Washington, DC, Congressional Research Service, The Library of Congress, 2003.

7. Ayesha Siddiqa-Agha, p. 13.

8. US Congress, Washington, DC, "Annual Report of the Military Power of the People's Republic of China", *Annual Report to Congress* (Pursuant to the FY 2000 National Defense Authorization Act), May 2004. Available online at http://www.dod.gov/pubs/d20040528PRC.pdf.

9. "Myanmar: Where the Indian and Chinese Navies Meet", *Stratfor Commentary*. Also available online at http://www.stratfor.com/asia/commentary/m0001272141.htm; and "India Challenges China in South China Sea", Stratfor Global Intelligence Update, 7 December 2000.

10. "How Russia Pits One Friend Against Another", Stratfor Commentary 001106, 6 January 2000. Also available online at http://www.stratfor.com/CIS/commentary/001160020.

11. Cooperative Maritime Security could be interpreted in the context as the endeavours to develop naval access, basing, posture, doctrine and alliances of extra-regional powers could develop with regional littoral powers.

12. Elizabeth Roche, "India forging special unit to operate nuclear arsenal", *Agence France Presse*, 30 September 2002.

13. Srikanth Kondapalli, "Chinese Navy in the Indian Ocean", *Journal of Indian Ocean Studies*, Vol. 8, Nos. 1 & 2, August 2000.

14. Hans Kristensen, "Preemptive Posturing", *Bulletin of Atomic Scientists*, September–October 2002.

15. Yoash Tsiddon-Chatto, "Non-Classified Realities Affecting Israel's Air Force 2005–2010", Policy Paper No. 136, Ariel Center for Policy Research, 2002.

16. Ibid.

17. Vern Clark, "Sea Power 21", *Proceedings of the United States Naval Institute*, Vol. 128, No. 10, October 2002.

18. Robert J. Peterson, "Missile Defence Exposes Real Fears", *US Naval Institute Proceedings*, February 2001, p. 78.

19. Michael T. Klare, "The New Geography of Conflict", *Foreign Affairs*, May–June 2001, pp. 49–61.

20. Karl W. Eikenberry, "Explaining and Influencing Chinese Arms Transfers", *McNairPaper No. 36*, Institute for National Strategic Studies, National Defense University, Washington, DC, 1995, pp. 5–15.

21. Girish Luthra, "Sea-Based Missile Defence and Regional Security", *Indian Defence Review*, October–December 2002, pp. 89–96, and P.K. Ghosh, "Naval NMD: The Concept of Expanding NMD Seawards", *Strategic Analysis*, Vol. XXV, No. 8, November 2001, pp. 897–918.

22. "Pakistan and India Vying for Regional Influence", Stratfor Commentary, 1 May 2002. Available online at http://www.stratfor.com/asia/commentary/0105021845.

23. Vijay Sakhuja, "Sea Based Deterrence and Indian Security", *Strategic Analysis*, Vol. XXV, No. 1, April 2001, pp. 21–32.

24. "The nuclear scenarios outlined by Humphrey Hawksely seems to have sound relevance", Humphrey Hawksely, *Dragon Fire* (New Delhi: Macmillan, 2000).

25. Michael Moodie, "Cooperative Security: Implications for National Security and International Relations Albuquerque", *Occasional Paper No. 14* (SAND 98-0505/14), Sandia Labs Cooperative Monitoring Center, January 2000.

26. Rajesh Pendharkar, "The Lahore Declaration and Beyond: Maritime Confidence-Building Measures in South Asia", *Occasional Paper No. 51*, The Henry L. Stimson Center, Washington, DC, February 2003.

27. Ayesha Siddiqa-Agha, "Maritime Cooperation Between India and Pakistan: Building Confidence at Sea", *Occasional Paper No. 18* (SAND 98-0505/18), Sandia Labs Cooperative Monitoring Center, November 2000.

28. Pendharkar, 2003.

29. Vijay Sakhuja, "Maritime Order and Piracy", *Strategic Analysis*, Vol. XXIV, No. 5, 6 August 2000, p. 935.

30. Rohan Kumar Gunaratna, "The Asymmetric Threat From Maritime Terrorism", *Jane's Navy International*, October 2001, p. 28.

II. *The Regional Maritime Challenges*

Chapter 5

Some Reflections on Maritime Boundary and Territorial Disputes in the Asia-Pacific with a Focus on the South China Sea

Peter Cozens

Introduction

Over the past 50 years the international community has increasingly sought to draw lines in the seas and oceans of the world to define boundaries of various sorts for reasons of sovereignty, economic and security purposes. The Third United Nations Convention on the Law of the Sea (UNCLOS III) that deliberated from 1973 to 1982 provided a comprehensive set of principles and rules. Although the intentions of its many architects may have been to devise a universal code, it has opened a sea of troubles that today manifest as maritime and territorial boundary disputes. However, there are many safety valves in the system whereby differences can be resolved, including pragmatic mutual agreement or in the case of a desperately contested dispute, by the International Court of Justice. In the Asia-Pacific region there are many maritime boundary delimitations to be fixed. A picture so they say, is worth a thousand words. A look at a schematic drawing of the Asia-Pacific illustrates approximate

111

Exclusive Economic Zones (EEZs), sea-lanes of communications, strategic waterways, other communication facilities and even the boundaries of the Treaty of Rarotonga. It dramatically underscores the importance of understanding the region. It also illustrates a number of potential trouble spots. This author acknowledges freely a debt to the National Geographic Society for such a forceful depiction of so many complexities in a single graphical image. Such a diagram raises the not inconsiderable problem of how do we humans manage our way through such a maelstrom of complexities. Furthermore, the world is changing with bewildering speed and what we took to be certainties just a little while ago now appear to be ephemeral and transitory. See Figure 1.

The purpose of this chapter is to briefly discuss contemporary issues of boundaries, focussing on the EEZs, in the region and in particular the South China Sea and to fit them into a broader historical perspective. The formula for the various boundaries is simply depicted in the attached schematic in Figure 2.[1] The actual drawing or the delimitation of boundaries in coastal regions is complicated by geography as illustrated in the diagram in Figure 3.[2]

Where did EEZs come from and why was the distance of 200 miles chosen? In January 1971, Kenya made a proposal to the Asian–African Legal Consultative Committee and in the following year to the United Nations Sea Bed Committee concerning exclusive use of the sea neighbouring the coast — these proposals being supported by a number of developing nations. Concurrently, some Latin American countries also developed a similar concept of the "patrimonial" sea. The two strands of thinking on the matter received active support from many Afro-Asian countries and also from some developed coastal states.[3] A prime motivator from many of these countries was to reduce the perceived depredations of Distant Water Fishing Nations (DWFN) in waters adjacent to their shores and to gain more control over fish stocks in particular. The actual distance of 200 miles appears to have been based on rather flimsy evidence. According to A.L. Hollick, and quoted directly from Churchill and Lowe:

> The figure of 200 miles seems to be something of an accident. Chile's claim was motivated by a desire to protect its then new offshore whaling operations. The whaling industry only wanted a fifty-mile zone, but was advised that some precedent was necessary. The most promising precedent appeared to be the security zone adopted in the 1939 Declaration of Panama. This zone was wrongly thought to have been 200 miles in breadth: in fact it varied and was nowhere less than 300 miles.[4]

Figure 1 Maritime areas in the Asia–Pacific

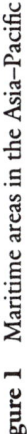

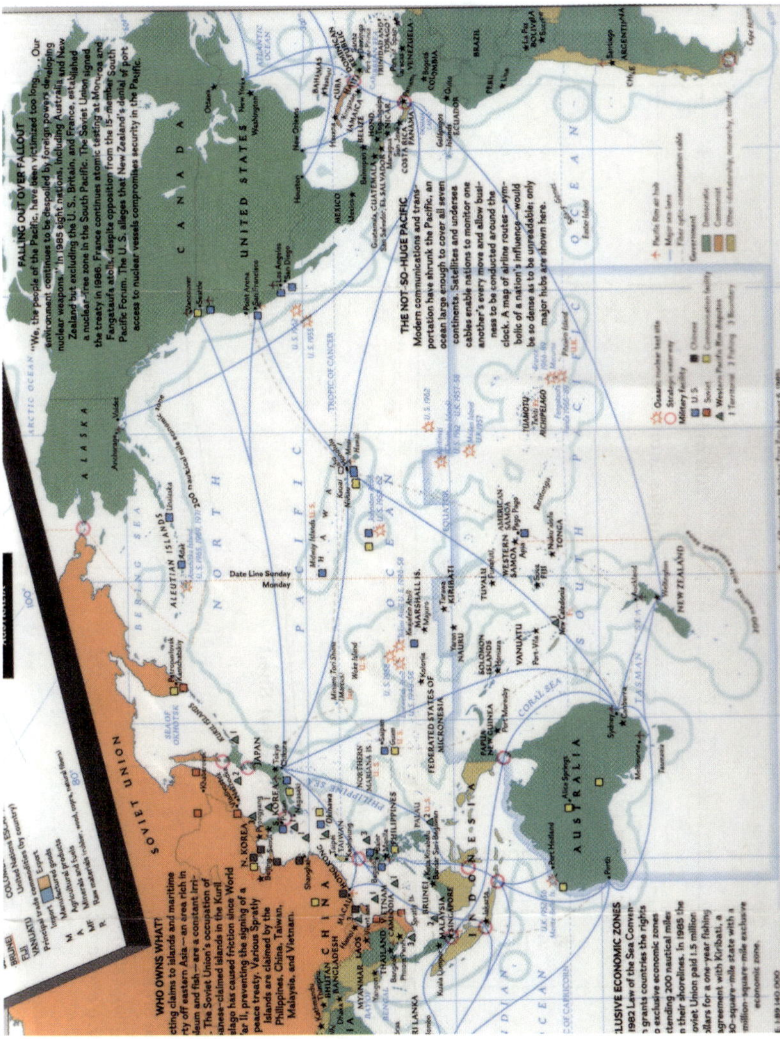

Source: Supplement to the *National Geographic*, November 1989, Vol. 176, No. 5 — Asia–Pacific, p. 558 A.

Figure 2   Maritime zones

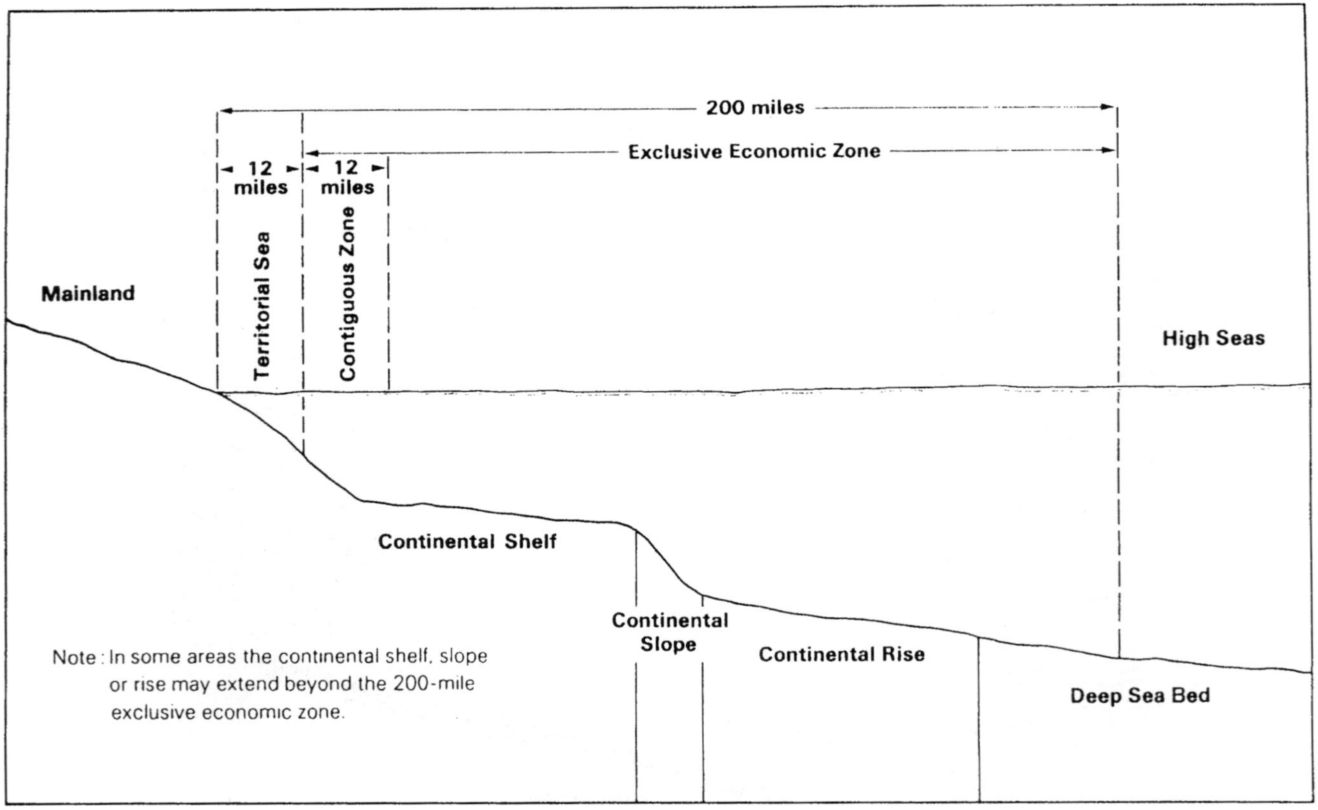

Mainland

Territorial Sea

12 miles

12 miles

Contiguous Zone

12 miles

Continental Shelf

Continental
Slope

Continental Rise

200 miles

Exclusive Economic Zone

High Seas

Deep Sea Bed

Note : In some areas the continental shelf, slope
or rise may extend beyond the 200-mile
exclusive economic zone.

Source: Churchill R.R. and Lowe A.V., *The Law of the Sea*, Third Edition, Melland Schill Studies in International Law (Manchester: Manchester University Press, 1999), p. 30.

Figure 3 The construction of baselines

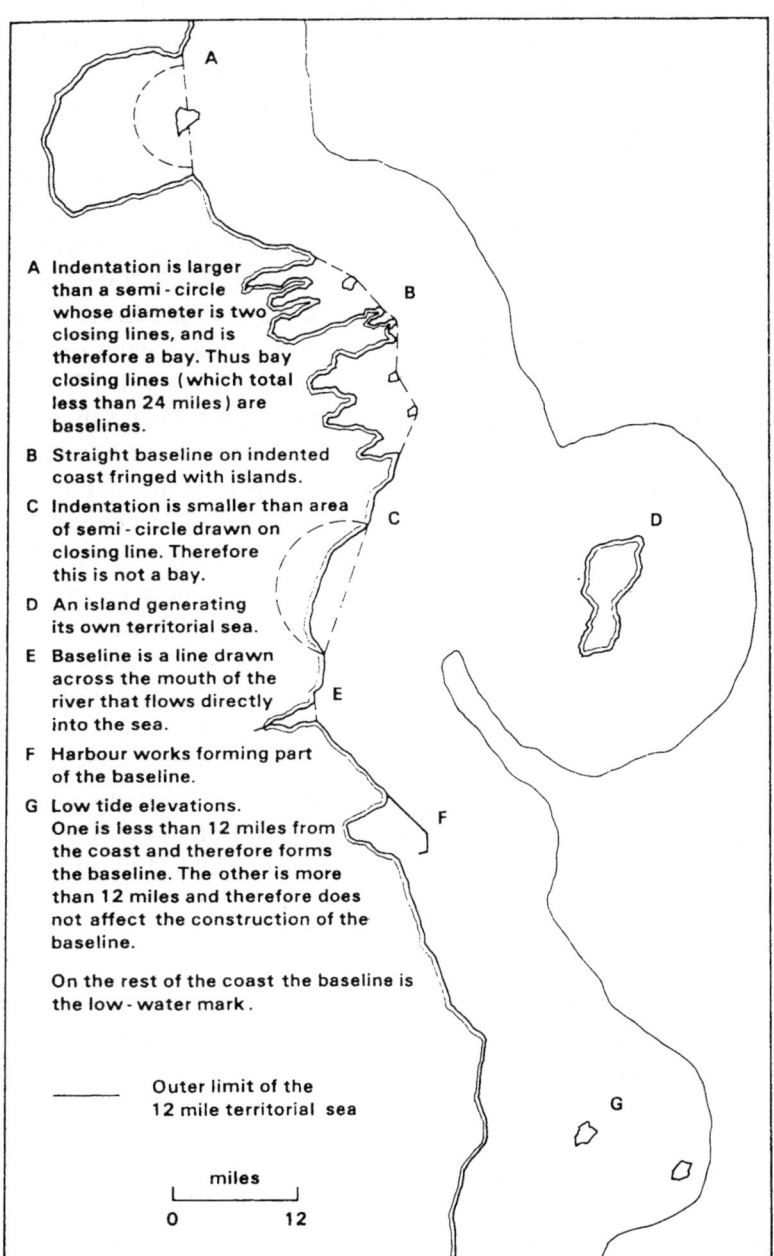

Source: Churchill R.R. and Lowe A.V., *The Law of the Sea*, Third Edition, Melland Schill Studies in International Law (Manchester: Manchester University Press, 1999), p. 36.

An idea of why some sort of regulation or claim to fishing zones was considered necessary can be gauged by the large number of fishing boats actively engaged in fishing activities around the world. For example, the Japanese Government had to undertake negotiations worldwide with 32 coastal states to secure access for their ships to fish in the new zones after many states declared 200 mile EEZs in the late 1970s.[5]

During the mid to late 1970s countries around the world declared 200-mile zones with astonishing frequency. India declared a zone on 28 May 1976 and the Mexicans in June 1976.[6] The French Cabinet issued an official communiqué on 16 June 1976 announcing a draft law to establish a 200 nautical mile economic zone.[7] The Canadians intended their 200-mile EEZ to come into force on 1 January 1977, as did Norway and the United States on 1 March 1977. Britain also intended the same thing for 1 January 1977 but faced delimitation talks with France, Denmark and Iceland.[8] What is important to recognise in the development of the Law of the Sea is that it has diluted the privileges of Western Nations who were the principal architects of the original law. This bias is revealed in the principles of the so-called "freedom of the seas", that is, freedom of navigation, freedom of fishing, freedom to lay submarine cables, and pipelines, and freedom to fly over the sea. Furthermore, the high seas in legal terms had been kept as large as possible by restricting the width of territorial seas — the idea of the cannon shot suited the powerful maritime nations as they could then influence and control what went on ashore.[9] An unfortunate outcome of UNCLOS III is that it has complicated relationships in those waters where several countries have competing claims as in the South China Sea and the archipelagic waters of South East Asia.[10] Major beneficiaries of the EEZs in the region are Indonesia, New Zealand, Australia, Japan, Kiribati and Papua New Guinea as Table 1 illustrates.[11]

Boundaries and Disputes

Where the claims of two or more coastal states intersect for reasons of territorial, contiguous, EEZ or continental shelf delimitation it raises a complexity of issues in coming to some sort of agreement. One might very reasonably ask why is it necessary to establish these boundaries. Some answers are provided by Dr Clive Schofield who cogently argued in a CSCAP Maritime Working Group meeting last year, that maritime boundary delimitation assists in providing jurisdictional *clarity* and *certainty*. A lack of agreed boundaries could hamper effective *international* cooperation thus reducing maritime security

Table 1   Leading EEZ beneficiaries

State	Area of 200-mile zone (square nautical miles)[55]	Offshore oil production 1992 in '000 tonnes (proven reserves in million tonnes)	Offshore natural gas production 1992 in million cubic metres (proven reserves in billion cubic metres)	Fish catches or estimated potential (EP) in 200-mile zone (million tonnes)
1. USA	2,831,400	35,308 (707)	103,471 (1,189)	5.5 (1994)
2. France	2,083,400	0	0	Not available
3. Indonesia	1,577,300	57,270 (286)	7,236 (1,447)	6.7 (EP)
4. New Zealand	1,409,500	797 (18)	2,998 (82)	0.7 (1995)
5. Australia	1,310,900	24,153 (258)	16,952 (538)	2.5 (1995)
6. Russia	1,309,500	10,558 (41)	10,337 (17)	3.0 (1994)
7. Japan	1,126,000	697 (1)	286 (0)	6.5 (1994)
8. Brazil	924,000	26,145 (631)	7,236 (2)	0.6 (1995)
9. Canada	857,000	498 (162)	0 (298)	0.8 (1995)
10. Mexico	831,500	85,656 (5,712)	11,370 (1,926)	1.2 (1995)
11. Kiribati	770,000	Not available	Not available	Not available
12. Papua New Guinea	690,000	0 (37)	0 (314)	Not available
13. Chile	667,300	847 (54)	569 (65)	7.5 (1995)
14. Norway	590,500	89,640 (2,364)	32,044 (3,088)	3.0 (1995)
15. India	587,600	35,856 (1,047)	6,202 (430)	2.0 (EP)
Total all States	37,745,000	909,398 (37,276)	355,697 (25,393)	91.9 (1995)

and furthermore that rational exploitation of resources could similarly be compromised. Clearly, it is not in anyone's interest to contribute to a "tragedy of the commons".[12] It is the *international* element that is important. Unlike some coastal states that have no or insignificant international boundaries it is *cooperation* that is the critical ingredient of successful use of space and the sustainable and equitable use of resources by those states with several intersecting boundaries with others that is important.

A significant dispute is brewing over access to hydrocarbons in the Timor Sea between the newly independent state of Timor L'Este and Australia. The coordinates of the maritime boundaries have yet to be fixed but powerful commercial and state interests are involved in the outcome. On the one hand, Australia is committed to a "strong and productive relationship with East Timor" but then, on the other, the Timor Sea Treaty is seen by some as being too generous.[13] It looks as if the dispute will have to be settled by an extensive process of litigation which is not necessarily in the best interests of Timor L'Este's exchequer.[14] The new state will have planned much of its new development on hydrocarbon revenues but until a satisfactory position is established there will be little investment. Copies of two opinions that illustrate the complexities of it all are in Annex A and B, respectively.

Boundary delimitation in Oceania is yet a long way from resolution. These small states simply do not have the largesse and expertise to invest in the exercise. It should be noted that the State of Kiribati has the 11th largest EEZ in the world but little in the way of infrastructure to finance the exercise. However, it appears that the Pacific Island Forum, of which Kiribati is a member, is anxious, at long last, to start a process to develop an Oceans Policy in which boundary delimitation is a vital part.

Boundary delimitation in the South China Sea is complicated by claims of a historical nature by China and also the occupation of certain small islands from which territorial, contiguous, EEZ and continental shelf limits can be drawn. There is no doubt that China has exercised a significant influence over this sea since antiquity and continually used it for commercial purposes. Distinguished scholars ranging from Professor Wang Gungwu, and his seminal work, "The Nanhai Trade: The Early History of Chinese Trade in the South China Sea", published in the 1950s, Anthony Reid's, "Charting the Shape of Early Modern Southeast Asia", to Deng Gang's "Chinese Maritime Activities and Socio-economic Development c. 2100 BC–1900 AD", underscore and support this assertion. Nonetheless, historical claims are extremely tricky tools to use as a basis for international law.

One cannot view modern boundary disputes in the South China Sea without a brief look at contemporary Chinese maritime history of say, the past 50 years or so. At the end of the Chinese Civil War, the Nationalists or Guomindang (GMD) evacuated their forces and a huge amount of imperial treasure to offshore islands in 1949, principally to Taiwan. The communists were soundly beaten with huge causalities when the People's Liberation Army (PLA) attempted invasion of some of these islands. This caused much intro-spection by Mao and his generals — he is reported to have said, "We must build a Navy capable of defending our coastal areas and effectively guard-ing against possible aggression by the imperialists".[15] The imperialists in this case were considered to be the Americans. The Chinese leadership, however, merely considered the Navy to be an adjunct of the Army and to be used to provide a first line of defence to limit an invading enemy's operations whilst ground forces were manoeuvred to best advantage. The strategy was known as *jinhai fangyu* — its primary purpose was to adopt guerrilla-type tactics against an invading force but under the direction of local military commanders — it was in effect for some 30 years notwithstanding the ambitions of a highly motivated and expansionist naval cadre who had been trained and influenced by the Russians at the Voroshilov Naval Academy in Moscow.

When Deng Xiao Ping assumed the mantle of leadership in 1978, PLA theorists and planners began thinking in terms of four specific types of war:

1. small confrontations at the frontier, e.g., Siachen Glacier;
2. medium-sized conventional wars;
3. full-scale conventional wars under the condition of nuclear deterrence;
4. nuclear war.

It was the first two types of war that were considered the most likely, with Vietnam and India being the opponents.[16] However, one must also examine this against the recent expansion of the Soviet Navy at that time — the estab-lishment of port facilities in Cam Ranh Bay and Da Nang in Vietnam, which were, in effect, a continuance of the border conflict between the USSR and China into a maritime dimension.[17] We must not forget the Chinese takeover of the Paracel Islands in 1974 — a naval operation — it was exquisitely accomplished by the Chinese leadership during a time of rapprochement between the Chinese and the United States — the understanding being that the United States would not intervene. It was perhaps factors of this nature that opened the minds of the communist leadership to the need for a compre-hensive maritime strategy and the tools with which to do it. Deng Xiao Ping's modernising influence marks a shift from a purely territorial defensive strategy to one of a maritime nature. The build-up of the Soviet Navy and Merchant fleet under Admiral Gorshkov in the 1960s and 1970s also helped to convince the Chinese leadership that there really was something useful in this maritime sphere after all.

Also at this time one must not overlook developments in UNCLOS III. The opportunity to claim a 200-mile EEZ and to formalise a historical claim to the Spratly Islands and therefore access and ownership of significant fishing and minerals resources (particularly hydrocarbons) gave Chinese naval planners much more muscle in arguing their case for a greater share of the national defence budget. But the Spratlys were not, and are still not, the only islands to which Beijing wants to lay claim. The islands to the north of Taiwan, the Diaoyudao or Senkakus, are on the edge of the continental shelf of China and there are reports of significant deposits of hydrocarbons there. However, both Japan and Taiwan lay claim to the same area. UNCLOS III in terms of EEZs, therefore, gave China a sense of the importance of local maritime resources and their security that may not have been that prominent in earlier Chinese strategic circles. However, those odd bedfellows of "influence and security" began to stir the imagination of China's leadership in ways that had not necessarily been previously considered throughout Chinese history. The leadership perceived the need to establish China as a major regional sea-power and to deter competition from India and Japan as well as from the United States and the USSR.

The first Chief of the Chinese Navy was Admiral Xiao Jingguang, who advocated a "light-type navy capable of coastal defence", essentially to support continentalist army manoeuvre operations. Although he did try to convince Mao of the necessity to have a blue-water capability it found little favour. It was his successor, Admiral Liu Huaqing, who pushed the Chinese Navy beyond the coastal. Admiral Liu had been educated in Russia and was deeply influenced by Gorshkov who had set about changing the Soviet Navy from coastal defence into a real deep ocean and blue-water capability. Admiral Liu commended all his officers to very carefully read Gorshkov's book, "Seapower of the State".

Admiral Liu introduced the idea of a "green water" zone. That is the littoral between the brown water of the coast and the deep blue sea beyond the island chain off the coast of China. His slogan was "*Jijide jinhai fangyu zhanlie*", which roughly translated means active green water defence. This is quite different from the idea of the light-type navy of Admiral Xiao. In China's case the area stems from the Chinese waters adjacent to Vladivostock in the north, to the Straits of Malacca in the south, and from the island chain stretching from the Ryukyu Islands and Japan in the north, through Taiwan and the Philippines. These distances are in some cases more than 1000 nautical miles from the Chinese mainland. Admiral Liu's ideas represented a quantum leap forward in China's maritime thinking and strategy. During the 1990s the People's Liberation Army Navy (PLAN) invested considerable resources in overseas bases, navigational facilities including hydrography, oceanography, meteorology, magnetic field intensity and nautical charts. China now lays claim to a coastline of 18,000 kilometres and a vast expanse of ocean spanning some 3.6 million square kilometres. There are, as we know, a number of problems to be resolved in the South China Sea with other countries including, Brunei, the Philippines, Malaysia, Indonesia and Vietnam. Other factors integrated into China's maritime strategy include the exploitation of the mineral wealth of the sea off the Chinese continental shelf — it is now a major preoccupation of the Chinese leadership. Geologists report huge hydrocarbon deposits — they represent some 40 percent of China's gross potential yield. Some studies conducted by the PLAN Staff look towards using the sea as a method of generating tidal electric power and this must be factored into matters of oceans governance and the effect it has on neighbours as well. The PLAN has also assumed responsibility for deterring any local crises in the coastal regions where much of China's new industrial base is located. One must also include, in a maritime strategic context, the security of China's foreign trade — there are some 3700 ships on the Chinese register, totalling over 22 million tonnes much of which transits the South China Sea. The volume of goods has approached some 500 million tonnes per annum. Sea Lanes of Communication (SLOC) protection has therefore become a major pre-occupation for the PLAN. There is also the protection of China's burgeoning fishing fleet. China intends to achieve the catch level of South Korea and Taiwan in the near future.[18]

What is important to appreciate is that the PLAN has reached the second stage of its development envisioned by Admiral Liu Haoqing — it is now capable of controlling the "green sea". China has many other problems to solve of a maritime nature — nonetheless there is sufficient evidence to suggest that the Chinese leadership, after a somewhat languid start, is beginning to appreciate the benefits of a maritime orientation to its grand strategy. In this respect it colours questions of boundary delimitation off the whole of the Chinese coast.

A recent paper by Peter Kien-Hong Yu discusses the matter of the Chinese U-shaped line in the South China Sea and some considerations that ought to be factored into understanding the positions of both China and Taiwan.[19] This is the traditional southern Chinese maritime boundary. However, its traditional or historical significance is one issue but whether or not it actually fits with UNCLOS III and the claims of the four or five regional coastal states is another. These two dynamics form the basis of the ongoing tussles. Nonetheless, the Chinese Government signed on 4 November 2002, after what has been a protracted series of negotiations over many years with ASEAN and in several different forums, a multilateral agreement or declaration on conduct in the South China Sea.[20] Unfortunately, disputes between some of the ASEAN claimants also complicate the picture. This document is but a first step in providing a base for further negotiation and compromise between ASEAN and China. Should we look at this as some commentators suggest as a watered down agreement without substance or is it another of a long series of agreements between China and the states of Southeast Asia?[21] Lessons from history provide a degree of comfort that the agreement is but yet another step in a long lasting *"dance macabre"* where each of the actors understand their own role. Martin Stuart-Fox, writing in a recent issue of Contemporary Southeast Asia contends that,

> Though the ASEAN states may prefer to deal with China as a group, it is upon their bilateral relations regimes that they will ultimately have to rely — and these are deeply influenced by history and culture. Southeast Asian leaders are thus likely to give China what they believe the Chinese want — due deference, status as a great power, recognition of China's interests even while pursuing their own — in return for non-interference in their internal affairs and fair trading relations.[22]

We should not, therefore, view the Declaration on the Conduct of Parties in the South China Sea as a toothless agreement, it is but part of a long unfolding historical process.

Other viewpoints tend to underscore this contention but offer the reality of new institutions in the development of East Asia's economic performance and the development of a fabric of international cooperation in the region. Such concepts as the clear delineation of property rights and the public provision of information on which business and investment decisions are made are clearly in the interests of all. David Kang writes about Southeast Asian countries "bandwaggoning" on China's rise rather than "balancing" and feeling threatened.[23] A further feature in the regional security architecture is China's New Security Concept (NSC). In essence it seeks "to rise above one-sided security and seek common security through mutually beneficial cooperation. It is a concept established on the basis of common interests and is conducive to social progress".[24] A commentary by Denny Roy provides a measure of comfort; that the competing interests will not be resolved by resort to armed conflict. He writes that,

> The NSC promotes cooperative security, an expanded understanding of security that includes threats beyond traditional state vs. state military conflict, and security cooperation that is aimed at promoting trust among states rather than targeting specific countries considered potential adversaries.

> The NSC advocates multilateral dialogue, confidence building measures, arms control and non-proliferation, and expanded economic interaction as policies that will reduce international tensions. It denounces the use or threat of force to settle political disputes and calls on large countries to treat smaller countries with equality and respect.[25]

The précis of the precepts noted above are very much in line with the concepts of Comprehensive and Cooperative Security advocated by the Council for Security Cooperation in the Asia-Pacific.[26] Although the NSC may reflect China's growing confidence, Denny Roy suggests that, "If the NSC can be considered a harbinger of Chinese intentions, the Chinese seem to believe at present that they will be able to achieve security and prosperity without forcing their will on their neighbours". In terms of resolving disputes in the South China Sea perhaps there is some cause for optimism. Nonetheless, there has to be a drawing of boundaries if for no other reason than to provide for good order at sea and to provide jurisdictional *clarity* and *certainty*. No matter how much China and ASEAN countries may agree to cooperate at various levels of dialogue, the absence of specified boundaries reduces the effectiveness of a regime of *international* cooperation. This will impair maritime security, lead to misunderstandings and compromise the sustainable use of natural and mineral resources to the detriment of all in the region. It is therefore imperative that the various methods of defining and delimiting these important boundaries are applied for the benefit of all.

Notes

1. R.R. Churchill and A.V. Lowe, *The Law of the Sea*, Third Edition (Melland Schill Studies in International Law) (Manchester: Manchester University Press, 1999), p. 30.
2. R.R. Churchill and A.V. Lowe, p. 36.
3. R.R. Churchill and A.V. Lowe, p. 160.
4. R.R. Churchill and A.V. Lowe, p. 163.
5. Edward L. Miles, ed., *Management of World Fisheries: Implications of Extended Coastal State Jurisdiction* (Seattle: University of Washington Press, 1989), pp. 298–299.

6. The Gazette of India, New Delhi, Friday, 28 May 1976, Bill No. XXVIII of 1976, The Territorial Waters Continental Shelf, Exclusive Economic Zone and other Maritime Zones Act 1976.

7. New Zealand Archives PM 106/22/16, 24 June 1976.

8. New Zealand Archives PM 106/22/16, circa July 1976.

9. Bynkers-hoek in his book, *De domino maris*, proposed that a nation should exercise dominion over the adjacent seas only to the extent that she could defend them from the shore, which was taken as the existing range of a cannon, and agreed to be three miles. See Peter Kemp, ed., *The Oxford Companion to Ships and the Sea* (Oxford: Oxford University Press, 1998), p. 863.

10. K. Suter, "The New Law of the Sea", *Contemporary Review*, Vol. 267, No. 1554, July 1995.

11. R.R. Churchill and A.V. Lowe, p. 178.

12. Clive Schofield, Unpublished paper presented at the CSCAP Maritime Cooperation Working Group/PECC Meeting, Manila, 6–7 September 2003.

13. Vivian Loius Forbes, *Timor Sea Treaty and Related Agreements*, available at http://www.aph.gov.au/house/committee/jsct/timor/subs/sub15.pdf (accessed 16 May 2004).

14. Jeffrey Smith, *Offshore Jurisdiction of the Timor Lest in the Timor Sea*, available at http://www.etan.org/et2003/march/01/07offsho.htm (accessed 16 May 2004).

15. Tai Ming Cheung, "Growth of Chinese Naval Power, Priorities, Goals, Missions and Regional Implications", *Pacific Strategic Papers*, Institute of Southeast Asian Studies, Singapore, 1990, p. 4.

16. John Wilson Lewis and Xue Litai, *China's Strategic Seapower — The Politics of Force Modernization in the Nuclear Age* (Stanford, CA: Stanford University Press, 1994), pp. 214–219.

17. Tai Ming Cheung, "Growth of Chinese Naval Power, Priorities, Goals, Missions and Regional Implications", in *Pacific Strategic Papers*, Institute of Southeast Asian Studies, Singapore, 1990.

18. You Ji, "The Evolution of China's Maritime Combat Doctrines and Models: 1949–2001", *Working Paper No. 22*, Institute of Defence and Strategic Studies, Singapore, May 2002.

19. Peter Kien-Hong Yu, "The Chinese (Broken) U-Shaped Line in the South China Sea: Points, Lines and Zones", *Contemporary Southeast Asia*, Vol. 25, No. 3, December 2003.

20. Leszek Buszynski, "ASEAN, the Declaration on Conduct, and the South China Sea", *Contemporary Southeast Asia*, Vol. 25, No. 3, December 2003.

21. Ralf Emmers, "Keeping Waters Calm in South China Sea", *The Straits Times*, 21 November 2002.

22. Martin Stuart-Fox, "Southeast Asia and Chian: The Role of History and Culture in Shaping Future Relations", *Contemporary Southeast Asia*, Vol. 26, No. 1, April 2004, p. 136.

23. David Kang, "Hierachy, Balancing, and Empirical Puzzles in Asian International Relations", *International Relations*, Vol. 28, No. 3, Winter 2003/4.
24. See http://www.chinaembassy.org.au/eng/jmhz/t46228.htm (accessed 16 May 2004).
25. Denny Roy, "China's Pitch for a Multi-polar World: The New Security Concept", *Asia Pacific Centre for Security Studies*, Vol. 2 No. 1, May 2003.
26. CSCAP Memorandum No. 3, The Concepts of Comprehensive Security and Cooperative Security.

Annex A

[SUBMISSION NO. 15]

Timor Sea Treaty and Related Agreements
Joint Petroleum Development Area
Issues and Implications

Vivian Louis Forbes
MA, PhD
Adjunct Associate Professor, Curtin University
Map Curator, The University of Western Australia

Geopolitical Expediency

That Australia is committed to a strong and productive relationship with East Timor is admirable especially in the context of the traumas that the East Timorese have experienced over the past three decades. Australia has established a substantial post-independence aid programme for East Timor that includes projects which cover education, health, infrastructure and governance, water supply and sanitation and rural development. The Australian Federal Police is providing assistance as part of the Civilian Police Force and the Australia Department of Defence is providing support to East Timor's Defence Force.

The *Timor Sea Treaty* (TST) and Related Agreements are a significant milestone in the development of this relationship. The related documents are a *Memorandum of Understanding* concerning an internationalisation unitisation agreement for the Greater Sunrise Field and an *Exchange of Notes Constituting an Agreement*. The Treaty and the two documents were signed on 20 May 2002 within about twelve hours of East Timor becoming a sovereign state, the first in the 21st century.

The TST will enter into force once Australia and East Timor ratify the document. The TST establishes a Joint Petroleum Development Area (JPDA) that replaces Zone of Cooperation "A" (ZOCA) which was established in the Timor Gap Treaty between Australia and Indonesia in 1989. Australia and East Timor (at Government levels) have commenced their ratification processes and are committed to expeditious entry into force of the TST.

That being said, it is suggested that:

- political expediency has been paramount in initialling the TST;
- the TST is far too generous;
- due process of consultation with user groups is a shortcoming of the Government; and
- the text of the TST is vague on a number of issues, in particular on sovereign rights to the marine biotic resources within the confines of the JPDA.

There are many issues and implications that need to be discussed before Australia takes the next step, namely that of ratification of the TST. However, events behind the scene may force Australia to reconsider the terms of the TST and indeed, those of the *Perth Treaty* of March 1997 between Australia and Indonesia.

Factors

Let us consider what factors were taken into account in drafting the TST. They include:

- Application of Article 83 of the 1982 *Law of the Sea Convention* that makes provision for "...the delimitation of the continental shelf between two states ... shall be effected by agreement on the basis of international law in order to achieve an equitable solution";
- A desirability of Australia and East Timor to enter into a Treaty;
- A desire to promote East Timor's economic development;
- Maintaining security of investment for existing and planned petroleum activities;
- Perceived benefits to flow to both countries by providing a continuing basis for hydrocarbon exploitation activities;
- Importance of developing hydrocarbon resources;
- Minimising damage to the marine environment;
- Maintaining economic sustainability of hydrocarbon resources;
- Promoting further investment;

- Contribution to the long-term development of both countries; and
- To provide an arrangement of a practical nature that does not prejudice a final determination of the seabed delimitation (TST, Article 2).

Summary of the Treaty

The key elements of the *Timor Sea Treaty* are:

- The new treaty will have a duration of 30 years; it may be renewed; activities may continue even if TST is no longer in force (Article 22);
- Deferral of delimitation of a permanent seabed boundary without prejudice to Australia's and East Timor's rights or entitlements in international law (Article 2);
- Joint control, manage and facilitate the exploration, development and exploitation of petroleum resources of the JPDA (Aticle 3);
- A revenue split of 90 per cent for East Timor and 10 per cent for Australia from petroleum development activities in the Joint Petroleum Development Area (JPDA) [Article 4];
- Agree on a joint fiscal scheme (Article 5);
- Regulatory bodies will include Designated Authority (DA), a Joint Commission (JC) and a Ministerial Council (MC) [Article 6];
- Australian jurisdiction over the planned pipeline from the JPDA to Australia (Article 8);
- Maintenance of the contractual terms of the existing petroleum/gas projects (*Bayu-Undan, Greater Sunrise and Elang-Kakatua*) [Article 9];
- Unitisation of the *Greater Sunrise* field (which straddles the JPDA and an area under Australian jurisdiction) on the basis that 20 per cent of the field lies within the JPDA and 80 per cent of the field lies within Australian jurisdiction (Article 9); and
- Australia has also agreed to provide additional financial support to East Timor of A$8 million per year with effect from 2005, to assist with petroleum resource development;
- East Timor will realise financial benefits (six billion dollars) from 2003.

Issues and Implications

Australia over-generous in 1989, 1997 and 2002

Australia has not adopted a firm stand over its rights to the resources of the continental shelf in the northern waters of Australia evident in the suite of Treaties that Australia has initialled with Indonesia, since the late-1980s and most recently with East Timor. Yet Australia allocates vast sums of money, expertise and time on research in the southern waters, in particular, to the southeast sector of its maritime domain.

The provisions of the TST offer enormous concessions to East Timor in addition to foreign aid. The generosity is akin to that of the 1958 Agreement between Bahrain and Saudi Arabia, in which the latter oversees much of the administration of the Joint Development Zone and the former receives the benefits accrued from the exploitation of the hydrocarbons within the Zone in the Gulf.

The JPDA includes the *Bayu-Udan Gas and Oil Field* and portion of the *Greater Sunrise Gas Field*. The latter is also the subject of dispute between two rivals, Shell and Phillips. Shell wants to use a floating platform to export oil and gas and Phillips want to pump the product to Darwin. Development of the Bayu-Undan has begun. If these and the other fields are put on hold for an extended period, it could shift the focus to the hydrocarbon developments in Papua New Guinea or elsewhere further away.

Indonesia and Australia signed the 1997 "Perth Treaty" to delimit maritime boundaries in the Timor Sea and in the northeast sector of the Indian Ocean. Both countries, pending its entry into force are observing the 1997 Treaty's terms. Ratification/entry into force is not "imminent" but should occur in the foreseeable future (Personal communication with DFAT, 17 June 2002). In this Treaty, Australia determined seabed and water column boundaries, delineated an extensive "grey area" (in colour coding and in reality) and defined a maritime boundary that lies much closer to Christmas Island which is much too close for comfort. The vast "grey area" now excludes Australian fishing industry from operating therein.

The Perth March 1997 Treaty delimiting a seabed boundary and a water column boundary with Indonesia is unusual and has created anxiety, insurmountable problems and uncertainty for the future for those in the fishing industry and in the exploration and exploitation of the hydrocarbon resources in the Timor Sea.

Have the politicians given away our seabed rights?

The TST is similar in content to the *Timor Gap Treaty* except that in the former there is a 90/10 ratio whereas with the latter the royalties were to be split 50/50.

There is good argument on this basis alone that Australia has been generous. It now appears that East Timor is seeking complete control of the JPDA and indeed, goes further with claims for larger areas, east and west of the JPDA, than is defined in the TST.

Who has rights to the biotic resources in the water column of the JPDA?

The TST is silent on this matter. Likewise the Australian Government is silent and dismisses any questions on the issue. This matter raises concerns to those engaged in the practicalities of the fishing industry.

Has precedence been set?

The Zone of Cooperation created precedence that was different from the conventional thinking of the continental shelf principle that governed much of the Arafura Sea and parts of the Timor Sea and indeed in the Coral Sea and elsewhere that Australia had delimited its maritime boundaries.

If Australia agreed to extend the limits of the JPDA at some later stage or caves in to East Timor's demands, it would have to revise a whole suite of its maritime boundary negotiations. One could not envisage Indonesia accepting the terms of the 1997 Treaty. There could also be claims from Papua New Guinea and the Solomon Islands. What will New Zealand demand when it negotiates its maritime boundary with Australia in the Tasman Sea?

Will the provisions of the Treaty create a problem for our future negotiations?

If Australia compromises its stand it runs the risk of placing the giant *Laminaria Gas and Oil Field* into the quagmire of the Australian/Indonesian "grey zone".

Have the geoscientist given their input and is the information on the geology of the substratum and geomorphology of the seabed fully understood? Is the Government heeding the advice of the geoscientists and political geographers?

It is hoped that in both instances the answers are positive and that the negotiations were not based purely on political expediency. There are areas in the world where similar cases exist and generally one Government will not submit so easily to another.

The Geography

- A distinct trough — Timor Trough — separates the Australian continent and the island of Timor. The two landmasses **do not** share a natural continental shelf. The continental shelf — out to the 200-metre isobath — is a narrow strip along the southern sector of Timor Island whilst being broad off the northern coast of Australia. The legal continental shelves of Australia, as indeed of East Timor and Indonesia, have yet to be defined in accordance with the 1982 Law of the Sea Convention.

- The substratum of the Timor Sea is regarded as a highly prospective hydrocarbon reserve region containing substantial condensate and gas reserves.

- Geological features are the Bonaparte (main) and Browse Basins.

- The area of the Timor Sea is administered by the Northern Territory, Western Australia and the Joint Petroleum Development Authority (JPDA) on behalf of Australia and East Timor.

- The Northern Territory Government administers the Ashmore/Cartier Islands Adjacent Area (on behalf of the Commonwealth Government) and the NT Adjacent Area.

- The Timor Sea is the focus of attention. *Bayu-Undan, Sunrise* and *Evans Shoal gas* projects and recently completed major oil developments include the *Elang/Kakatua, Laminaria/Corallina* and *Buffalo* projects have the potential to generate wealth to the sovereign state.

- Exploration commitments offshore are high, with the expectation of further oil and gas discoveries in the future which would be stimulated by gas markets in Australia and overseas.

History

- Exploration commenced in the early 1960s.
- Thirty-two wildcat wells (rank exploration wells) were drilled to 1975. There were several oil and gas strikes although no commercial developments resulted.
- Seabed boundaries delimited in the Arafura and Timor Seas in 1971 and 1972.
- Exploration in the Timor Gap area was suspended in 1975 due to the unresolved seabed boundary between Australia and Indonesia.

- A Provisional Fisheries and Surveillance Enforcement Line (PFSEL) aligned approximately on a median-line principle was defined and incorporated in 1981.
- Signing of *Timor Gap Treaty* in 1991 that established the Zone of Cooperation and award of production sharing contract areas in 1992 hailed the start of the exploration "boom" in the region.
- Portugal takes Australia to the ICJ in 1995; sought Treaty as void; Indonesia not a party to the ICJ.
- East Timor opts out of Indonesia in September 1999; becomes an independent state in May 2002; and
- Zone of Cooperation extinguished and ZOC Area "A" replaced by Joint Petroleum Development Area (JPDA). ZOC "B" and "C" have been abolished.

The Arafura and Timor Seas are marine regions that are "over-the horizon" for Canberra-based politicians to gain an appreciation of the potential problems that have been created by Australian Governments, both past and present, in signing the 2002 *Timor Sea Treaty*, the *Perth Treaty* March 1997 and the *Timor Gap Treaty* of 1989. If the intentions were honourable at the time of signature, so be it. However, the process of consultation prior to signing the treaties leaves a lot to be desired. The adverse comments raised in the Joint Senate Standing Committee into the 1997 Treaty speak volumes.

On geographical reality, historical facts, and traditional and conventional international law alone Australia must insist on its inherent rights to harvest the marine biotic and exploit the mineral resources of the Timor and Arafura Seas and to manage the marine environment of the region. A cooperative approach is welcomed but administration must at all times be seen to be even-handed.

It may be too late to suggest that Australia should not ratify the TST. It would appear that Australia will be open to criticism if it ratified the TST or sought to draft another Agreement with East Timor. There is no doubt that there is pressure from East Timor to re-negotiate on terms that best suits that country, but that could be a short-term solution. If Australia permitted East Timor, and later Indonesia, to dictate the alignment of maritime boundaries — lines of resource allocation — in the Timor Sea it will create many more problems than could be suggested in this brief submission.

The Australian Government has been warned, in the past, that our northern waters are open to abuse by aliens; that it has taken a softly-softly approach to a number of major issues, such as illegal fishing and illegal trade in people smuggling; and has had a weak policy on so called "traditional mode of fishing".

Annex B

The Offshore Jurisdiction of Timor Leste in the Timor Sea

Summary Opinion

March 2003

Prepared by:

Jeffrey Smith of LINDSAY KENNEY Barristers & Solicitors Vancouver, Canada T +1 604 687 132 F +1 604 687 2304

Introduction

Timor Leste, known also as East Timor and Timor Loro Sa'e, became the world's newest State in May 2002. It achieved its independence with an undefined maritime jurisdiction and is now in the fortunate position of not being bound by any pre-existing offshore boundaries. The importance of this for energy development in the ocean area to the south of Timor cannot be understated, given significant reserves of oil, gas and condensates in the continental shelf. Timor Leste's maritime jurisdiction, both north and south of its territorial land areas, remains to be defined. The new State's jurisdiction is capable of certain determination with the application of criteria found in several decisions of the International Court of Justice, arbitration awards, State practice and developments in customary international law. The recent decisions in the Eritrea/Yemen and Qatar/Bahrain cases support the delimitation of Timor Leste's maritime boundaries in areas outside of the restrictive Timor Gap Treaty Zone of Cooperation, now the Joint Petroleum Development Area of the pending Timor Sea Treaty (1).

This paper discusses Timor Leste's maritime jurisdiction in the Timor Sea. From reasons of brevity, it does not address the new State's jurisdiction in the Ombai and Wetar Straits to the north.

Present Boundaries in the Timor Sea

There is presently only one formal maritime boundary in the Timor Sea. It is the continental shelf boundary established by treaty between Australia and Indonesia in 1972 (2). A gap was left in the boundary, between its delimited points A16 and A17, because Australia could not obtain the agreement of Portugal to complete the seabed delimitation. The position of Portugal was pragmatic it would wait to conclude a seabed boundary until further development of the law of the sea. Portugal did not agree that the doctrine of natural prolongation applied to determine the boundary position along the south slope of the Timor Trough, as had Indonesia, notwithstanding Australia's reliance on the doctrine following its application in the 1969 North Sea Continental Shelf cases. In 1989, after a decade of negotiations, the closing lines and area of the Timor Gap Treaty Zone of Cooperation were agreed upon by Australia and Indonesia. It must be recalled that the Timor Gap Treaty is expressly not a maritime boundary treaty. Nevertheless, the "lateral" (i.e. east and west) closing lines of the Zone of Cooperation were based on lines of simple equidistance extending seaward from the coastline of Timor and small Indonesian islands to the east. A second boundary treaty in the Timor Sea was concluded in 1997 between Australia and Indonesia has not been subsequently ratified (3). The 1997 Treaty was intended, in part, to delimit a water column boundary between the two states across the entire Timor Sea. The resulting boundary followed an equidistance line generally from east to west, some 140 nautical miles from Timor and the north coast of Australia. Apart from the 1997 Treaty not having been ratified, Timor Leste would not be bound to succeed to it for other reasons, although the delimitation effected by it is supportable and reasonable under the current law of the sea. The 1997 so-called "EEZ" delimitation stands in obvious contrast to the more restrictive continental shelf boundary defined by the 1972 Treaty.

There are obvious flaws in the locations of the 1972 continental shelf boundary and the closing lines that define the Zone of Cooperation, now the Joint Petroleum Development Area of the Timor Sea Treaty. Those flaws are not supportable under international law as it now applies. The 1972 boundary encroaches spatially on Timor Leste's continental shelf entitlement. That an independent Timor Leste has an entitlement to an exclusive economic zone (EEZ) larger than the Timor Gap and the present Zone of Cooperation (4) is evident from geography, decisions of the International Court of Justice and the past conduct of Australia and Indonesia in the Timor Sea. First, the Timor Gap, defined as the undelimited area between points A16 and A17 of the 1972 Treaty is demonstrably too narrow (5). It constrains Timor Leste's coastal projection to the south, whether such projection extends directly south or, more obviously on the basis of local geography, in a more general southeast direction.

Second, the 1972 Treaty has a diminished basis in international law. There is no precedent for it in state practice or any recent ICJ and arbitral authorities. The application of seabed geomorphology as a delimitation criterion is manifestly wrong and, without it, the 1972 continental shelf boundary would have been drawn further to the south. This was implicitly recognized in the 1997 Treaty between Indonesia and Australia for an unadjusted median "water column" boundary. Timor Leste's full maritime jurisdiction does not so much depend on recognizing that the 1972 Treaty boundary should be properly disregarded or at least shifted south as it does on the enlargement of the overall area at issue. Third, the 1972 Treaty expressly acknowledges that the interior boundary segments A15-A16 (in the east) and A17-A18 (in the west) would subject to adjustment or roll-back possibly on the request of Portugal. This opening up of the Timor Gap would have a clear result in the west. In the east it would be of little significance. Here, however, developments in the law of the sea, including state practice and recent decisions of the International Court of Justice and the Permanent Court of Arbitration reveal that Timor Leste's ocean area is encroached upon by the restrictive lateral closing line of the Zone of Cooperation. The lateral closing line is simply an unadjusted median line that accords full effect to the disparate Indonesian islands east of Timor. This is manifestly contrary to the treatment of islands in the law of the sea, where small offlying islands or island groups are invariably accorded reduced weight or coastal projection into the offshore.

It must also be recalled in considering the lateral closing lines which define the Zone of Cooperation that the Timor Gap Treaty was, if not illegal, a discredited treaty instrument and its supersession by delimitation has been expressly recognized by Australia. Moreover, it exacerbates the obvious encroachment of the 1972 continental shelf boundary by repeated application of simplified and unadjusted geographic features. Delimitation in the Timor Sea.

There are several interrelated factors that support Timor Leste's EEZ extending to a median line with Australia and over areas wider than the former Zone of Cooperation and the pending Joint Petroleum Development Area. These factors are supported by state practice and through decisions of the ICJ. The first, extension of an EEZ to the median line between Timor Leste and Australia, is straightforward especially given decisions of the ICJ (6) and also as a matter of state practice in the Timor Sea (7).

Second, a widening of the Timor Gap from east to west can be done by adjustment of the boundary segments between points A15 and A16, and points A17 and A18, on the 1972 Treaty boundary, a matter provided for at Article 3 of the Treaty. This adjustment a widening of the Timor Gap — is particularly relevant to the drawing of a western EEZ "lateral" line which, with regard to generalized equidistance between the coast of Timor Leste and Indonesia, will seaward extend from terminus of the land boundary at the Masin River through point A18 on the 1972 continental shelf boundary to terminate just east of point Z40 on the 1997 Treaty line. As noted, above an Article 3 adjustment done in the east is less marked, largely because the 1972 Treaty gave full effect or weight in setting point A15 on full geographic application of the Leti Islands.

Accordingly, the median line and western lateral boundaries of Timor Leste's EEZ are relatively simple to define. It should be expected that they will conform to generally equidistant courses and not require adjustment to account for geographic or other features.

Those factors that will determine the orientation of the eastern "lateral" line of an EEZ to extending seaward from the Wetar Channel include: (1) the geographic effect or weight to be given to the Leti Islands; (2) the opposing coastlines of Timor Leste and Indonesia across the Wetar Channel; (3) the encroachment of maritime areas generated by Indonesia's baselines on the offshore jurisdiction of Timor Leste; and (4) the application of the equitable delimitation method of proportionality to illustrate the non-encroachment of Timor Leste's EEZ into Indonesian and Australian waters.

In the area south of the Wetar Channel a lateral EEZ boundary will be drawn to continue seaward from the boundary between opposing coastlines in the Wetar Strait to the north of Timor. The lateral boundary, as it follows a course seaward out of the Strait, will pass through a mid-channel point at 8 20′ south, 127 28′ west, midway between the opposing coastlines of Jaco Islet and Leti Island (8).

The course of the lateral boundary further seaward will be contingent on the four factors above. The ICJ decisions suggest that small, disparate islands must be given diminished effect in their weight on delimitation. This is the case with the Leti Islands to the east. Their size and limited coastal presence/pdf3 must necessarily be a factor in delimitation. By giving only half or reduce/d effect to the geographic presence of these islands an equitable result is achieved by adjusting the lateral boundary further east (9). This minimizes the encroachment of the islands into a constantly radiating and uniform coastal façade generated by Timor Leste southeast of the Wetar Channel.

Without such an adjustment, the lateral boundary drawn as a perpendicular (and essentially parallel to the western lateral boundary) would pass through or a few miles to the east of Point A15 on the 1972 Treaty boundary (10). A basic equidistance line that does not account for the limited geographic presence of the Leti Islands would follow an azimuth of between 155 to 160. This encroaches on Timor Leste's more pronounced coastal reach.

The two most recent delimitation decisions support the equitable requirement for reduced effect to be given to the Leti Islands. The Eritrea/Yemen decision confirms that small groups of islands can be discounted (that is, be accorded reduced weighting or effect) in the drawing of a median line (11). It is now well recognized that "mid-sea islands", if accorded full effect, can have a disproportionate result in delimitation. This is readily evident in delimitations between opposing coasts. In the present situation, even if it can somehow be characterized as one of mixed oppositeness and adjacency, it should be straightforward to apply to the islands in question the principle of reduced effect or weight.

It is the degree of reduced weight to be given to the Leti Islands (and therefore the baseline drawn across their southern periphery) that is possibly controversial. Although the ICJ decisions support half effect reduced weighting, this would result in a marked shift of the present Zone of Cooperation/Joint Petroleum Development Area closing line. A more acceptable result might be to accord three-quarter effect to the islands. This would result in a lateral boundary following a course generally close to a true opposing boundary between the east part of Timor and the Leti Islands. The coincidence of these boundaries is a further test of their equitableness. No state's maritime area is unduly encroached upon; an overriding concern in every maritime delimitation.

The justification for such an eastward shift of the lateral boundary can also be taken from the International Court of Justice's most recent decision in Qatar/Bahrain (12). The Court fixed a single equidistant maritime boundary which extended almost perpendicularly seaward from the interior embayment area between the two states. The Court was careful to assess whether any equitable criteria required an adjustment of the provisional median line. None merited any application.

Further certainty can be achieved by the application of the equitable delimitation method of proportionality. This doctrine suggests that no encroachment on the respective states' maritime areas results from an opposite line or three-quarter effect delimitation, as the ratios of coastlines involved to maritime areas delimited are generally equivalent.

The Law of the Sea Next Steps

The criterion for maritime boundary delimitation, and therefore the determination of offshore jurisdiction is overwhelmingly distance based. At play is the geography of the coastlines at issue. Maritime states are entitled to claim EEZs up to 200 nautical miles from their shores. Conceptually and legally, the EEZ extent of a state is defined by different criteria than is the continental shelf. For this reason, because of the obvious advantages in establishing a proper maritime jurisdiction, it would be highly advisable for Timor Leste to claim the EEZ it has in national legislation. This EEZ, on the basis of state practice and the caselaw, should be larger than Area A defined by the former Timor Gap Treaty and now the same Joint Petroleum Development Area under the pending Timor Sea Treaty. In asserting the claim, Indonesia and Australia would have to recognize its merits and the settled law in support of it. The preferred result would be a negotiated delimitation, desirable under the 1982 Law of the Sea Convention and a result to be achieved by conciliation or the good offices of a fourth state.

Notes

1. Treaty on the Zone of Cooperation in an Area between the Indonesian Province of East Timor and Northern Australia, 11 December 1989, (1990) 29 ILM 469 (in force 9 February 1991) (the Timor Gap Treaty).
2. Agreement between the Government of the Commonwealth of Australia and the Government of the Republic of Indonesia establishing certain seabed boundaries in the area of the Timor and the Arafura Seas supplementary to the agreement of 18 May 1971, Aus. T.S. 1973, No. 32 (9 October 1972) (the 1972 Treaty).
3. Treaty between the Government of Australia and the government of the Republic of Indonesia establishing an Exclusive Economic Zone Boundary and Certain Seabed Boundaries, (1997) 36 ILM 1053 (not yet in force) (the 1997 Treaty). The median line followed by this treaty is the course of the Provisional Fisheries Surveillance and Enforcement Line agreed upon between Australia and Indonesia in 1981.
4. Or the Joint Petroleum Development Area that is defined by the nominal successor to the Timor Gap Treaty, the July 5, 2001 Arrangement on the Timor Sea.
5. The south coast of Timor Leste generates a maritime projection into the Timor Sea somewhat perpendicular to the geographic orientation of the Island of Timor. This projection, derived from the extrema of a simplified national coastline has a simplified width of 158 to 162 nautical miles, including the territorial sea east of Jaco Isle in the centre of the Wetar Channel. This projection is oriented southeast along an azimuth of about 155. If the profile of the south coast is considered differently a direct projection south from the two extrema of Timor Leste's land area, in the mid-point of the Wetar Channel and the Masin River, will result in a narrower width to the coastal front of about 142–144 nautical miles. In contrast to these coastal projections the Timor Gap defined by points A16 and A17 of the 1972 Treaty is only 130 nautical miles wide.
6. The leading decisions now being Greenland/Jan Mayen, (1993) ICJ Rep. 8, Qatar/Bahrain, 40 ILM 743 and Eritrea/Yemen (2001), 40 ILM 750 (Permanent Court of Arbitration).

7. It is not possible for Timor Leste and Australia to each realize the maximum extent of their jurisdictional claims to 200 nautical mile EEZs (or a continental shelves) in the Timor Sea. Absent the options of maintaining the status quo under the July 5, 2001 Arrangement on the Timor Sea or some other settlement a delimitation of the area must result. This has influenced all attempts to settle jurisdictional claims in the Timor Sea since 1972, and as recently as the negotiations for the 1997 Treaty. It is likely that the geographic basis for the boundary defined in the 1997 Treaty will be recognized allowing adoption of the basepoints detailed in that treaty to be used in a formal median line delimitation. There is no encroachment that occurs from the adoption of the 1997 median line as a provisional mid-sea boundary between the EEZs of Timor Leste and Australia.

8. See the attached chart. The commencement point is merely the continuation of an opposing delimitation extending through the Wetar Strait as it progress seaward into the Timor Sea [chart is available at http://www.etan.org/etanpdf/ pdf3//timor_map_12B.pdf].

9. A half effect was given, among other decisions, to small offshore islands in the Gulf of Maine case, supra note at paragraph 222 and in the Tunisia/Libya decision, (1982) ICJ Rep. 18 at paragraph 128. The reduced and half effect weighting of islands is common in bilateral treaty practice, something recognized by the ICJ in Tunisia/Libya.

10. This result is consistent with the operative provisions of the 1972 Treaty, which set point A16 as the eastern terminal point of the Timor Gap with allowance for it to be adjusted to account for any continental shelf boundaries proposed by Portugal.

11. Supra note 6 at paragraph 117.

12. Supra note 6.

Chapter 6

The Modernisation of Naval Forces in the Asia-Pacific: A Focus on Three Northeast Asian Navies

Derek da Cunha

Introduction

For the most part, defence expenditures by countries in regions around the world have largely been in decline since the end of the Cold War, as countries, particularly those in Europe, have wanted to benefit from a "peace dividend" brought about by the end of the ideological confrontation between East and West. However, the peace dividend has generally not been apparent in the Asia-Pacific region where conventional security issues — ranging from the standoff on the Korean peninsula, to the tensions across the Taiwan Strait, to overlapping jurisdictional claims to island territories across the region — still remain prominent. The Asian financial crisis of 1997/98 did put a brake on defence expenditures, especially that of a number of Southeast Asian states, but since then those expenditures have rebounded and continued to rise steadily, aided by national economic expansion. What is noteworthy is that since the early 1990s a greater share of national defence budgets have been given over to building-up the capabilities of navies/maritime forces as against the other component arms of military forces throughout much of the

Asia-Pacific region. That trend highlights two issues:

- navies in the region have tended to lag behind other service arms, particularly armies, and governments have since decided to redress that imbalance; and
- issues related to maritime security have risen in prominence, especially over the last decade, with countries now wishing to provide themselves with a means to meet the multifaceted challenges posed by maritime security.

These two broad features of the process of robust modernisation, and indeed expansion, of naval forces, in the Asia-Pacific only partly explain what is going on. Other reasons that have specifically underpinned that process include:

- the vast growth in global seaborne trade, a great proportion of which is conducted through and within the Asia-Pacific region;
- the China–Taiwan standoff and its ripple effect across Northeast Asia and into Southeast Asia;
- the spectacular rise of a regional hegemon, China, with its potential to upset the regional balance of power;
- perceptions of a reduced US military presence, and commitment to security, in the Asia-Pacific region;
- bilateral disputes and tensions between a number of countries, most notably in Southeast Asia, exemplified between Malaysia and Singapore;
- the requirement for enforcement of national jurisdiction over maritime domains covered by the UN Convention on the Law of the Sea (UNCLOS);
- a plethora of overlapping claims to island territories across the Asia-Pacific;
- the increasing incidence of piratical attacks at sea, especially in Southeast Asian waters; and
- the simple growth in the stature and geopolitical significance of a number of regional states and their desire to underline their increasing influence regionally.

All these factors illustrate the point that whereas in Europe the notions of balance of power, self-help (arms buildups) and conventional deterrence have largely lost their relevance in the post-Cold War order, in the Asia-Pacific they remain centrally relevant. And they do so even if transnational issues, such as international terrorism, the spread of infectious diseases, international crime and the illegal movement of people across national borders, have also now come to the fore in the Asia-Pacific security calculus. More specifically, the factors enumerated above have spurred the modernisation and expansion of naval forces by most of the Asia-Pacific states. This chapter will examine that phenomenon. The coverage here will not be comprehensive in nature, but will examine some of the more salient aspects of the modernisation of naval forces by three Northeast Asian states: China, Taiwan and Japan. Taken together, these states exemplify the factors that have been spelt out to account for naval development in the Asia-Pacific in recent times.

Definition

In definitional terms, the "modernisation" of naval forces means more than just the upgrading of equipment or the introduction of new platforms (not just afloat, but also airborne, i.e. naval aviation) into navies. It also includes the adoption of new operational concepts that allow navies to engage in a panoply of missions in peace time, crisis situations or in major conflict. This aspect is often absent in the analysis of naval capabilities in the Asia-Pacific. As a generalisation, the practice by defence analysts in the region has usually been simple bean counting, the kind of approach whose utility in understanding the purpose, existence and development of navies is rather doubtful. And, here, it is also worthwhile noting that when more than just bean counting is adopted as analysis there has generally been a tendency by some observers to judge the quality and capabilities of Asia-Pacific navies against the standard of Western navies, more especially the US Navy. This constitutes a major error, as wrong assumptions or conclusions are the end result. The US Navy — which is a superpower navy — has a global role, and, as such, its capabilities are comprehensive in nature so as to allow it to carry out the entire spectrum of missions required to secure US national interests (which also includes the interests of America's allies). On the other hand, the navies of the Asia-Pacific, which are much smaller and less capable in comparison, have either a localised or, at most, a regional role. That localised or regional role would be considered sufficient in securing individual national interest. And, indeed, that localised or regional role might, at least in theory or on paper, be sufficient in countering the American superpower navy in the localised theatre-of-operations. Here, one refers specifically to the navy of China, the People's Liberation Army Navy (PLAN), which is the focus of the section that follows.

The PLA Navy

Since the early 1980s, the PLAN has slowly but most assuredly been given increased importance and resources relative to the other service arms — the army, air force and strategic missile forces. By the mid-1990s, observers began to note the significance of the change. For instance, the London-based International Institute for Strategic Studies' *Military Balance 1995–96* contended: "There is growing evidence that the Chinese Navy is now its [the PLA's] paramount service". Since the early 1980s, the PLAN's fleet components — North Sea, East Sea and South Sea — have tended to develop unevenly as a consequence of the twin factors of PLA doctrine and Beijing's shifting threat perceptions.

For much of the 1970s, the PLAN had concentrated its best units in the North Sea Fleet, towards the Soviet Union's Far East and that country's Pacific Fleet. In the 1980s, however, as a result of the establishment of a Soviet naval presence in the South China Sea out of Vietnam's Cam Ranh Bay, the South Sea Fleet was accorded greater attention in terms of improved hardware and increased numbers of personnel. This attention remained until the early 1990s when, with the disappearance of the Soviet threat, the focus appeared to shift towards the East Sea Fleet, and oriented towards the Taiwan contingency.[1] The most notable manifestation of this new focus has been twofold in nature: most of the newest warships the PLAN has been acquiring from Russia — such as Sovremenny-class destroyers (re-designated by the PLAN as Hangzhou-class destroyers) and Kilo-class diesel-electric submarines — have now been assigned to the East Sea Fleet; and, the vast bulk of multi-role Su-27 Flankers the PLA Air Force (PLAAF) has either acquired or produced locally under license from Russia have been located in geographical proximity to East Sea Fleet installations. In exercises conducted in recent years, Su-27 Flankers have been staging out of their operational bases in Anhui Province to cover the emergence of the East Sea Fleet into the East China Sea. That is a vivid demonstration of the PLA's application of the maritime-air operation (MAO). It is also a clear indication of how the PLAN intends to fight if conflict breaks out across the Taiwan Strait. PLA fleet units will fight largely under the cover of land-based air power. (The PLAAF now has within its inventory more than 100 Su-27 Flankers. This force is deployed and designated as frontline Category A units with operational readiness levels of between 60 and 70 percent, as against 25–50 percent for much of the rest of the air force. Annual flying hours for Flanker pilots is roughly 180, as against half that time for pilots of other PLAAF aircraft types.) This would allow the Chinese to send into combat two full Flanker regiments at short notice, constituting sufficient critical mass for the conduct of offensive operations. That would also indicate the relatively short range of Chinese fleet units. Despite impressive peacetime voyages — intended as "goodwill" visits — around the globe, in periods of crisis or conflict the vast proportion of the PLAN would largely be operating relatively close to shore installations. PLAN units would surge out of their bases to attempt to strike at enemy formations and then return to their operational bases for re-supply, refueling and rearmament. A war across the Taiwan Strait, however, will likely see the PLA's strategic missile forces as China's main strike component. More than 500 M-9 and M-11 ballistic missiles — which can be fitted with a range of ordnance from conventional high-explosives to fuel-air explosives and chemical warheads — had by late 2004 been deployed and are operational with PLA brigade-level strategic missile force units in the southeastern coastal regions from where they are within strike range of Taiwan. (This is more than ten times the number of missiles that were deployed at the time of the Taiwan Strait crisis in March 1995.) By the end of 2005, it is expected that the Chinese would have deployed more than 700 M-9 and M-11 missiles against Taiwan, suggesting a stepped rate of deployment.

While missile strikes will be intended to smash Taiwanese resistance, the mission of the PLAN and PLAAF will likely be to counter the US Navy in its bid to forestall or smother any Chinese amphibious assault on Taiwan. Here, the lessons for the Chinese of the 1996 Taiwan Strait crisis are apparent. As the Chinese carried out aggressive missile and naval exercises intended to intimidate Taiwan in the run up to its presidential election, Washington deployed two carrier battlegroups close to the Straits in an attempt to deter the PLA from moving beyond mere intimidation. It is said that the Chinese navy slunk away in the face of the deployment of American naval power. The Chinese have since vowed never to allow such a humiliation to occur again, and part of the PLAN's modernisation process has been intended to achieve that objective. The initial order for two Sovremenny-class destroyers from Russia was actually made in advance of the Taiwan Strait crisis, but their acquisition took on new significance in the wake of that crisis. That crisis also prompted Beijing to acquire at least two further Sovremennys. The Sovremenny is a warship largely designed for surface warfare. It was conceived during Soviet times as a platform to counter US aircraft carriers. Armed with eight SS-N-22 Sunburn supersonic ship-to-ship missiles (SSMs) — without at-sea re-load capability — the Sovremenny would, in the event of any Taiwan-type crisis involving the US Navy, likely take station off US aircraft carriers, shadowing those carriers during the period of crisis. Here, one has the scenario of the game of "chicken" in mind. Effectively, who seizes the initiative by launching a strike first on either ship will destroy or severely damage the target. It would be useful to elaborate on this point to underline the significance of Chinese naval modernisation, even if it includes just a few, but very capable, platforms.

The sheer proximity of a Sovremenny-class destroyer to an American carrier and its battlegroup would effectively degrade by a significant margin the battlegroup's otherwise all-round superiority. It would take a mere few seconds for the Sovremenny's SS-N-22 Sunburn SSMs to saturate the battlegroup's anti-air defences and strike at its central target, the aircraft carrier. The very short distance would not give the US battlegroup's surface-to-air missile (SAM) batteries sufficient time to engage and destroy the incoming missiles. The same would apply to the battlegroup's electronic countermeasures, i.e. chaff cloud, which would also be ineffective as a result of the short time-towards-target dilemma posed by the incoming anti-ship missiles. The only counter available would be the aircraft carrier's last line of defence — the close-in-weapon system (CIWS), i.e. gatling guns. But here, even if CIWS succeeded in destroying incoming SS-N-22 SSMs, the missiles' resultant explosion and the speed with which they had been traveling would ensure that the enormous luminous fireball would continue to roll towards the carrier, engulfing it, killing or injuring personnel on deck, destroying or damaging exposed assets such as aircraft, and most importantly destroying the carrier's external antenna arrays of radar and communications equipment. That latter kind of loss would effectively degrade the aircraft carrier's capabilities to such an extent that it would not be able to operate effectively, leaving its commander with little choice but to withdraw from the battle zone.

This scenario is credible but is often overlooked, not contemplated or not understood by most observers who seem to be overly mesmerised by US military power and have not thought through the kind of tactical issues or problems that could emerge in an operational context. The point emphasises how in specific situations a relatively inferior force, if it seizes the initiative during the period of crisis leading up to the commencement of hostilities, could achieve a major tactical objective over a superior force. And that is precisely what PLA strategic planners have been putting their minds to since the Taiwan Strait crisis of 1996.

Acquisition of big-ticket hardware such as destroyers and submarines from Russia only provide a partial picture of Chinese naval modernisation efforts. The PLAN has also systematically been retrofitting a range of high-technology

Russian and Western weapons and electronic systems — such as anti-ship missiles, communications suites and radar — onto existing warships as a cost-effective means to extend the service life of warships listed in the Chinese navy's operational order-of-battle. Similarly, the Chinese themselves have an ambitious warship building programme of their own that includes an open-building line for two destroyer classes — the Luhai (Type 54) and Luhu (Type 52), and the Jiangwei-class frigate. Although, overall, there has been a slight increase in the number of major surface combatants listed in the PLAN's total order-of-battle since 2000, the new warships that are being brought into service are largely intended as replacements for older vessels earmarked for phased retirement: these include Luda-class destroyers and Jianghu-class frigates. The same rationale — force modernisation — lies behind China's construction of a Type 93 nuclear-powered attack submarine (SSN), which in design is based on Russia's Victor III-class SSN, and Type 94 nuclear-powered ballistic missile submarine (SSBN): these boats are to eventually replace the Han-class SSN force and the single Xia-class SSBN currently in operational service.

Probably far more significant for contingencies related to Taiwan are developments in naval aviation. The most significant development for the PLAN Air Force (PLANAF) has been the bringing into service of fairly large numbers of Su-30 MKK and MK3 multi-role fighters. These aircraft are navalised versions of the Su-27 Flanker. Some 60 Su-30s are currently in service with the PLANAF, and they are being serially armed with the Russian supersonic Kh-31A (NATO reporting name, Krypton, AS-17) anti-ship missile, which has a *maximum effective* range of 70 km (maximum range of 130 km). (Some of the latest versions of the Kh-31A are said to employ both track-via-missile and video-data-link technologies in an effort to maximise chances of spoofing enemy electronic countermeasures.) The Su-30s have significantly boosted the PLAN's surface warfare capabilities. They would constitute a significant threat to enemy surface units.

From the above picture one might get the impression that since the 1990s the modernisation of forces within the PLAN has been of a scale that has transformed the force completely out of proportion to what it was previously and that within waters familiar to it the PLAN might be able to stand up to even a major opponent such as the US Navy. That is not entirely the case. The acquisition of new warships, anti-ship missiles, communications and radar systems, and also the adoption of new tactical concepts such as the maritime-air operation, while significant, have still not been able to propel the PLAN to surmount long-standing operational weaknesses. Among the weaknesses, the ones that stand out the most are deficient command, control, communications and intelligence (C3I) systems that make integration of forces for large-scale operations over the spatial scope of several hundred nautical miles difficult to achieve. This is compounded during bad weather where, as exercises continue to demonstrate, PLAN and accompanying PLAAF units have had to withdraw and return to bases prematurely. Another weakness has been problems with integrating state-of-the-art weapons and equipment on older platforms: the interfacing of the two has thrown up difficulties that have not entirely been rectified. Further weaknesses include only a marginal capability in anti-submarine warfare (ASW), and not much better in anti-air warfare (AAW). This tends to underscore the point that the PLAN has placed inordinate focus on surface warfare (primarily to target US surface units), highlighting that, as it is currently structured, it is largely a sea-denial, rather than a sea-control, force. A more broad-based weakness for the PLAN is its generally low level of operational readiness. For instance, many of the Romeo and Ming-class diesel-electric submarines continued to be listed on the PLAN's total order-of-battle are in actual fact not operational. (This is a reason why in addition to the four Kilo-class diesel-electric submarines currently in service with the PLAN, another eight have been ordered from Russia.) Considering that all the above weaknesses are fairly rudimentary to any 21st century navy, they call into question the PLAN's ambitions to eventually acquire aircraft carriers with all the complexities that would be entailed in operating such warships. For the medium term, steady force modernisation and a focus on specific and immediate challenges — such as the Taiwan contingency — will likely be the PLAN's priorities.

Where the Chinese could affect the geopolitical balance at sea to a significant degree would be if they acquired between 80 and 120 (i.e. two or three regiments) of the navalised version of the formidable supersonic Tu-26 Backfire bomber from Russia. Armed with the AS-4 Kitchen anti-ship missile, if deployed in strength, Tu-26 Backfires would be a very effective counter to US carrier battlegroups. However, for a range of reasons, mostly political and strategic, the Russians have declined to supply the Chinese with the Tu-26, although Moscow has not had similar qualms with respect to India.

Republic of China Navy — Taiwan

The main island of Taiwan, sitting astride mainland China, is separated by the Taiwan Strait, which, at its widest point is 220 km, and, at its narrowest, 130 km. It has been said that if not for that strait, which effectively serves as a large moat, the PLA would have marched into Taiwan more than half-a-century ago. This illustrates how geographical factors have a salutary role in a state's ability to defend itself. Considered a rebel province of China, Taiwan has been likened by some defence analysts as an aircraft carrier that is bristling with weapons systems, allowing it to defend itself with some degree of success. On the other hand, there is the view that because of the US commitment to the security of Taiwan as enshrined in the 1979 Taiwan Relations Act, Taiwan has largely relied on the United States to ensure its security from aggression by an external power, whether that "external" power is perceived as the People's Republic of China or some other country. Under the Taiwan Relations Act, the United States is allowed to sell Taiwan weaponry, but these must be of a "defensive" nature. As a truism, what is defensive to one party might, however, be construed otherwise by another. And so that was how Beijing viewed the Bush Administration's April 2001 announcement of a package of military technology and weapons systems it would sell to Taiwan. That package was the largest US announced sale of weapons systems to Taiwan since 1992 (under the administration of George Bush Sr.). All but two of the significant line-items in the package had to do with maritime defence. The maritime-related items were:[2]

- four second hand Kidd-class destroyers;
- eight diesel-electric patrol submarines;
- twelve P-3 Orion ASW maritime patrol aircraft;
- MH-53 minesweeping helicopters;
- AAV7A1 amphibious assault vehicles;
- submarine and surface-launched torpedoes.

Seen in context, these weapons systems can at best be only considered as a modest addition to Taiwan's burgeoning defence requirements in the face of the buildup of adjacent Chinese military power, particularly the ballistic missile buildup. In terms of major surface combatants, the reactivation and refurbishment of four mothballed Kidd-class destroyers and their eventual transfer to the ROC (Republic of China) Navy will not ease the navy's need for capable surface warships. A large proportion of the 30 or so major surface combatants in the ROC Navy's order-of-battle list in early 2004 were ex-US Navy vessels, some of which have over-extended their service life despite constant attempts at weapons and equipment refits. Only the ROC Navy's 6 Kang Ding-class frigates (which is effectively the French La Fayette-class stealth frigate) can be considered up-to-date warships. One of the main missions of these warships, like the rest of the ROC Navy, would be to prevent a blockade of Taiwan by the PLAN. The US arms package will help in that mission but only to a modest extent. The eight diesel-electric patrol submarines are the only aspect of the package that suggests not just modernisation for the ROC Navy but indeed a buildup of its submarine capabilities. There are currently only two operational (Hai Lung-class) diesel-electric submarines in the ROC fleet and a further two boats (Hai Shih-class) employed for training purposes. The eight new diesel-electric boats when they are eventually acquired and become operational with the fleet will therefore result in a quantum leap in its sub-surface capabilities. In a clear sign of arms racing across the Taiwan Strait, shortly after the US arms package was made public, Beijing announced that it was acquiring a further eight Kilo-class attack submarines from Russia to add to the four already in its fleet. This ever-present dynamic — of arms racing — appears to have been one reason why Washington decided against supplying Taiwan with four Arleigh Burke-class destroyers equipped with the formidable Aegis area defence system, which would have allowed the Taiwanese to deploy these ships in a tactical anti-ballistic missile mode. (But the official explanation was that the ships were too technologically sophisticated for the Taiwanese to operate.) The transfer of these vessels to Taiwan would have been construed by Beijing as a major provocation and escalation, which, in turn, would have prompted it to engage in a response. Equally, politics were at work here for the United States, as the Bush administration seemed to have decided against further damaging relations with China, which had taken a tailspin as a result of the E-P3 episode in early April 2001, when a US Navy E-P3 reconnaissance plane was forced to land on Hainan Island by PLAAF aircraft after it had collided with one of the Chinese fighter aircraft. The Arleigh Burke destroyer issue has still been placed on-hold as Sino-American ties have improved in the wake of the September 11, 2001, terrorist attacks on the United States, as Beijing decided to signup to Washington's global anti-terror campaign.

As it stands, the current force structure of the ROC Navy would allow it to carry out all its patrol functions in peacetime in securing Taiwan's coastline and maritime jurisdictional area. It would also have some capability in keeping open key Taiwanese ports in the event of a PLAN attempt to engage in aggressive mine laying in the waters leading to those ports. However, without significant support from the US Navy, the ROC surface fleet, would be vulnerable to the depredations of the PLAN submarine fleet, which, just by sheer force of numbers in an operational deployment area not too distant from logistical bases, would likely exact a toll on the ROC surface fleet.

It is precisely because it faces a large PLAN submarine fleet that the ROC Navy has been prodded to modernise and buildup its capabilities in ASW. The inclusion of P-3 Orion ASW aircraft in the announced US arms package to Taiwan is intended to meet that effort. So too are efforts to acquire advanced ASW technology from a number of sources and to retrofit them onto existing at-sea and airborne platforms.

The ROC Navy does have a stated programme to modernise its forces, but it has so far had mixed results. Called Kwang Hua (Glorious China) Naval Modernisation, the programme consists of a number of projects, some of which are:[3]

- *Kwang Hua Project I*: eight Cheng Kung-class frigates (based on the US Perry-class). As of early 2003, seven of the frigates have been delivered and are operational.
- *Kwang Hua Project II*: 16 Kang Ding-class frigates (La Fayette-class). Six vessels have been delivered to date.
- *Kwang Hua Project V*: The construction of 1500–2000 ton patrol vessels as a second strike component to the principal strike force of major surface combatants. This project has been delayed due to budgetary and technical reasons.

The domestic production of frigates (such as the Cheng Kung-class) and smaller patrol vessels provide the ROC Navy some degree of self-reliance in its attempts at modernisation when many other capable naval shipbuilding countries are holding back in supplying the navy to avoid any fallout from offending Beijing. As currently structured, the ROC Navy is a relatively capable brown-water force. Its main problem is that it is adjacent to its primary adversary — the PLAN — which is far larger in size and can throw into battle more assets even if the attrition rate on its forces was to be high. (High attrition rates have never previously held back the PLA from prosecuting war with adversaries, whether it was during the Korean War in the early 1950s, the territorial conflict with India in the early 1960s and the border war with Vietnam in 1979.) This is why, notwithstanding attempts at naval modernisation, the security link with the United States is still the cornerstone of Taiwan's security policy. This is also the case with Japan, to which the next section will focus on the modernisation of the Japanese Maritime Self-Defence Force.

The Japanese Maritime Self-Defence Force

During the Cold War era, the Japanese Maritime Self-Defence Force (JMSDF) had been tasked to play two key roles, among others. One was to close off the three key straits (Soya, Tusgaru and Tsushima) leading into the Sea of Japan, in an attempt to bottle-up a large part of the Soviet Pacific Fleet based at Vladivostok and secondary naval bases located on the Soviet Far Eastern coastline fronting the Sea of Japan. That was a mission largely for Japanese submarines, two of which were to deploy at the entrances to each of the three straits, once an order to deploy was sent out. The second role was to have the large Japanese destroyer force providing an ASW and AAW screen for US fleet striking carrier battlegroups advancing towards the Soviet coast in an explication of the US Maritime Strategy enunciated by the then US Navy Secretary John Lehman. Much of the development of the JMSDF during the 1980s had therefore to do with these two key roles. With the dissolution of the Soviet Union, and therefore disappearance of what was the formidable Soviet threat, the JMSDF has effectively lost the key *raison d'etre* to justify its relatively large size and highly capable units. But its numbers have only been marginally reduced. The JMSDF has re-cast its role for a post-Cold War environment in the Asia-Pacific that is more fluid in nature and where challenges to Japan's security interests originate not from a single source but from multiple sources.

JMSDF roles now include the following:

- To secure Japanese maritime traffic by defending sealanes of communications (SLOCs) out to 1000 nautical miles from Japan's main islands (a role that was apparent during the Cold War era but has since been reemphasised with greater significance ascribed to it).
- The defence of Japanese territory, which includes contested islands — the Senkakus (which is claimed by China and referred to by it as the Diaoyutai); and Takeshima (claimed by South Korea and referred to by it as Tokdo).
- To ensure that Chinese naval power does not grow to such an extent that it overshadows the JMSDF and underlines China's primacy in the Asia-Pacific.
- To extend logistical support to US naval forces in the event of an outbreak of hostilities across the Taiwan Strait, and as now dictated by guidelines in the mid-1990s revitalisation of the US–Japan Security Treaty.
- To support a new activist Japanese regional and international diplomacy, which raises Japan's non-economic profile in the Asia-Pacific region and signals Japan's readiness to assume the mantle of a "normal" country and in consonance with its economic weight and technological prowess.

These are multiple roles for multiple contingencies/objectives. In combination they provide iron-clad justification not merely for the existence of the current Cold War force configuration of the JMSDF but also its measured modernisation and expansion.

The development of the JMSDF is dictated by the National Defence Programme Outline (NDPO), which sets out Japanese security policy and goals over the medium term and is modified about once every 8–10 years, with further modifications allowed under Mid-Term Defence Programme reviews. The current NDPO was adopted in 1995 and the next one will be released later in 2004. In the current NDPO the JMSDF diesel-electric submarine force has remained at the same numbers as under the previous NDPO, i.e. 16 boats. As to the surface fleet, outside the US Navy the JMSDF possesses the second largest force of destroyers in any navy. The current NDPO has a provision for 50 destroyers, down from 60 from the previous NDPO. Naval aviation has also witnessed cuts in force strength, from a force of about 100 P-3C Orion ASW aircraft in the previous NDPO to the current force of 80 P-3C Orions. The cut in the number of P-3Cs is symptomatic of the significantly reduced submarine threat the JMSDF faces. The previous Orion force was geared almost exclusively to deal with the huge submarine force deployed with the then Soviet Pacific Fleet. These quantitative force reductions in destroyers and naval aviation, however, mask significant aspects of qualitative modernisation that has significantly boosted the capabilities of the JMSDF.

The most significant aspect of modernisation is the steady induction into the destroyer force of Aegis-equipped Kongo-class destroyers (which in displacement and armament is actually the equivalent of cruisers in other navies) at the rate of one new ship every 2–3 years. Each of the current four operational Kongos serve as the core element of what the JMSDF calls "escort flotillas". In other words, the Kongos each act as command ships in what are effectively major surface action groups each comprising a formidable array of two or three air-defence destroyers, five or six ASW destroyers and two frigates. This complement of escort vessels is even larger than the US Navy accords to the defence of its aircraft carriers. A further two Kongo-class destroyers are expected to enter service with the JMSDF in the near term.

In July 2003, it was reported in the media that the JMSDF would acquire two small aircraft carriers.[4] The two warships will be designed to deploy STOVL (short takeoff and vertical landing) aircraft on inclined flight decks. Even though the ships will have a displacement of 13,500 tons and will carry fixed-wing aircraft, the JMSDF has chosen to refer to them by the euphemistic term "aviation-capable destroyers". Observers have suggested that the acquisition of such warships is a further indication that Japan "is shedding its pacifist cocoon in which it has wrapped itself since its devastating defeat in World War II", and that the ships will provide the JMSDF with "a modest capability to project power into sea lanes that are vital to Japan's economy".[5] According to reports, funds for the first vessels have been included in Japan's budget for fiscal year 2004 commencing on 1 April 2004, with funding for the second ship included in fiscal year 2005. The media reports on Japan's desire to acquire STOVL-equipped light aircraft carriers have, however, been disputed by Japanese officials.

A robust domestic naval shipbuilding programme — led by the Kawasaki and Mitsubishi shipyards — will witness Improved Murasame-class destroyers being brought into the JMSDF. The first two ships in this class were laid down in April 2000. Troop-carrying transports — landing-platform docks (LPDs) — of the Osumi-class are also being constructed to potentially support Japan's increasingly activist international role (i.e. peacekeeping operations), and, if need be, for amphibious landings to enforce Japanese jurisdiction on islands whose sovereignty is disputed by China and South Korea.

The above is only a sketch of the kind of modernisation currently being undertaken within the JMSDF. It is clear that ships like the Kongo-class and the potential "aviation-capable destroyers" will transform the nature of the JMSDF into a more powerful force that can deploy further afield. Growing Chinese naval power — which the Japanese have been monitoring closely through yearly counts of PLAN vessels close to, or intruding into, Japanese territorial waters — simultaneous with a perceived decline in US naval power in the Asia-Pacific is a major factor spurring the JMSDF's modernisation programme. Despite all its advances, however, the JMSDF is still largely tethered to operating close to its home islands due to political considerations — domestic opposition at home, and negative reaction by regional states who contend that Japan has never really come to terms with its World War II record of brutality, preferring instead to cast itself as a victim of that war. Until and unless Japan addresses those concerns, the deployment of its warships — which, since 1954, have flown the World War II rising sun ensign with its 16 rays — will not be accepted by most Asia-Pacific states as having a legitimate regional role.

Conclusion

The modernisation of naval forces in the Asia-Pacific is a dynamic process. And, as the above examination has tended to convey, it is also a very interactive process. Clearly, it has been an interactive process among the three navies that have been looked at in this chapter. Regional navies have attempted to keep up with one another for a range of reasons, not least to ensure that their own force capabilities do not fall too far behind those of their neighbours. While the process of modernisation of naval forces has generally been impressive and robust, and has now provided regional navies with a greater range of options on the deployment of naval assets, some longstanding challenges remain. The ability to project power beyond a few hundred nautical miles and to engage in at-sea sustainability is doubtful for most Asia-Pacific navies. And despite the proliferation of anti-ship missiles, which have equipped surface, sub-surface and airborne platforms, targeting remains a major problem for most of the navies, even for the three that have been examined here. The problem is how to pick up over-the-horizon targets from the dense background clutter that is especially apparent in heavily trafficked seas, such as the East and South China Seas. The next phase of naval modernisation in the region will have to address these and other challenges in a more systematic fashion if regional navies are to be considered credible arms enforcing state policy. Until such time, the dominance of the US Navy will continue to be apparent, even if there are mixed signals about the extent of its regional visibility over the medium to long terms.

Notes

1. Derek da Cunha, "Southeast Asian Perceptions of China's Future Security Role in its 'Backyard'", in Jonathan D. Pollack and Andrew Nien-Dzu Yang (eds.), *In China's Shadow: Regional Perspectives on Chinese Foreign Policy and Military Development* (Santa Monica, CA: Rand, 1998), p. 118.
2. Kelly Wallace, "Bush Pledges Whatever it Takes to Defend Taiwan", *CNN*, 25 April 2001. Also available online at http://www.cnn.com/2001/ALLPOLITICS/04/24/bush.taiwan.abc.
3. "Taiwan: Navy Modernisation", *GlobalSecurity.org*, 19 April 2004. Also available online at http://www.globalsecurity.org/military/world/taiwan/nay-mod.htm.
4. Richard Halloran, "Warships Suggest Discarded Pacificism", *The Washington Times*, 13 July 2003. Also available online at http://www.washtimes.com/world/20030712-104212-6831r.htm.
5. Ibid.

Chapter 7

Terrorism in the Early 21st Century Maritime Domain

Rupert Herbert-Burns

Introduction — A Superfluity of Targets

International terrorism throughout its history is a phenomenon that has been conceptualised of, strategised towards and executed largely in the terrestrial parts of the world. Likewise, the bulk of the strategies and means directed to counter terrorism have been logically land-focused in accordance with this axiom. However, we live in a world where the potential scale of terrorist destruction and disruption has become a 21st-century variant of a quasi-"first strike" weapon with putatively *strategic* capabilities, properties and implications. In considering the reality of this young but nevertheless dangerous paradigm, politicians, intelligence services and security forces, the media, commercial maritime businesses and experts in the epistemic community have all begun to take serious note of the potential of the maritime domain as an ideal environmental complex that can simultaneously incubate, facilitate, and be the target of, a sophisticated, highly motivated and tactically adroit terrorist organisation and its far-flung cellularised detachments or proxies.

On the 24 April 2004, three small vessels — a dhow and two nimble speed boats — executed a "multiple attack" on the Bakr and Khawr al-Amaya oil terminals located 100 nautical miles from the port of Umm Qasr, 9 nautical miles offshore. The assault fortunately did not yield the scale of intended destruction on the facilities themselves; nevertheless, it cost the lives of three coalition servicemen, the wounding of several others, a spike in oil prices and some US$ 28 million in lost oil revenue.[1] This recent example of the very real capability of terrorists to attack and inflict damage upon vulnerable and critical infrastructure in the maritime domain serves another "wake-up call" for the international community. If the attack had and netted the intended results and the suicide craft had managed to detonate alongside a berthed tanker loading crude, the scale and cost of the attack in all respects would have been severe in the extreme, to say nothing of the propaganda dividends for those responsible.

This chapter, split into five main sections, will initially discuss the sheer magnitude and expanse of the maritime realm in which terrorist operatives can function and conceal themselves. By way of extension, the second examines the scale and the suitability of the commercial shipping milieu as the ideal medium within which, through which and from which terrorists can manoeuvre and project offensive operations. The third section assesses the contemporary threat picture, which encapsulates the major components of maritime terrorist capabilities; considering the existence and importance of logistical and financial activities as well as attacking methodologies and tactical flair. The fourth section harnesses the revelations of the preceding section and considers how this veritable "tool box" of skills can be applied by way of extrapolation to assess the shape of putative terrorist operations in the maritime domain likely to darken our future. Lastly, the chapter turns to consider the various strategies that are arguably best-suited to confront and mitigate both the existential and likely future manifestations of terrorist action in this environment with a philosophical and methodological approach that emphasises the fusion and inter-dependence of intelligence, international and transnational cooperation, and risk management.

Regardless of the outcome of the Basra operation, this was an attack in one small, though admittedly important and brittle part of the world; in considering the sheer multiplicity of vulnerable targets around the globe, let us turn to consider the vastness of, and the opportunity afforded by, the playing field that terrorists have to work with, and by extension the concomitant scale of the problem faced by those around the world tasked with confronting and mitigating this dangerous threat. A well-chosen, effectively executed attack against a major target in the maritime domain could, in addition to potentially causing appalling loss of life, initiate a chain reaction through the world's trading economy with incalculable financial costs and systemic disruption.

Global Maritime Expanse — Strategic Reach and Geographical Flexibility

Viewed in aggregate the planet's oceanic expanse encompasses a vast 139,768,200 square miles — 2.42 times the planet's terrestrial surface area. Of this, the vast majority are international waters, which are by definition and nature anarchic, sparsely patrolled and beyond the strict jurisdiction of any one of world's sovereign states. These waters, which are to all intents and purposes "over the horizon", are fringed and linked by a complex lattice of territorial waters, which in terms of internationally recognised jurisprudence are distinct and independent. They are comprised variously of littoral waters, estuaries and complex river systems. The scope of this environment offers terrorists virtually unparalleled opportunity for "strategic reach" and "geographical flexibility" in terms of the range of targets, the freedom to manoeuvre and the ability to disperse and deploy assets. Accordingly, the world's coastline totals some 356,000 km, which is connected by 6591 ports and harbours, which affords the ill-disposed a powerful medium for inter-connectivity, logistical support and attack projection. Lastly, given the sheer volume and vitality of global seaborne trade (which amounted to some 5.8 billion tons in 2001 or 80 percent of world trade by volume)[2] and the large number of crucial ports, transhipment nodes and several vital trading links, the maritime environment offers an almost limitless range of tempting, high pay-off targets, many of which are fringed by densely populated urban conurbations.

By any definition, the scale of the space outline above is vast, which affords the terrorist with the necessary and relevant skill-sets, assets and connections, the ability to hide, move and strike in a way not possible on land. The advantages the maritime environment confers upon the suitably endowed and motivated terrorist are reflected inversely and proportionately as impediments to governments and their intelligence services and security forces as they endeavour to confront and neutralise this threat.

Perhaps the best confirmation of the opportunities offered by the maritime environment as space in which terrorists can move, disperse within and attack from is revealed in the sufficiently large number of groups that have at some time in the recent past or present demonstrated a capability and willingness to operate within and attack targets located in the maritime environment. To date some 36 terrorist groups, dispersed across Europe, Central and South America, the Middle East, Africa, the Sub-Continent and Southeast Asia, have conducted maritime attacks, have the capacity to do so or routinely use the maritime domain for logistical and financial support. Of these, some of the better-known organisations include: Abu Sayyaf Group (ASG), Al Qaeda, Egyptian Islamic Jihad (EIJ), Euskadi ta Askatasuna (ETA), Fatah Tanzim, Gerakin Aceh Merdeka (GAM), Hamas (Izz al-Din al-Qassam Brigades), Hezb'allah, Jaysh Aden Abyn al-Islami (Aden Islamic Army), Jemaah Islamiya (JI), Kurdish Workers Party (PKK), Laskar Jihad, Liberation Tigers of Tamil Elam (LTTE), Moro Islamic Liberation Front (MILF), National Liberation Army (ELN), Palestinian Islamic Jihad (PIJ), Popular Front for the Liberation of Palestine-General Command (PFLP-GC), Provisional IRA, Revolutionary Armed Forces of Colombia (FARC) and the Revolutionary United Front (RUF).

The combination of the enormous scope, variety and "room for manoeuvre" offered by the physical and geographical realities of the planet's maritime environment and the large number of geographically dispersed, well-established, accomplished and highly motivated terrorist groups presents a sobering and uncomfortable reality for those attempting to mitigate this existential threat. However, what compounds this reality further is that the commercial milieu that simultaneously affords them the ability to deploy, finance operations, conceal tactically, provide logistical fluidity and provide a wealth of targets of opportunity is itself numerically vast, complex, deliberately opaque and in a perpetual state of flux. Before considering the state of the contemporary threat picture in detail, let us examine the business and trading milieu that affords maritime terrorism at once both its means and its shield.

The International Commercial Maritime Domain — The Means and the Shroud

The modern commercial maritime and shipping business milieu is arguably the most dynamic, endemic and peculiarly esoteric of all the world's international commercial systemics. In assessing its overall relationship with the physical environment outlined above, the two phenomena could be viewed as somewhat of a complex within a complex. The commercial maritime systemic is rendered such ideal operational and tactical cover for terrorists by virtue of the ontology and inter-relationship of its component parts.

Initially, it is revealing to consider numerical scope. On any one day in the year there are approximately some 52,000 merchant vessels either preparing to sail or already at sea.[3] There are currently well over 6500 port and harbour facilities around the world, serviced by approximately 112,000 merchant vessels of numerous varieties (manned by over 1,227,000 officers and ratings[4] of every conceivable nationality, religion and ethnicity) and in excess of 45,000 shipping companies and maritime businesses, both of which link roughly 225 maritime trading nations, dependent territories and island states.[5] This international maritime trading systemic is responsible for the perpetual motion of approximately 5.8 billion tons of goods (80 percent of world trade by volume), including an estimated 15 million containers that collectively registered a staggering 232 million point-to-point and transhipped movements in 2001.[6] This collective high-speed trade ballet is facilitated by an aggregate average of some 3.6 million vessel movements every year, on occasion as many as 12,000 moves every 24 h.[7]

If locating a handful of maritime terrorist or organised criminal operations amidst this daunting canvas seems problematic at best and seemingly impossible at worst, then it is important also to consider that the shipping operations that reside amidst this vast collection of fluxing component parts are themselves afforded a range of complex interlocking mechanisms that enable anonymity, the ability to circumvent intrusive forensic audits and the freedom to operate sub-standard vessels crewed by poorly trained and salaried crewmen, many with inaccurate or even forged documentation.

International maritime corporate and business practices — viewed alternatively as the "corporate veil" — represent the most potent and flexible range of measures that can be used by an individual or shipping entity to conceal their true identity and, by extension, the real motivations behind their activities and holdings. Anonymity can be affected by the utilisation and interlocking of three operational components: the employment of the various business modalities that ensure the beneficial (ultimate) owner remains unknown; the manipulation of the institutional mechanisms that facilitate the formation of corporations; and the diligent selection of an appropriate flag of convenience (FOC) that whilst nominally represents the legal legitimiser of a vessel's commercial operations also serves to incubate and shroud the previous two mechanisms.

Individual anonymity can be achieved through the utilisation of one or several commonly recognised propriety features, namely: bearer shares, nominee shareholders, nominee directorships and business intermediaries. Of these, the holding and transference of bearer shares is perhaps the most effective and most commonly used method. Beneficial ownership is conferred merely by the possession of the certificates, which do not bear the name of the owner. In the event of a putative investigation, the transfer of these documents is facile and guarantees obscurity. Alternatively, in private companies with typically few shareholders, the beneficial owner can appoint "nominee shareholders" to represent their interests, effectively masking their involvement. Similarly, nominee directorships can represent the ultimate owner's interests operationally while shielding beneficial identity. Some jurisdictions even permit whole corporations to function as nominee directors, further exacerbating the complexity of the structural picture. Lastly, additional layers can be created by the utilisation of intermediaries such as formation agents, trustees and lawyers. These intermediaries are both common and intrinsic to offshore financial havens, where they function as local agents and provide service in the form of "brass plate" front companies. Moreover, company lawyers can always conceal the identities of their clients though the attorney–client privilege protocols implicit in established jurisprudence.

Leveraging institutional devices is the other effective method of obscuring corporate identities, holdings, activities and personalities. This can be achieved by establishing one or an aggregation of the following: Private Limited Companies (PLCs), International Business Corporations (IBCs), trusts, foundations and partnerships. PLCs tend to be undisclosed by nature, are not listed on public stock exchanges and generally free from stringent regulatory inspections or forensic audits.[8] Many of these types of companies are often formed to function as "shell" companies, and are ideally suited to placement in offshore financial havens. IBCs are recognised as the principal mode for the enabling of transnational business dealings, and can be set up easily and rapidly in the world's best-known offshore havens. Because IBCs can only do business outside the territory of incorporation, they are not usually required to submit annual reports, pay taxes and are thus freed from monitoring or inspection.[9]

These realities, added to the inevitable use of bearer shares and nominees, renders obscurity a virtual certainty. Trusts are specifically designed as a means of separating legal ownership and beneficial ownership, and are thus also widely used to protect identities. Foundations, though not operationally or structurally best-suited to functioning as a shipping company, can be formed virtually anywhere and have no listed owners or shareholders. Though nominally intended to perform private functions, many jurisdictions, for example, Panama, allow foundations to execute commercial dealings. Although foundations are unlikely to be used by terrorists for operational purposes, they are highly suited for the anonymous generation of revenue. Lastly, partnerships, though effective in concealing individuals and operations, are not ideal as a single method of operating vessels because of their limited corporate status; however, they could be utilised as a component layer of a holistic masking scheme.

Status of dependencies, overseas territories and free trade regimes represent a generic third layer that could be utilised to complicate and confuse the search for a terrorist operating in the shipping and maritime milieu in harmony with many of the other methods outlined previously. Examples include: Gibraltar, the Cayman Islands, New Caledonia, the Channel Islands, the Netherlands Antilles and Antigua & Barbuda; however, there are many others. Though these entities garner legitimacy from association with their parent sovereign guardian states, they also have identifiable distinctions in terms of regulations regarding the investigation, or rather the lack of permissible investigation, of corporations based within their jurisdiction. Many of these territories operate ship registries of their own.[10] When owners and corporations are based inside free trade areas such as the European Union, institutional disjuncture and areas of uncoordinated jurisprudence can obstruct and complicate legal proceedings directed against targeted persons or corporations, thus allowing the criminal time and opportunity to evade further intensive investigation.

Vessel registration is both an intrinsic feature of shipping practice and can potentially function as another significant layer of concealment for terrorists and criminals seeking to conceal their identities and shipping operations. This is achieved because many open registers effectively function as an incubator and shroud for the mechanisms examined above, and many if not all of the aforementioned corporate mechanisms are used for establishing an anonymous shipping operation. Thus, the result is a veil within an external mantle — the flag. Indeed, many registries, in addition to permitting irresponsibly lax strictures regarding crewing conditions and training, port state control and documentation requirements, actively promote the appeal of their service by making the registration process straightforward, completely anonymous and inexpensive.

Flags of convenience are widely utilised, as they offer owners/operators a range of important benefits enabling them to operate free from costly and intrusive strictures. These may include the following: greatly reduced or zero taxation on profits; less stringent requirements concerning crewing regulations and safe working practices; the ability to register a shell (or paper) company in that country for the purposes of registration, but maintain the beneficial company in another; the ability to use bearer shares for ownership transactions (which facilitates the obscuring of the beneficial owner) and remain exempt from audit in that country.

In the wake of September 11 and the elevated security imperatives associated with the war on terrorism, officials within the commercial maritime world and national intelligence and security officials concerned with maritime security have become far more anxious about the ability of ship owners, operators and criminal organisations and even terrorists to obscure their maritime operations behind the cloak of flags of convenience. Ideally, a reputable and compliant flag state should demonstrate the following characteristics:

- Ratification of an extensive range of International Maritime Organisation (IMO) and International Labor Organisation (ILO) conventions.
- Maintenance of complete records of the beneficial ownership of vessels in its registry, including disclosures of identity.
- Ability and willingness to carry out inspections of vessels and casualty investigations under its own capacity.
- Maintenance of a registry that does not design and codify its operational strictures only in terms of greater income generation.
- Establishment of effective sustained certification and welfare arrangements for seafarers.
- Formulation and codification of jurisprudence that unambiguously protects the rights of seafarers employed onboard the vessels in its registry regardless of their country of origin.
- Funding and monitoring of the registry of a level sufficient to maintain the standards set for the number of vessels registered.
- Willingness to enforce the chains of responsibility on ship owners and operators as they interact with and report to other official bodies that act on behalf of or in conjunction with the flag state, such as Memorandum of Understanding (MOU).

The above list represents a best-case scenario and should be used as an ideal against which registries can be judged. Many of the registries in existence are designed and operated in order to facilitate obscurity, thereby attracting owners and operators wishing to function in anonymity.

Paradoxically, the masking effectiveness of registries is actually codified in the first article of the United Nations Law of the Sea Convention that pertains to the registering of ships. Article 91 dictates that there "must exist a genuine link between the State and the ship";[11] however, there is no reference at all to a requirement for a declaration of ownership. With this caveat in place to assist beneficial owners in achieving at least partial concealment within even the most scrupulous and transparent of registries, the difficulty in detecting would-be terrorists becomes apparent. The most "useful" flags for those with criminal and/or terrorist intent, in addition to permitting the existence of fringe operators due to a lack of onerous operating standards, further fortify the ability of clients to remain concealed by permitting many if not all of the following: corporate ownership of ships, undeclared nationality, establishment of IBCs, undeclared owner identity, use of bearer shares, nominee shareholders and directors, and being absolved from submitting annual reports.

It is critical, therefore, to any effort in maritime counter-terrorism to pierce this "corporate veil" and gain visibility into the behaviour and characteristics of vessels and their owners and managers. Otherwise, intelligence agencies and security forces are effectively operating blind, with no real knowledge of exactly who is bound for and transiting their ports, the vessel's past activities, the owner's corporate composition, what the master's intentions may be and what their over-the-horizon activities entail. Terrorists thus far have demonstrated a preference for the Tongan, Honduran, Cypriot, Panamanian, and Liberian flags among others.[12] In the wake of recent arrests and detentions of vessels with alleged links to Al Qaeda, there is likely to be a shift towards the more respectable flags that nevertheless enable the requisite anonymity. Terrorist and criminal organisations now have a logic-driven need to ensure their vessels are as nominally respectable as is feasible, so as to avoid intrusive inspections and unwelcome surveillance that are inimical to their operational effectiveness. Adopting a diligently — calibrated *registry–classification society–company location* — matrix with just the right balance of respectability, seeming operational transparency and anonymity will be the formula likely to be embraced.

Contemporary Threat Picture — Methodological Variety and Tactical Flair

Terrorist activity in the maritime domain began to emerge in the 1980s with various operations being conducted by the IRA, the Palestine Liberation Front and of course the LTTE to name a few. However, from the mid-1990s terrorism in this arena began to show signs of increasing frequency and levels of sophistication. To date, terrorist groups of numerous typologies have demonstrated the ability to execute the following operations: hijack passenger ships at sea with well-armed cells; generate revenue to support operations ashore by means of "legitimate" maritime trade; seize hostages from vessels at sea and precipitate sizable ransoms (especially in Southeast Asian waters); attack the world's most sophisticated warships with suicide craft packed with shaped explosive charges; cripple a laden Very Large Crude Carrier (VLCC) as she was making way using a suicide craft offshore; deliver large consignments of weapons, explosives, ammunition, training personnel and tech-support by sea; develop underwater delivery/attacking craft and "stealth" boats; and transport terrorist operatives by sea inside containers. In order to capture some of the specifics of the phenomenon, what follows are four case studies, some familiar, others less so, which reveal the sobering reality of what terrorists have accomplished and attempted in the maritime realm. The case studies highlight the need for a perpetual, updated appreciation of the threat that exists within, employs and targets the maritime realm, which can otherwise be referred to as *maritime terrorist threat acuity.*

Vessel as a high-impact target of opportunity

At 0915 on 6 October 2002, the 299,364 DWT VLCC, *M/V Limburg* (since re-named *M/V Maritime Jewel*)[13] was struck by a small, fast fibreglass boat that was subsequently deliberately exploded as the tanker was preparing to take on a pilot to approach the single mooring buoy (SMB) at the Ash Shihr Terminal off the coast of Yemen.[14] The vessel was lifting 297,000 barrels of crude at the time of the attack. The estimated 100–200 kg TNT shaped charge punched a 26-feet oval-shaped hole through both the inner and outer hulls at the waterline thereby breaching the No. 4 starboard cargo tank, the contents of which were instantly ignited. In addition to the explosion and the cargo fire, an estimated 50,000 barrels of Iranian crude (loaded at Kharg Island) spilled into the waters surrounding the stricken vessel. The attack claimed the life of one of the crewmen, Atanas Atanassov (a Bulgarian national), who jumped overboard and drowned, and forced the hospitalisation of 12 others.

This maritime terrorist attack is both compelling and revealing for a number of reasons. Firstly, it demonstrates the extreme vulnerability of this class of merchant vessel to waterline suicide attacks by small, agile and fast-moving craft that can take advantage of a large tanker's inability to manoeuvre rapidly enough to avoid danger (technically referred to as "vessel restricted in ability to manoeuvre"), especially when at reduced speed and/or in the process of embarking a pilot whilst in confined (or pilotage) waters. Secondly, the attack highlights the vulnerability of the littoral waters in this region, especially off the coast of Yemen, which are margined by a multiplicity of coastal villages and towns that are ideal bases from which to prepare and launch attacks of this kind. (It is thought that the Abdel Hakim Baa'thiv-led cell of the Aden-Abyan Islamic Army,[15] which executed the attack, used a village harbour in the Hadhramut region as a base from which to launch their assault.) The third area of interest concerns the effect of the explosion itself. On the one hand, the damage to the hull itself demonstrates the effectiveness of a medium-sized shaped explosive charge in punching through a tough double-hull flank structure and inducing a fire. However, on the other hand, the location along the hull of the detonation reveals an interesting paradox.

It has been thought that the attackers may have had intelligence that revealed which of the vessel's 14 cargo tanks were filled, thereby enabling them to target that part of the vessel that would supposedly yield the most damage. However, in this instance there is an argument that the attackers got it wrong; in targeting part of the tanker filled with an incompressible liquid mass the explosive force was dampened somewhat in its effectiveness and could only ever induce the *liquid-state* cargo to burn. Had the attackers deliberately (or inadvertently) struck a void tank the structural damage would have been greater and the likelihood of the explosion detonating residual petroleum vapours inside the tanks would have increased significantly. The combination of both the explosion, conspicuous structural deformation and the cargo fire would likely have rendered the Limburg effectively a *constructive total loss* (CTL). Fourthly, the incident is revealing for its impact upon the oil industry, the Yemeni economy, and maritime insurance premiums and cargo-related indemnity rates. Oil prices spiked briefly and then re-stabilised; however, this re-settling would not have been quite so swift had this incident occurred in the immediate approaches to the Suez Canal and the damage to the vessel been more pronounced. The effects on the Yemeni economy were more prolonged, which was losing an estimated $3.8 m per month in the aftermath of the attack because of the added insurance premiums in the form of war risk surcharges (WRS) imposed upon vessels using Yemeni ports, thereby forcing many to divert to terminals in other countries. Lastly, the incident was edifying in that though the Al Qaeda-directed operation had initially sought to target a warship (which have changed their procedures and tactics in the wake of the attack on the *USS Cole*), the operation was effective, fairly well executed and ultimately revealing in confirming Al Qaeda's stated intention to attack Western oil interests:

> ... By exploding the oil tanker in Yemen, the holy warriors hit the umbilical cord and lifeline of the crusader community, reminding the enemy of the heavy cost of blood and the gravity of losses they will pay as a price for their continued aggression on our community and looting of our wealth[16] (Alleged Bin Laden statement).

Vessel-use for logistical support

A useful example demonstrating the level of capability of terrorist groups is the *Abu Hassan* incident which occurred on 22 May 2003, when Israeli

Naval commandos boarded and seized the 16-meter Egyptian-registered fishing boat, 35 nautical miles off Rosh Hanikra near Haifa, some 19 nautical miles south of Lebanese territorial waters. The vessel was deemed suspicious after surveillance revealed atypical behaviour for a vessel of her type. She was not behaving like a fishing vessel but more like a coastal/short-sea general cargo vessel given that she was in shipping lanes in international waters. The naval team towed the fishing vessel into Haifa, where subsequent inspection revealed that the *Abu Hassan* was being used to ferry a consignment that comprised of complex weapon components and training materials, namely: 25 fuses for 122 mm Qassam surface-to-surface rockets; 15 electronic time-delay fuses; timer programming units; a radio-activated initiation device for explosives; a training video that instructed on optimum methods for carrying out a suicide bombing on a bus using strategically placed training mannequins; and two sets of 36 CD-ROMs containing detailed bomb-making training manuals.[17]

Though interrogation revealed that of the eight men captured, six turned out to be ordinary Egyptian fishermen who were apparently not privy to the details of the operation and were used simply to operate the vessel, while the other two were Hezbollah operatives. The Egyptian captain/owner of the *Abu Hassan* had been recruited by Hezbollah and trained specifically to carry out maritime support missions. It is believed that he had also been active in recruiting crew members for the *Karine-A* operation. However, it was the eighth man who turned out to be the sole reason for the operation; he was identified as Hamad Masalem Mussa Abu Amra, an explosives, ordnance and tactics expert. Interrogations also revealed the complexity of the operation.[18]

After sailing west from the Egyptian port of Rasheed on 16 May, the *Abu Hassan* first put into Marsa Matrou (also in Egypt), where after she sailed for Lebanon, arriving off Beirut on 20 May.[19] During dawn that morning, Abu Amra, accompanied by an armed Hezbollah cell, rendezvoused with the *Abu Hassan* at sea, where after she proceeded south. Had the vessel not been intercepted, the intention was to ferry Abu Amra to Egypt (most likely to the coast north of El Arish) from where he would be infiltrated with his equipment into the Gaza Strip via an underground tunnel. Finally, the Israelis concluded that the geographical diversity and operational scale of the mission could only have been orchestrated by an organisation with considerable reach and contacts. This was confirmed by the revelation that the operation's most likely architects were Fathi Razam, the Palestinian Authority's (PA) deputy chief of Naval Police, and Adal Al-Mugrabi, who is responsible for weapons smuggling projects for the PA.[20]

The incident is significant for several reasons: (1) it shows that in the wake of the failure of the larger *Karine-A* operation, the Palestinians were keen to attempt a transfer of a consignment of more manageable, less conspicuous proportions with a significant qualitative technical/instructional component; (2) it demonstrates not only the desire and the necessity to use maritime methods of transfer, but also an ability to manage an operation at long range that brings together different terrorist cells operating in both blue water and littoral environments; and (3) the operation will stand as an example of the utility of transnational maritime support missions in support of terrestrial operations.

Attacks in maritime domain for purposes of generation of critical finance

At 1330 hours local time on 10 August 2003, eight Gerakin Aceh Merdeka (GAM) rebels onboard a fishing vessel, armed with assault rifles (both AK-47s and M-16s) and a rocket propelled grenade launcher (RPG-7), opened fire on the 740 GT Malaysian-flagged product tanker, the *M/V Penrider* (8617615), in position 2°47.5′ N, 101°05.3′ E.[21] The assailants were all dressed in military-style clothing. The tanker was lifting 1000 tons of fuel oil from Singapore to Penang in northern Malaysia when she was attacked. After having taken heavy fire to the superstructure and bridge, the master ordered the vessel to stop, thereby enabling the guerrillas to board the Penrider whilst she was still some 12 nautical miles from Port Klang.

After the ship's crew were assembled and centrally controlled, the master was ordered to sail the vessel towards Pulau Jemor (2°52.7′ N, 100°34′ E). Subsequently, the master, chief engineer and second engineer (all Indonesian nationals) were removed from the Penrider and taken hostage. During the attack, the guerrillas also seized cash, cell phones, ship documentation, crew certificates and clothing from the crews' quarters and the bridge. The rebels demanded $100,000 for the return of the three officers. Following their release (off an island inside Indonesian territorial waters), Captain Djunaidi Nawawi informed investigators that though he and his officers had not been provided with any food during their captivity, they had not suffered any injuries. The ransom eventually paid amounted to the equivalent of $52,000.[22]

Initially this attack was not deemed to be the work of GAM because the location of the assault and because the coastal site chosen by the assault commander as the hostage transfer point was not only some way from Acehnese territory but closer to waters more regularly patrolled by Indonesian naval forces. However, subsequent questioning of the crew in the aftermath of the incident revealed that the assailants spoke the Acehnese language; moreover, after having been transferred to a rebel camp in Aceh, the assailants voluntarily admitted to belonging to GAM.[23] The significance of these various and rather unexpected geographical realities lies in the fact that GAM cells are operating further away from their base camp areas and realms of geo-tactical dominance than previously thought. Moreover, they have demonstrated the capability to retain control over a maritime assault and kidnapping operation that also has an important and logistically complex terrestrial hostage-control and ransom negotiation phase. Though this incident lies astride the blurred line between an act of piracy and a terrorist incident in the maritime domain, it could be argued that though it most certainly is an act of violent piracy, it could be defined as an example of a *terrorist-support (logistical/financial) operation*.

Vessel leveraged as a "weapon system"

In February 2003, following the interrogation of Al Qaeda's Abdelrahim al-Nashiri, it emerged that a highly complex and far more potentially lethal Al Qaeda maritime operation than the Cole and Limburg attacks using a "mother-ship" and "multiples" had been narrowly averted. Using a series of front companies, al-Nashiri's procurement arm in the United Arab Emirates had managed to acquire a coastal/short-sea general cargo vessel and several small fast attack boats. Following the fitting of a special lifting rig to the weather deck of the vessel, the plan called for the loading of smaller craft packed with shaped explosive charges aboard the freighter, which would then be put to sea in the shipping lanes in the Straits of Hormuz.[24] Once in position near passing US warships, the smaller attacking suicide craft were to be lowered over the side and dispersed in order to mount a combined (or "multiple") assault on the passing target. In order to create a redundancy (back-up) component to the operation, the freighter itself, ladened with explosives (presumably above the waterline and/or inside the perimeter of the superstructure/hull), would then approach the shipping lanes and self-detonate as close as was feasible to a transiting warship. (It is important to keep in mind that the rigging of freighters to detonate and sink and destroy surrounding targets is a perfected LTTE standard operating procedure.) In this instance, the sheer size of the proximate explosion and resulting shrapnel plume would be sufficient to cause the sinking or crippling of the target vessel. It was later learned that the plan called for the attack to coincide with those in the United States on 11 September. However, fearing that the operation's coordinators were under surveillance, the attack was aborted.

Though aborted, the attempted "multiple"-style attack by Al Qaeda's maritime division represented a major escalation in destructive intent on the part of the organisation's maritime/Arabian Peninsula cells. It demonstrated several important realities. In the wake of the failed attempt on the *USS Sullivans* (*DDG 68*) and the partial success of the *USS Cole* (*DDG 67*) attack, al-Nashiri specifically designed an operation with tactical flexibility, flair and a built-in system for redundancy. This ensured (had the operation been initiated) that the target in question would have suffered far greater levels of damage if not being sunk altogether, with a concomitant elevation in casualties. The plan also demonstrated a wide grasp of nautical skill-sets, explosive-charge design, command and control, and the ability to substitute or coerce the mothership's officers and crew. The choice of target-strike location was also highly significant; the sinking of the freighter and potentially the target as well vessel would have severely disrupted regional trade by disrupting passage of shipping through this pivotal strategic conduit. Viewed holistically, any maritime terrorist strike operation of this scale on a geopolitical/trading chokepoint represents a strategic-level escalation in terms of its implications; especially so had the attack successfully coincided with the 11 September strikes in the United States. Of greatest importance, however, is that the operation was abandoned due to sensitivity to surveillance, detection and operational compromise. This is a critical sensitivity to note and to take advantage of when crafting responses to this form of threat and in developing best practices in maritime security — the potency of *intelligence deterrence*. This case study is a valuable example of the potent value of *intelligence deterrence* in thwarting a terrorist operation in its preparatory, logistical non-lethal phase. Whilst terrorists with suicide intentions and capabilities will not be deterred by threats of counter violence or death, they are most certainly deterred by the threat of mission failure, especially if opportunities for attacking "time windows" and applicable resources are finite as is usually the case.

Future Threat Scenarios — Extrapolation and Application of Recent Past and Current Terrorist Intent, Capability and Opportunity

Intent is defined as the strategic goals set forth by the organisation. *Capability* is the presence of adequate knowledge, expertise and resources — both material and human — to plan, support and conduct operations. *Opportunity* is defined as the vulnerabilities we present to our enemies — opportunities that are rife within the maritime domain and port security environment.

The scenarios in the previous section, when assessed against the backdrop of the enormity, complexity, fluidity and range of cover afforded by the geo-commercial maritime environment, can be distilled to form a rather impressive maritime terrorist capability "tool box" or "skill-set menu". The declared strategic *intent* of the world's most currently notorious and implacable international terrorist organisation — Al Qaeda — is well documented and reported. The *capability* similarly can no longer be called into question. Terrorist operatives have at their disposal a vast omni in the form of the planet's maritime realm, which affords them both *strategic reach* and *geographical flexibility* when supporting operations, selecting targets and initiating strikes. Additionally, this commercial systemic affords them perfect cover for all of their activities — supporting or tactical. At the operational level, numerous groups have demonstrated accumulation of the necessary levels of fire-power, ingenuity, tactical acumen, adroit command and control, logistical connections, technological embrace and nautical knowledge to execute attacks and supporting operations, even if some have been only partially successful or uncompleted. With this in mind, it is logical and responsible to conceive of what operations could conceivably be in the pipeline.

However, before this can be done, let us consider the levels of *opportunity* available to the protagonist. The magnitude of the stain of piracy at sea is proof both of the number and vulnerability of merchant ships to attack. As described in an earlier section of this paper, the geographical synapses that link trading nations, oceans and strategic bodies of water vital to the mobility and deployment of naval forces are painfully vulnerable to disruption. Chokepoints, by definition, tend to be shallow, constricted, adjacent to geopolitically brittle regions, and perpetually densely populated with transiting vessels. In the event of blockage by mining, sunken obstruction, naval action and now terrorist action, these vital links are not easily circumvented; in some cases their compromise would impair movement completely. Indeed, they represent the geographical "Achilles heal"[25] of the global economy. There are six critical chokepoints: the Bab el-Mandab Straits, the Bosporus, the Panama Canal, the Suez Canal, the Straits of Hormuz and the Straits of Malacca. Of these the last two are the most vital. A strike on either one would seriously disrupt the supply of the bulk of the world's crude petroleum shipments from the Persian Gulf and throttle the flow of trade to the developed economies of Southeast Asia, China and Japan, respectively. The third category of targets of opportunity for terrorism are the thousands of port facilities around the world, many are critical transhipment nodes such as Singapore, Hong Kong, Rotterdam, Dubai, Gioia

Tauro, Malta, Kingston, New York and Los Angeles/Long Beach. Hundreds are also imbedded within, or fringed by, densely populated urban-industrial conurbations. It is these that are likely to be the most highly sought after as targets for a major future maritime terrorist operation; disturbingly, the majority remain highly vulnerable to infiltration and attack.

Attacks against ships at sea will continue for as long as there are inadequate laws and security regimes, multilateral cooperation and assets to prevent them. Low-level maritime terrorist logistical support and selective suicide attacks will also continue. However, what is becoming increasingly certain is that at some point in the not too distant future there will be an attack launched from the maritime realm against a target with strategic value located within it. On this front there is some good news and some less so. An operation of this kind is complex to put together and will remain beyond the capabilities of all but a few of the most sophisticated groups, thus narrowing the probabilities. An attack of this scale will have to be delivered in the form of either a prefabricated nuclear, radiological, chemical or biological weapon of mass destruction; conveyed either inside a 20' or 40' container, or concealed within an ordinary break-bulk consignment aboard a general cargo vessel. Alternatively, a vessel lifting a large bulk cargo of dangerous, toxic and/or flammable liquids or solids could be deliberately leveraged for its lethal properties and turned into an initially un-noticed but un-stoppable "guided weapon-system" of enormous destructive potential. Such an operation would certainly require a high degree of technical and nautical skill, privacy of preparation and a rich understanding of explosives and bulk-charge detonation requirements; nevertheless, these shipments are at sea every day and startlingly vulnerable to seizure. All that is required is the right shipping/cargo intelligence, the skill-set and necessary preparation time. Commentators further agree that one of the very large tankers or bulk carriers could be used affectively as a ramming or momentum weapon. This form of attack could be spectacularly effective against a coastally exposed port/urban complex or refining facility, or in blockading a vital chokepoint; the world's two main canals (Suez and Panama) and the Bosporus are particularly vulnerable to this form of attack because of their narrow apertures.

Al-Qaeda's long-range maritime support operations

Distinct from al-Qaeda's prowess at delivering suicide tactical-level attacks at sea, are concerns regarding its control and/or ownership of some 15 merchant vessels;[26] thought to be predominantly coastal/short-sea general cargo vessels. Other reports have also hinted at there being a bulk carrier or two within the fleet. Intelligence reports emanating from the United States have suggested that the bulk of this fleet is likely to be operating in the Red Sea and in the waters off the Horn of Africa, but that it has been difficult to maintain a fix on the ships as they are likely to have been given new names, re-registered,[27] and "sold" to new ownership structures or within existing ones. However, the arrest of the *M/V Sara* and the *M/V Twillinger* off Sicily and Trieste, respectively, demonstrates obvious movement through the Suez Canal, and the Sara's regular trade moves through the Bosporus prior to her arrest is potentially indicative of the organisation's interest in, and coverage of, the Black Sea region, long a medium for maritime trafficking of contraband and weaponry. These vessels, similar in specification to the *M/V Sky-1* (that was allegedly involved in conveying the explosives used in the 1998 East Africa embassy bombings), are not usually associated with trans-oceanic trade; however, the other as yet unidentified al-Qaeda vessels of this class could indeed venture long range across the Atlantic and Indian Oceans with prudent passage-planning and bunkering allowances. Thus far, however, there is no indication that the ships have been deployed in this way. What is of greater concern is that if indeed, as it appears, the organisation has operatives or sympathisers with well-developed seamanship and navigational expertise, and experience at remaining concealed within the merchant shipping world, they have the ability to use this acumen as purchase for a bolder use of other forms of merchant ships. Vessels that may be used in the conveyance of dangerous cargoes or the routine shipment of privately owned TEUs stuffed surreptitiously at the furthest reaches of the container supply chain.

Symmetrical and Asymmetrical Threat Mitigation — The Fusion of Intelligence, International and Transnational Cooperation and Risk Management

Bluntly stated, there is no quick fix or easy remedy for the dangers posed by terrorism in the maritime domain. The environment is too vast, has too many vulnerable targets, is highly populated with vessels, affords too much operational cover and is devoid of sufficient patrolling and interdicting forces to be adequately secured. So what do we do? The answer comes in the form of three distinct but interlocking parts: the generation of intensive and endemic maritime intelligence; vigorous international and transnational cooperation among maritime trading governments, security forces and the appropriate public and private bodies within the maritime industry; and holistic risk management. This maritime security "triangulation" is variously symmetrical and asymmetrical in nature depending upon the circumstances, the level of operational application and the typology of the enemy target.

Intelligence

During the Cold War, East and West faced off with vast, conspicuous military assets and formations; interestingly, however, though the intelligence effort on both sides was sizeable indeed there were an abundance of potential enemy targets to choose from and thus the effort required at the point of initiation was relatively small on an effort-to-target basis. However, today the game is different and the application of intelligence effort-to-target in the war on terrorism is vastly complicated, indeed the calculus is reversed. Today, the potential target cell is tiny and leaves a correspondingly small "operational footprint". Thus, the effort that must be applied in order to have any chance of identifying and interdicting a maritime terrorist cell (or cells) hidden within the vastness of the domain at hand must be large and sustained. The diagram below represents the paradigm shift.

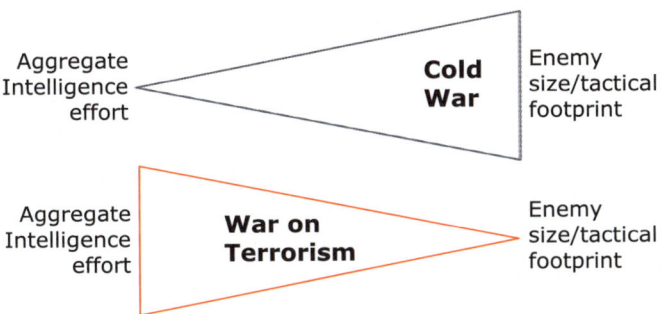

From a qualitative standpoint, the intelligence effort must embrace penetration into the commercial maritime and shipping realm as well as harnessing the considerable capabilities of more traditional military intelligence perspectives and foci. It is no use simply knowing a vessel's latitude and longitude, course and speed, there must also be a focused and sustained effort to seek out identities, operational histories and capabilities of vessels, shippers, freight-forwarders and terrorist groups with recognised maritime capabilities. These are the indices that bestow thorough appreciation. It should be stressed that the projection of "intelligence deterrence" is a proven way of compelling terrorists to delay or abandon their operations.

International and transnational cooperation

This component comes in a variety of forms. The most obvious and topical manifestation is the International Ship and Port Facility Security Code (ISPS), which came to force on 1 July 2004. Notwithstanding the hurdles and inevitable discrepancies in levels and timeliness of compliance, this regime regardless of its imperfections must not be allowed to fail or become institutionally diluted. Moreover, when initial endemic compliance has been achieved, the task has only just begun; the Code will be meaningless unless it can be enforced worldwide and if convincing punitive action is meted to those found to be in contravention. Ultimately, ISPS will only be as strong as the weakest link. Thus far the US-led Container Security Initiative (CSI) is the best answer to the problem of securing the world's cellularised trading matrix; the faster this regime proliferates and the more intrusive it becomes the more likely it will be that a containerised WMD, terrorist operative or a consignment of tactical-level weapons can be intercepted. The industry itself, at both state and private sector levels, must start to de-cloak all of the mechanisms that enable the concealment of shipping operations. This will not be straightforward; however, with the correct balance of financial incentives and punitive action, progress can be made. Naval and military forces, including coast guards and maritime police units, have a critical role to play; recent collaborative exercises and operations in the Malacca Straits, the Proliferation Security Initiative (PSI) and Operation *Active Endeavour* are testament to the effectiveness of the deployment and application of force at sea where necessary. Lastly, the private sector has a role to play, whether as security consulting and training agents, as monitors of shipping activity, in the provision of physical port security, or as instigators of regulatory reform in the commercial shipping and trading complex.

Risk Management

As demonstrated above the scale and complexity of the maritime environment, the sheer number of vessels that service it and the momentum of the global trading systemic render even the best efforts of intelligence gathering agencies at all levels and the effectiveness of participating military and security forces only a partial answer. Total security intrusion would retard and even cripple operations along vital trading links and at port facilities; clearly this is not acceptable for the economic well-being of nations and the global economy. Thus, the risk posed by terrorists must be managed through the constant and diligent screening and vetting of vessels as they come into ports, the crews that man them and the companies that own and operate them. This approach allows ports to continue to function whilst affording realistic protection. This simultaneously passive/active strategy is the responsibility both of port state control and security agencies and concerned bodies within the private sector. The diagram below captures the operational and structural sense of the overall approach to mitigating the threat residing within the maritime domain.

Symmetrical/Asymmetrical Threat Mitigation – M³

Conclusion

Currently, terrorist *attacks* in the maritime domain are fortunately comparatively infrequent and dispersed. However, terrorist *activity* in this arena is most certainly ongoing, well-concealed and has the potential to develop both in terms of sophistication and amplification of consequence. This chapter has sought to highlight and analytically address five main inter-related fields of concern: (1) the nature and properties of the global maritime expanse and the opportunities and complications this space confers upon terrorists and security forces, respectively; (2) an appraisal of the ontology of the international commercial maritime domain as both a means and the shroud for terrorist operatives; (3) a capture of the contemporary threat picture; (4) a projection of possible future terrorist scenarios founded upon an extrapolation articulated according to an understanding of declared *strategic* intent, the latent and existential capabilities exposed, and the vast range of vulnerable targets of opportunity that exist within the maritime domain; and lastly (5) an argument in favour of a "triangulation" of three symmetrical and asymmetrical, mutually reinforcing strategies aimed at threat mitigation — intelligence, international and transnational cooperation, and risk management.

The absence of philosophical and operational clairvoyance is an unfortunate shortcoming for those tasked with confronting terrorism. Nevertheless, agile and diligent cognitive preparation, monitoring, cooperation, force application and risk management are most certainly within the capabilities of those committed to confronting terrorism in the maritime domain. If this strategy is found wanting, even for just a short while, a well-prepared and tactically competent terrorist cell at sea could amplify the already considerable advantages conferred upon him by the environment at hand and exact a terrible price in the form of a strategic-level attack on a major port or vital maritime chokepoint.

Notes

1. Available online at http://www.guardian.co.uk/worldlatest/story/0,1280,-4020163,00.html.
2. Organisation for Economic Co-operation and Development, *Security in Maritime Transport: Risk Factors and Economic Impact* (OECD, July 2003).
3. Lloyds Marine Intelligence Unit.
4. Organisation for Economic Co-operation and Development, *Security in Maritime Transport: Risk Factors and Economic Impact* (OECD, July 2003).
5. The CIA World FactBook. Available online at http://www.cia.gov/cia/publications/factbook/geos/xx.html.
6. Organisation for Economic Co-operation and Development, *Security in Maritime Transport: Risk Factors and Economic Impact* (OECD, July 2003).
7. Lloyd's Maritime Intelligence Unit.
8. Organisation for Economic Co-operation and Development, *Ownership and Control of Ships* (OECD, March 2003).
9. Ibid.
10. Organisation for Economic Co-operation and Development, *op. cit.*
11. 1982 United Nations Convention on the Law of the Sea (UNCLOS).
12. Alex Vines, "Vessel Operations Under "Flags of Convenience" and National Security Implications", Statement before the House Armed Services Committee Special Oversight Panel on the Merchant Marine, 13 June 2002. Available online at http://armedservices.house.gov/openingstatementsandpressreleases/107thcongress/02-06-13vines.html.
13. Lloyds Marine Intelligence Unit.

14. "Investigators to board Yemen tanker", *BBC News*, 9 October 2002. Available online at http://news.bbc.co.uk/1/hi/world/middle_east/2312739.stm.
15. "Yemeni authorities identify Limburg attack mastermind", *International Policy Institute for Counter Terrorism News*, 26 February 2003. Available online at http://www.ict.org.il/spotlight/det.cfm?id=870.
16. Brian Whitaker, "Tanker blast was work of terrorists", *The Guardian*, 17 October 2002. Available online at http://www.guardian.co.uk/yemen/Story/0,2763,813411,00.html.
17. Available online at http://www.jinsa.org/home/home.html.
18. Ibid.
19. Available online at http://www.arabicnews.com.
20. Available online at http://www.jinsa.org/home/home.html.
21. ICC International Maritime Bureau, *Piracy and Armed Robbery Against Ships*, Annual Report, 1 January–31 December 2003.
22. International Maritime Organisation. Availalble online at http://www.imo.org/includes/blastDataOnly.asp/data_id%3D8084/40.pdf.
23. Kate McGeown, "Aceh rebels blamed for piracy", *BBC News*, 8 September 2003. Available online at Http://news.bbc.co.uk/1/hi/world/asia-pacific/3090136.stm.
24. Available online at http://www.guardian.co.uk.
25. Jean-Paul Rodrigure, *Straits, Passages & Chokepoints: A Maritime Geostrategy of Petroleum Circulation*.
26. Peter Grier and Faye Bowers, "How Al Qaeda might strike the US by sea", *The Christian Science Monitor*, 15 May 2003. Available online at http://www.csmonitor.com/2003/0515/p02s02-usgn.html.
27. John Mintz, "Al-Qaeda fleet takes terrorist threat to sea", *SMH.com*, 1 January 2003. Available online at http://www.smh.com.au/articles/2002/12/31/1041196641696.html.

Chapter 8

Maritime Terrorism, A Risk Assessment: The Australian Example

Catherine Zara Raymond

Introduction

"Just enough — just in time" — the buzzwords of a 21st century world trade system. One which is characterised by free-flowing international trade within a truly globalised economy. A system that has developed over the years to be as open and frictionless as possible in order to spur even greater economic growth. A system where efficient production processes have reduced inventory-holding to a very minimum, hence the phrase "just enough — just in time". A system fundamentally dependent upon a large and heterogeneous fleet of ocean going vessels, reduced trading barriers and decreases in tariffs.

A system that on one tragic day in September 2001 would be irrevocably changed.

Immediately following the shocking September 11th World Trade Centre attacks in New York, governments around the world hurried to assess their vulnerability to highly organised terrorist groups willing to sacrifice thousands of lives to achieve their aims. Although the initial focus was on the vulnerability of the air transport system, attention soon turned to the maritime sector — that is, the vulnerability of port infrastructure and commercial shipping to a maritime terrorist attack. A threat the international naval community is still largely unfamiliar with.

This issue became all the more pressing since the major shipping countries agreed that by July 2004 they would have carried out risk assessments on their maritime sectors, and implemented the new security plans set out in the International Ship and Port Facility Security Code (ISPS Code). The ISPS Code is one of a number of amendments to the 1974 Safety of Life at Sea Convention (SOLAS). It contains detailed security-related requirements for Governments, port authorities and shipping companies together with a series of guidelines about how to meet these requirements.

In light of these developments, this chapter will seek to examine whether maritime terrorism poses a threat to commercial shipping in transit or at port, and port facilities, and if so, to what extent. Although the focus of the article is on the threat to Australian shipping and ports, the findings of this risk assessment are applicable on a regional level.

The chapter, split into five main sections, begins with a brief introduction and definition of maritime terrorism; it then goes on to outline the historical context of the phenomenon; an analysis of Australian ports and commercial shipping follows; the terrorist groups and their capabilities are then examined; and the final section is the risk assessment itself.

Maritime terrorism is, unlike piracy, a new phenomenon compared to other violent activities that take place in the marine environment. Where it has occurred, it has largely been in the context of civil war or wars of succession and has as a consequence remained the business of the affected state. Thus, the international naval community has remained to a large extent unfamiliar with the threat of maritime terrorism.

There is, as shall be shown below, no international agreement regarding most maritime violence or sea robbery. As a result there is also no internationally agreed definition of maritime terrorism.

What is found in fact is that even within one organisation there can be differing emphases within definitions of the term *maritime terrorism*. For example, the Council for Security Co-operation in the Asia Pacific (CSCAP), which is a forum for non-governmental "track-two" multilateral security dialogue, has used a number of definitions of the term maritime terrorism. In 2002, the CSCAP Working Group on Maritime Co-operation used a relatively broad definition:

> Maritime terrorism refers to the undertaking of terrorist acts and activities
> (1) within the maritime environment, (2) using or against vessels or fixed

platforms at sea or in port, or against any one of their passengers or personnel, (3) against coastal facilities or settlements, including tourist resorts, port areas, and port town or cities.[1]

However, in a CSCAP memorandum the definition of maritime terrorism is: "The use of violence at sea or to a ship or fixed platform for political ends, including any use of violence for the purpose of putting the public or any section of the public in fear".[2]

For the purposes of this chapter, maritime terrorism shall be defined as any illegal act directed against ships, their passengers, cargo or crew, or against sea ports with the intent of directly or indirectly influencing, for political purposes, a government or groups of individuals.[3]

At this point a definition of piracy would also prove useful. Not only to distinguish piracy from maritime terrorism but to illustrate how the two phenomena overlap to some extent.

According to the United Nations Convention on the Law of the Sea, piracy consists of:

(a) any illegal acts of violence or detention, or any act of depredation, committed for private ends by the crew or the passengers of a private ship or a private aircraft, and directed:
   (i) on the high seas, against another ship or aircraft, or against persons or property on board such ship or aircraft;
   (ii) against a ship, aircraft, persons or property in a place outside the jurisdiction of any State;
(b) any act of voluntary participation in the operation of a ship or of an aircraft with knowledge of facts making it a pirate ship or aircraft;
(c) any act inciting or of intentionally facilitating an act described in sub-paragraph (a) or (b).[4]

The problem with this definition when applied to Southeast Asia is that most pirate attacks occur within the 12-mile limit. That is, within the territorial sea of the state and not on the high seas. Therefore, such incidences are not legally considered piracy and there is therefore no international agreement regarding most maritime violence or sea robbery.

To overcome this problem the International Maritime Bureau (IMB), which tracks piracy world-wide from London, has adopted the following broad definition:

Piracy is an act of boarding any vessel with the intent to commit theft or any other crime and with the intent or capability to use force in the furtherance of that act.[5]

This wider definition, "which has no status in international law, covers all acts regardless of the location of the vessel. It includes not only acts against vessels underway but also against vessels alongside in port or at anchor".[6]

The Phenomenon Explained

The incident that first brought the phenomenon of maritime terrorism to the world's attention was the hijacking of the cruise liner *Achille Lauro* by Palestinian terrorists in 1985. The incident took place in Egyptian territorial waters. The crew and passengers were held hostage, and were threatened with death should a group of Palestinian prisoners detained in Israel not be freed. In the course of the incident a disabled American citizen was murdered and his body and wheelchair were thrown into the sea in full view of the international press. The Palestinian terrorists surrendered after 2 days and were captured through US military intervention when they were fleeing on board a commercial jetliner.[7]

Following this high profile incident, maritime states under the auspices of the International Maritime Organisation (IMO) drafted and approved the Convention for the Suppression of Unlawful Acts Against the Safety of Maritime Navigation in 1988 (the *Rome Convention*). The convention would extend the rights of maritime forces to pursue terrorists, pirates and maritime criminals into foreign territorial waters. A protocol to the Convention extends its application to offences committed on fixed platforms on the continental shelf (the Protocol for the Suppression of Unlawful Acts against the Safety of Fixed Platforms Located on the Continental Shelf). However, so far only 34 states are party to the convention — including the United States, Canada, major European countries, Australia, Singapore, China and Japan.

Other high profile maritime terrorist attacks have been the hijacking of a Greek freighter in Karachi in 1974, the suicide attack on the *USS Cole* in October 2000, killing 17 people, and the bombing of a Philippine ferry in February 2004, killing more than 100 people. Although these attacks have been well documented, attention is only now starting to turn to the implications these attacks have for international maritime security in general.

Apart from these somewhat isolated incidences of maritime terrorism, terrorist attacks against maritime targets are quite rare. They constitute only 2 percent of all international terrorist incidences over the last 30 years.[8] According to Dr Rohan Gunaratna, one of the few terrorism scholars who has been studying maritime terrorism for a number of years: "There has been no discernible trend or pattern in attacks against maritime targets".[9] They are also not isolated to any one particular region.

Terrorist groups that are known to have maritime capability are the Provisional Irish Republican Army (PIRA), Polisario, Abu Sayyaf Group (ASG), Palestinian groups, The Contras, Al Qaeda, and the Liberation Tigers of Tamil Eelam (LTTE). Over the years maritime terrorist attacks have taken different forms. They have been committed on board vessels or fixed platforms, for example, the armed attacks against Chinese, Indonesian and Korean vessels near Sri Lanka in 1997 resulting in the loss of the vessels, and the several hostage-taking incidents on a Shell oil-drilling platform in Nigerian waters in 1999.

The vessel itself may be used as a weapon against another. The best-known example of this is the attack on the *USS Cole* in 2000. The vessel was severely damaged by suicide bombers using a small dinghy to come into direct contact with the American navy destroyer. Maritime terrorist attacks have also been perpetrated against ports or coastal facilities, such as the bombing of two tourist resorts in Turkey in 1994, armed raids against two fishing villages in Cambodia in 1998, or the kidnapping of foreigners in Sipadan Island in 1999.

Maritime attacks can be carried out from land, sea and air. Terrorist tactics range from "employment of land-based teams — trained to place improvised explosive devices (IEDs) on ships — to terrorist divers, attack craft and sea mines. Maritime terrorist technologies range from scuba, sea scooters and speedboats to Global Positioning Systems (GPS)",[10] all of which are available on the open market.

By far the most high profile maritime terrorist group is the LTTE, which has been employing maritime terrorist tactics since the 1980s in their ongoing war against the Sri Lankan government. Since July 1990 they have carried out over 40 sea-borne suicide attacks against the Sri Lankan navy. They have also been responsible for boarding without permission, attacking, destroying, damaging or shipjacking a number of foreign-owned civilian vessels in the Sri Lankan waters. They have over the years "developed and operated an extensive and profitable network of freight forwarders and ship operators. Current estimates of the LTTE's fleet size range from 10–12 ... bulk freighters".[11] The LTTE is at the cutting edge of maritime terrorism, and their activities are potentially copycat models for other groups. However, according to Rohan Gunaratna: "In both classified and open literature there has been little systematic research on terrorist maritime capabilities".[12] The Sri Lankan case provides an "early example of emerging trends and patterns in maritime terrorism"[13] that has been dangerously ignored.

The Implications of 9/11 for Maritime Terrorism

The advent of 11 September 2001 changed world perception of terrorism considerably, and brought new issues to light. As a result, the perception of the threat from maritime terrorism has changed too. The attack on the Twin Towers in New York set new precedents:

> The enormity and sheer scale of the simultaneous suicide attacks on September 11 eclipsed anything previously seen in terrorism. Among the most significant characteristics of the operation were its ambitious scope and dimensions; impressive co-ordination and synchronisation; and the unswerving dedication and determination of the 19 aircraft hijackers who willingly and wantonly killed themselves, the passengers, and the crews of the four aircraft they commandeered and the approximately 3,000 persons working at or visiting both the World Trade Centre and the Pentagon.[14]

The attacks also demonstrated that ordinary means of transportation can be turned into lethal weapons of terror in the hands of determined terrorists. The fear of mass-destruction threats such as biological, chemical or nuclear attack has led to a massive oversight in international security. One which fails to see that this type of attack, using ordinary means of transportation, is a possibility.

What was made clear by the events of 9/11, was that the potential targets of terrorist groups had just got wider. According to David Claridge of Janusian Securities Ltd., Al Qaeda in particular has "started to shift its strategy towards economic targets".[15] This new strategy is made evident in this statement by Al Qaeda: "We, the fighters of the holy war, in general are hoping to enter the next phase ... It will be a war of killings, *a war against businesses*, which will hit the enemy where he does not expect us to".[16]

All of the above issues that came out of 9/11 — the skill and dedication of the terrorists in planning and carrying out their attack, the demonstration that ordinary transport can be used as a devastating weapon and the targeting of economic lifelines — mean that transportation security and economics can no longer be treated as an afterthought or tertiary issue post-9/11. The targeting of maritime infrastructure is a now a real possibility. According to the former vice-president of the Philippines, Teofisto Guingona: "The security environment that has emerged from the rubble of the 9/11 incident introduces new perspectives, and necessitates fresh approaches and new responses".[17]

One way which maritime security needs to change, according to Pottengal Mukudan of the International Maritime Bureau, is that rather than assessing risk and potential targets on the basis of the intrinsic value of the cargoes and the ships carrying them, "the main focus now has to be the strategic intentions of terrorist groups".[18] In addition, according to terrorism expert Dr Gunaratna "the 'hardening of land aviation targets will shift the threat to maritime targets, particularly to commercial shipping' ".[19]

Australian Commercial Shipping and Ports

At the regional level, Australia is located at the Southern tip of Southeast Asia. The region encompasses a huge maritime area. In fact, it has been argued that the region is situated at the centre of the world's sea network: in the central location of the Asia/Europe and the Asia/North America line (i.e. in the central latitude of the world) and the intra-trade of Asia.

However, the region's Sea-lanes of Communication (SLOC) are also well known for having numerous critical "chokepoints". In other words, "points of convergence and focus such as straits and other bottlenecks".[20] The most important of these being the Straits of Malacca, Sunda and Lombok. The "chokepoints" are created in part by the archipelagos of the Philippines and Indonesia, which are characterised by shallow, narrow waterways, but also by the large number of vessels passing through these waterways.

The region has over the past decade experienced the highest economic growth rate in the world: since 1990, the economic growth rate has kept a higher level than the world's total, including North American and the EU. One of the fundamental characteristics of this growth is that it is based on sea-borne trade. Thus, there has been a rapid increase in the amount of container traffic traversing the region's waterways. More than half of the world's trade passes through the Straits of Malacca. Or put slightly differently, the Straits of Malacca experience more than three times the traffic of the Suez Canal and well over five times that of the Panama Canal.[21]

Shipping routes have often been described as the arteries of the regional economy. In the Asia-Pacific, uninterrupted flow of shipping is critical to most regional countries economic health and prosperity, and to some countries' very survival. Australia's economy is a case in point. Last year, 76 percent of the value of Australia's trade was conducted by sea and 71 percent of the total value of all imports into Australia arrived by ship.[22]

Forty percent of Australia's sea trade passes through the narrow waterways of the Indonesian and Philippine archipelagos. Thus, the vitality of the Australian economy depends on free access to these sea-lanes. Australia is particularly dependent upon the Straits of Lombok, which it uses for the shipment of iron ore to China.

Australia has a vast coastline of 37,000 km, much of it remote and practically unpopulated, and an offshore maritime zone of 9 million square kilometres.[23] Australia has some 60 ports with international facilities, and over 300 port facilities.[24] Australia's ports range in size from Melbourne, which is one of Australia's three top ports, to smaller isolated ones such as Port Hedland. In 2001–02 the top three ports of Melbourne, Sydney and Brisbane combined handled approximately 44 percent of Australia's trade, with Melbourne and Sydney accounting for well over three-quarters of that.[25] In the year 2000–01, 3200 ships entered Australia from overseas, making more than 9600 calls at Australian ports. If coastal shipping is included, port calls rise to 21,500.[26] Australia's major ports are also leading destinations for cruise ships visiting the South Pacific. More than 100,000 travelers arrive at Sydney Port alone each year.[27]

From the information above, it is possible to conclude that Australia's maritime infrastructure, including both its port facilities and its sea-trade, are essential to Australia's economic vitality — yet at the same time aspects of Australia's maritime sector and its trade routes are a source of concern. These are the difficult routes Australian ships must often take, the vast coastline and the high number of foreign vessels entering Australian waters.

A number of other potentially vulnerable areas have also been identified in the maritime sector. However, before going on to examine these areas individually, the assessment given in the OECD/OCDE Report called *Security in Maritime Transport: Risk Factors and Economic Impact* of the maritime sector in general is a useful starting point:

> Here is a sector characterised by an extremely diverse international labour force, transporting a vast range of goods whose provenance, description and ownership are often left remarkably vague. This is a system were international transport chains involved thousands of intermediaries, on vessels registered in dozens of countries that sometimes choose not to uphold their international responsibilities and where some vessel owners can and do easily hide their true identities using a complex web of international corporate registration process.[28]

Ports

Ports themselves by their very nature are vulnerable; ports are extensive in size and accessible by water and land. Their accessibility makes it difficult to apply the kinds of security measures that, for example, can be more readily applied at airports. Also, as is the case for Melbourne and Sydney, ports are often located in or near major metropolitan areas: "their activities, functions, and facilities, such as petroleum tank farms and other potentially hazardous material storage facilities, are often intertwined with the infrastructure of urban life, such as roads, bridges, and factories".[29]

Inspection Rates

Due to the huge quantities of cargo coming into ports, even with the latest x-ray facilities (which are only available in the largest ports) only 5 percent of imported sea cargo containers are inspected.[30] Following 9/11, the US Customs Service launched the Container Security Initiative (CSI). The key features of CSI are the posting of US Customs officials at major foreign ports, the increased screening of designated "high-risk" containers at their port of loading and the use of "smarter", tamper-proof containers and container-seals. Another important initiative that has been introduced in conjunction with CSI is the "24-hour rule", which requires the transmission of container manifests 24 hours before loading. CSI offers members the reciprocal opportunity to enhance their own shipment security through the same system. However, Australia is currently not a member of CSI. This is a worrying situation when it is taken into account that total container traffic is expected to rise by 66 percent by 2010.[31] Also, the screening and inspection of passengers and their baggage, which takes place in the aviation industry, is not carried out during the boarding of cruise ships and ferries. Given that one cruise ship can hold almost 700 people, this is a cause for concern.

Container Shipping

Another weakness in maritime security lies in the containers on large vessels in which cargo is transported. Containers revolutionised the world of shipping and today some 200 million containers are traded annually. However, the containerisation of cargo has meant that ports and cargo handlers no longer see each piece of cargo they are transporting — only the containers. As was noted above, only 5 percent of containers are actually inspected; therefore, the only information there is on the contents of a particular container is that which the shipper has declared.

Even if the shipper is not engaged in illegal activity, the containers are in fact vulnerable to tampering and access into the container can be gained relatively easily. The weakness lies in the container seals. It is presumed that if a container seal is intact, then the container has not been opened. However, "the seals ... can cost anything between a few cents and hundreds of dollars each and are often vulnerable to pre-use tampering, manipulation, physical force, falsification, super-glue and heat".[32] As mentioned above, CSI addresses the problem of container-seal tampering. However, as was also stated above, Australia is not a member of CSI.

This lack of security at the ports in relation to container contents and the vulnerable nature of the container seals becomes all the more worrisome when the journey a container makes before arriving at its port destination is examined. According the OECD/OCDE Report, the container begins its journey at the manufacturer's premises where it is loaded with the cargo. It is then transported by road or rail to a port.

> While in transit, the container may be stationary for various periods of time as trucks are stopped on the roadside and/or container carrying trains are being assembled in freight yards. Once in port, the container is sent to a staging area before it is placed immediately next to the vessel at quay. Even within the port area, a container may be moved several times as required by the port operator and/or customs. After being placed on board a ship, the container can be removed and trans-shipped in another port onto another vessel before arriving at its destination port. Here again, the container may be moved several times...[33]

What is clear from this study of container movement is that the system has many flaws, making it relatively easily subverted from legitimate commercial purposes.

Information and Documentation

Maritime certificate fraud is a common problem in the maritime industry. The problem lies in the fact that it is possible to acquire, relatively easily, the legal documents needed to command a vessel, without any proof of qualifications.

Evidence of this is the existence of "phantom ships". "Phantom ships" are vessels that have been hijacked by pirates — the ship is then repainted, the crew dumped or killed, the cargo transferred or sold. The ship sails into a new port with a false name and false papers. They are used in various maritime criminal activities, such as to conduct pirate attacks and the smuggling of goods and people.

People

Crewmembers of commercial vessels belong to different nationalities and there can be up to 60 crewmembers on a ship. According to the IMB it is "virtually impossible to verify the authenticity of the identity of the crew. This is due mainly to the relative ease with which forged and/or falsified seafarer certificates and identity documents can be bought on the black market". In fact, it was discovered by the IMB that in the 54 maritime administrations it surveyed, more than 12,000 cases of forged certificates of competency were reported.[34] Therefore, it is relatively easy for people to pose as crewmembers using false documents, thus creating the potential for pirates or terrorists to board ships without being identified.

Vessels in Transit

Ships are particularly vulnerable to a breach of security when they are making their slow passage through narrow waterways like the Malacca Straits. The high degree of congestion of maritime traffic limits the vessel's ability to manoeuvre to avoid a potential threat and can provide cover for a perpetrator's attack. The tankers that lumber along at 11 knots are easy pray to smaller boats with outboard motors that can travel up to three times faster than the tankers. They are often only equipped with spotlights, fire axes and hoses, as the laws in many ports bar the equipping of tankers with deck guns. The many uninhabited, jungle-covered islands that border the straits, provide ideal launching points to attack passing vessels and also a refuge from law-enforcement units. Finally, the lack of visible maritime law-enforcement patrols in the region adds to the vulnerability of shipping, as deterrence is a key element in preventing the conduct of any criminal activities whether on land or sea.

Bulk Shipments

Given the information above on the vulnerability of vessels in transit, the potential for security problems becomes even greater in the case of bulk shipments. Although bulk shipments of highly volatile liquid compounds are subject to tighter security and have escort requirements, this is not the case for the bulk shipment of fertilisers such as ammonium nitrate. Ammonium nitrate is "widely used throughout the world as an agricultural fertiliser and is generally considered a safe and stable compound when stored and handled correctly. However, with some manipulation (e.g. through the addition of fuel oil) and triggered by a sufficiently large explosive catalyst, fertiliser grade ammonium nitrate can be used as a powerful explosive".[35]

Not only are vessels carrying dry bulk cargoes vulnerable to some sort of attack, but due to the significant number of vessels in the shipping industry in general that are operated as one vessel companies using opaque ownership mechanisms, the vessels and their potentially dangerous cargo could be used for illegal purposes.

Flags of Convenience

Most vessels in the region of Southeast Asia fly flags of convenience. The most common in the region is the Panama flag. Shipping companies use flags of convenience to "avoid heavy taxes and stringent inspections which would condemn their vessels to the wrecker yards. While the vessels' real owners can hide behind a wall of secrecy created by the dubious ownership structures, the crews are cheap foreign labour, with no rights".[36]

There is often little correlation between nationality of registration and the nationality of owners, and these factors often have little relationship to the economies shipping or receiving cargoes. The nature of flag of convenience shipping means that these vessels are often used to carry out illegal activity. For example, gun running and drug smuggling.

It was remarked by Australia's deputy Prime Minister John Anderson that; "Australia is a shipper nation and not a shipping nation".[37] This reflects the government policy to decrease the Australian flagged coastal fleet in favour of the cheaper flag of convenience shipping. With a high proportion of Australia's sea faring trade being carried out by flag of convenience vessels, the security of Australia's maritime infrastructure is potentially weakened.

Due to the maritime industry's preoccupation with "open participation" and the "unfettered flow of trade", and the huge quantities of goods and containers that get transported on large numbers of vessels, it has as a consequence left itself tremendously vulnerable in terms of security. This seems particularly true in the case of Australia, given its location next to some of the world's most pirate infested areas and sea-lane "chokepoints", and its governments policy of increasing the use of flag of convenience vessels.

The Terrorist Groups

At this juncture, it is important to point out that in order to be considered a threat, it is not necessary for a terrorist group to have already carried out a maritime terrorist attack against Australian shipping or port facilities, or even displayed an interest in carrying out a maritime attack. Terrorist groups that have targeted westerners or had connections with networks or groups that have targeted westerners and western interests will be sufficient criteria to merit an examination. As 11 September 2001 highlighted, terrorist groups are very unpredictable and should not be underestimated. As the perpetrators of 9/11, this is especially true of Al Qaeda. Thus, this will be the first terrorist group to be examined.

Al Qaeda

Al Qaeda ("The Base") has been labelled as the first multinational terrorist group of the 21st century. According to terrorism expert Dr Rohan Gunaratna, "Al Qaeda has moved terrorism beyond the status of a technique of protest and resistance and turned it into a global instrument with which to compete with and challenge Western influence in the Muslim world".[38] Essentially, Al Qaeda is an international terrorist network led by the infamous Osama Bin Laden, which seeks to rid Muslim countries of what it sees as the profane influence of the West and replace their governments with fundamentalist Islamic regimes. More specifically, it has vowed to cut the "economic lifelines" of the world's industrialised societies.[39]

Al Qaeda's targets have included American and Western interests as well as Muslim governments it sees as corrupt — this has most commonly been the Saudi monarchy. Apart from the attacks on the Twin Towers and Pentagon in 2001, terrorist attacks by Al Qaeda have included:

- The suicide truck bombings in 1998 against the US embassies in Nairobi, Kenya, and Dar es Salaam, Tanzania, in which over 200 people were killed.[40]
- The suicide attack against the *USS Cole* off the coast of Yemen in 2000, in which 17 American soldiers were killed.
- The Millennium bombings in Indonesia, on Christmas Eve 2000, in which 30 churches were targeted.[41] This attack is thought to have been carried out in conjunction with Jemaah Islamiyah, an Indonesian terrorist group.

- The suicide attack against the French tanker, *Limburg*, also off the coast of Yemen in 2002, which resulted in the death of one crew member.
- A bomb attack against the US Consulate in 2002 in which 12 people were killed.[42]

In his book *Inside Al Qaeda*, Rohan Gunaratna describes how Al Qaeda's modes of attack range from "low-tech assassinations, bombings and ambushes to experiments with explosive-laden gliders and helicopters and crop-spraying aircraft adapted to disperse highly potent agents. It will have no compunction about employing chemical, biological, radiological and nuclear weapons against population centres".[43] The variety and innovation of the tactics and equipment used by this terrorist network highlight the importance of lateral thinking when trying to estimate the threat it will pose in the future.

Also worthy of note is Al Qaeda's considerable financial support base. Not only does it benefit from "the largesse of Osama Bin Laden, its business and financial committee generates significant revenues from its companies, charities and world-wide investments".[44] It has penetrated one-fifth of Islamic NGOs, conducts business operations in the money and share markets and has in the past received funding from state sponsors. All of which have contributed to a financial strength rarely held by terrorist groups.

Despite the destruction of its bases in Afghanistan by the US government and the subsequent capture or killing of more than half of its leadership, Al Qaeda still has, according to the director of Australian Security Intelligence Organization (ASIO), Dennis Richardson "considerable, real global capacity".[45] This is especially true of its networks in Southeast Asia; "Except for Singapore, and to a lesser extent, Malaysia, and the Philippines, Al Qaeda's network in the Asia-Pacific has remained virtually intact in the wake of 9/11".[46]

Al Qaeda began making inroads into Southeast Asia in 1988. Osama Bin Laden personally forged the link with Adburajak Janjalani, the founder and leader of the Abu Sayyaf Group (ASG) based in the Philippines. As a result, ASG's organisation, ideology, target selection and tactics are deeply influenced by Al Qaeda. It also formed links with another Philippine group, the Moro Islamic Liberation Front (MILF).

Using the Philippines as a base, in the early 1990s Al Qaeda penetrated several other Islamic terrorist groups in Malaysia, Indonesia and Singapore. One of which was Jemmah Islamiyah or Islamic Group (JI) initially based in Indonesia. Al Qaeda developed JI into a pan-Asian network extending from Malaysia to Japan in the north and to Australia in the South. Following this JI has carried out a number of attacks in the region with support from Al Qaeda.

It is believed that Al Qaeda operatives, working in conjunction with its Southeast Asian networks, have stockpiled at least 12 tons of explosives in the region: (i) 4 tons in Malaysia; (ii) 4.6 tons in the Philippines and (iii) at least 4 tons in Indonesia".[47] There is also evidence to suggest that Al Qaeda had plans to carry out September 11 style attacks on buildings in Australia. A man, believed to be a member of Al Qaeda, was arrested and confessed to making these plans and receiving pilot training in Australia and Britain.

Attacks on maritime interests are known to have featured in Al Qaeda's ongoing terrorism plans. Apart from the attacks on the *USS Cole* and the *Limburg*, perhaps the most well publicised examples of Al Qaeda's maritime capabilities, it has been uncovered that Al Qaeda had plans to attack Malaysian and US naval vessels while they were on patrol in the Straits of Malacca.

Late in 2002, US intelligence officials identified approximately 15 freighters around the world that they believe are controlled by Al Qaeda and are used both for generating profit and for aiding terrorist attacks. However, the US-maintained list of suspected Al Qaeda ships, which was begun in September 2001 has varied from a low of a dozen to as high as 50 demonstrating the difficulties naval officials have in keeping track of vessels.[48]

Although international counter-terrorism efforts were given a boost in 2002 with the capture of Adb al-Rahim al-Nashiri an alleged mastermind of Al Qaeda's nautical strategy, the situation in the global maritime industry remains strongly in favour of the terrorists. One of the main problems is the extensive use of "flags of convenience" by maritime trade. US officials say that Al Qaeda has been using a shipping fleet flagged in the Pacific-island of Tonga and owned by the shipping company called *Nova* to carry out its terrorist activities.

In February 2002, eight Pakistani men jumped ship off one of the *Nova* freighters, the *Twillinger*, at an Italian port, after a trip from Cairo. US officials claimed that the men — who lied about being crewmen and carried false documents and large sums of money — had been sent by Al Qaeda. Then in August of the same year another Nova freighter, named the *Sara*, radioed to maritime authorities in Italy that 15 Pakistani men whom the ships owner had forced to take aboard in Casablanca, were menacing his crew. According to US officials, tens of thousands of dollars, false documents, maps of Italian cities and evidence tying them to Al Qaeda members in Europe were found amongst the 15 men, leading them to conclude that they too were possibly on a terrorist mission for Al Qaeda.

Al Qaeda has even made use of legitimate merchant vessels to carry out its terrorist activities: In October 2002, inspectors at an Italian port opened a shipping container bound from Egypt to Canada via Italy and discovered a suspected member of Al Qaeda. The container had been "converted into a portable hotel room, complete with bed, toilet, laptop computer, two mobile phones, cameras and enough supplies to tide him over during the three-week journey".[49] Very worrying was the fact that the man had in his possession a Canadian passport, airport maps and airline security passes for Canada, Thailand and Egypt.

Finally, it is believed by terrorism experts that Al Qaeda is "investing significantly in maritime technology and tactics, establishing diving schools, experimenting with various gases, trying to conduct surface attacks using boats laden with explosives but also using divers carrying explosives attached to hulls of vessels".[50]

Jemaah Islamiyah

Jemaah Islamiyah is a militant Islamic terrorist group active in several Southeast Asian countries, whose aim it is to establish an Islamic republic unifying Malaysia, Indonesia, Brunei, southern Thailand and Mindanao in the Philippines. Originally an Indonesian group, under Al Qaeda's influence JI established cells throughout the region, its plan being to carve out smaller Islamic states from within the existing state borders and later unify them in an Islamic republic. JI targets have included US and Western interests in the region. The group is believed to be part of the regional terrorist network that is controlled by Al Qaeda. JI is conceivably Al Qaeda's instrument connecting mainstream and renegade terrorist and guerrilla elements in the region. It now has some 200 members in Malaysia alone.[51]

The most notable of JI's previous attacks are:

- The 12 October 2002 Bali suicide attack in a nightclub that killed nearly 200 people; mostly Western tourists including 88 Australians.[52]
- The Marriott Hotel bombing in Jakarta on 5 August 2003 that killed 12 people.[53]
- The suicide bombing of the Australian Embassy in Jakarta on 9 September 2004, which killed nine people and injured more than 180.[54]

The attacks above show beyond doubt that JI is targeting Westerners and Western interests in the region. Following a statement released by JI after the latest Embassy bombing, it has become evident that Australian interests in particular are a target due to Australia's role in the war in Iraq.

Like Al Qaeda, JI has planned attacks against naval vessels in the region. In late 2001 JI had planned to target American military vessels at Changi Naval Base. However, these plans had to be put on hold as the Singapore JI members lacked the operational capacity to launch the attack. Renewed fears of a JI attack against maritime targets came after US Intelligence passed on warnings about a plot to hijack a vessel in the SLOCs of the region. The warnings, issued in September 2004, stated that activists from JI have been discussing plans to seize a vessel using local pirates.

Abu Sayyaf Group and the Moro Islamic Liberation Front

Abu Sayyaf Group (ASG) meaning "bearer of the sword" in Arabic, and the Moro Islamic Liberation Front (MILF) are both separatist groups active in the Philippines. MILF is currently the largest Islamic separatist group, with an estimated 15,000 members.[55]

Since the late 1990s, the MILF has been in peace negotiations with the Philippine government; however, the talks have been punctuated with violent outbreaks on both sides. The MILF has mounted attacks against both military and civilian targets, resulting in the deaths of over 210 people in 2003.[56] One such attack took place on a busy seaport in Davao City, in the Philippines, in April 2003. Seventeen people were killed in the attack.[57] The group has also carried out attacks on Philippine shipping, mainly placing bombs on domestic inter-island ferries being used to transport members of the Armed Forces of the Philippines and Christians to and from Mindanao.

ASG was formed by a group of terrorists who split from the MILF, it committed its first major attack in 1991. ASG has been responsible for abducting foreign nationals and holding them to ransom, bombings and assassinations. It has also made threats against the global petroleum industry. Examples of its attacks include:

- The kidnapping of 21 people, including Western tourists, from the Island resort of Sipadan, Malaysia, in 2000. Resolution of the incident came a year later when ASG received a $15 million ransom in exchange for the release of the hostages.[58]
- The kidnapping of 20 people from a tourist resort on Palawan Island, in 2001, in which several people were murdered including a US citizen.[59]

- The bombing of *M/V Superferry* 14 shortly after it left Manila Bay on 27 February 2004, killing more than 100 people.[60]

As I mentioned above, both the MILF and ASG have strong links with Al Qaeda. Their members are known to have trained in camps in Afghanistan that also provided training for Al Qaeda recruits. It is believed that Al Qaeda provides financial support to both groups to carry out their attacks. ASG also finances its operations through robbery, piracy and ransom.

Free Aceh Movement

The Free Aceh Movement or Gerakan Aceh Merdeka (GAM), as it is known in Indonesian, has been fighting for an independent Islamic state in Aceh, Indonesia, since the 1970s. Historically the group's maritime capability centred around the smuggling of people, weapons and supplies; in other words, maritime activities were primarily a source of revenue and resources. Since early 2001, there has been a significant rise in pirate attacks in Acehnese waters. The Indonesian Government blames GAM for these attacks; however, GAM denies the charges, admitting only to the June 2002 attack on a boat chartered by Exxon Mobil. These pirate attacks attributed to GAM usually take the form of robbery and/or kidnap of crewmembers for ransom.

GAM is known to have maritime forces capable of brown water (riverine) and green water (coastal) operations, and its targets have generally been the Indonesian military forces (TNI), Indonesian government officials and Exxon Mobile facilities, employees and infrastructure.

Some of the maritime attacks attributed to GAM are:

- The attack of *M/V Ocean Silver* on 26 August 2001. The attackers forced the ship to sail to Jambu Air in Aceh, where they held six crewmembers hostage for ransom. Following a failed rescue attempt by the TNI, the ransom was paid and the crewmembers released.[61]
- On 9 August 2003, attackers boarded the *M.T. Penrider*, which was carrying 1000 tons of fuel oil through the Straits of Malacca. The pirates robbed the ship of cash and valuables and took two crewmembers hostage for ransom. Despite demanding $100,000 for the return of the crewmembers, the sum eventually paid was approximately $52,000.[62]

It could be argued that these attacks, if perpetrated by GAM, constitute maritime terrorism. Although they exhibit much the same characteristics of a traditional pirate attack the motivation behind the attack is distinctly political.

A term coined by Rupert Herbert-Burns of the Maritime Intelligence Group for this type of maritime terrorism is "logistical-support terrorism".[63]

Terrorism in Southeast Asia represents a tangled web of networks, often making it nearly impossible to attribute — beyond doubt — an attack to a particular group. However, what is clear from the analysis above is that all the terrorist groups in the region have both the motivation and the potential capability to carry out an attack on Australian maritime interests.

It has increasingly come to the attention of researchers of maritime terrorism that there is a possibility, especially in Southeast Asia, that pirates and terrorists could join forces. Not as seen in the GAM example but through the dissemination of vital knowledge from pirate groups to terrorist groups. There is a possibility that pirates could sell assets such as maritime and littoral knowledge, stolen vessels (such as tugs) and stolen documentation to conventional terrorists, who could then employ these assets to carry out a large-scale terrorist attack. Therefore, it would be useful at this stage to give a brief historical overview of piracy, and trace its present trends.

Piracy has been a nagging problem across the world's waters for centuries. However, over the past 10–15 years it has evolved into an art form. Reported incidences have increased dramatically around the world, with more than 300 attacks taking place annually. According to the International Maritime Bureau (IMB) attacks on ships have tripled in the past 10 years. Already in the first half of 2004 there were 182 attacks on ships worldwide and 30 crewmembers killed. The number of deaths is twice as many as was reported in the same period last year.[64]

Southeast Asia is the most pirate-prone region of the world; between 1991 and 2001 there were 1567 actual and attempted attacks in the region — 66 percent of the global total.[65] The Malacca Straits and the waters around Indonesia, the Philippines and the South China Sea have become a haven for pirates. The main cause of this being the Asian financial crisis that began in Thailand in late 1997 and the political instability in Indonesia that followed, leading to the creation of thousands of unemployed people.

There are three main types of piracy: "Harbour/anchorage attacks, attacks against vessels on high seas/territorial waters and hijackings of commercial vessels on high seas (phantom ship phenomenon)".[66]

In harbour/anchorage attacks the vessel is surreptitiously boarded while it is stationary, allowing the perpetrators to commit acts of thievery or robbery. While underway, the vessel may be subjected to a short-term seizure lasting a few hours while the pirates take cargo or belongings; a long-term seizure lasting several days while the cargo is unloaded at ports selected by the pirate or transferred to another vessel; or a permanent seizure wherein the vessel is turned into a "phantom ship".[67]

Pirate boats are usually equipped with several outboard motors on the back, allowing them to go almost three times as fast as tankers. They often make use of modest radar systems to help them locate their targets. The pirates also use a low-tech version of stealth technology: they choose boats made of wood, which are hard to spot on radar.

From the analysis above, it is clear that contemporary pirates use much the same tactics and technology that maritime terrorists might use. If the terrorist groups of the region employed the knowledge and expertise of the pirates to carry out their maritime attacks this would be a very worrying development.

The Risk Assessment

Before beginning the assessment of whether or not maritime terrorism is a threat to Australian shipping interests and infrastructure, consideration should be given to the presence of existing preventative security measures to further establish the context within which the threat of maritime terrorism exists.

Most maritime security measures currently in place in Southeast Asia and Australia have been designed primarily to deal with the more conventional threats to maritime security, which include, for example, illegal immigration, drugs and arms smuggling, and piracy. The various governments whose states border the strategic waterways of the region share responsibility for patrolling the waterways with the US government. However, as was discussed earlier in the paper, there is no international legal agreement regarding most maritime crime or violence, therefore there are no multinational enforcement strategies.

Recently, there have been some minor developments aimed at addressing the region's maritime security issues. In June 2004, the partner states of the Five Power Defence Arrangements (FPDA), which include Australia, Malaysia, New Zealand, Singapore and the United Kingdom, agreed to widen the scope of the grouping's military exercises to include non-conventional security threats, including maritime terrorism. Also, the first trilateral coordinated maritime patrol of the Malacca Strait (known as operation MALSINDO) by Malaysian, Indonesian and Singaporean forces took place in late July of 2004. However, there is still much to be done.

According to Sam Bateman, a retired commodore of the Australian Navy, there is "a lack of trained maritime police, inadequate boats and equipment, and inexperience with complicated concepts of law enforcement such as the doctrine of hot pursuit".[68] This is particularly a problem in Indonesia, which has the lowest defence budget in Southeast Asia. Although developments such as the creation of MALSINDO are a step in the right direction they fail to address the most fundamental issues outlined by Sam Bateman above.

Australia itself has problems with its coastal security system. In its current state, Australia's "Coastwatch" system has only eight vessels and 14 aircraft that are immediately available.[69] The rest of its capability is divided amongst a number of different agencies, one of which is the Royal Australian Navy, which lend their resources to coastal surveillance. Michael O'Connor, executive director of the Australian Defence Association, argues that "the lack of a professional coastguard service with adequate resources means the whole process of external intelligence gathering and analysis, surveillance, detection and interception is shared by too many agencies".[70]

The Coastwatch's inadequacy was highlighted when in April 2003 a vessel with a cargo of 50 kg of heroin, which it was intending to offload, was able to remain anchored off the south coast of Australia for some days. According to reports, "the ship apparently entered Australian waters with no intention of port visits and with empty holds. There were no checks or balances. This underlies the vulnerability of our coastline".[71]

Following 9/11, governments around the world began to reassess their vulnerability to a terrorist attack — and none more so than the United States. Following requests by the United States, the IMO developed an international maritime security code that would address some of the perceived vulnerabilities found to be present in most states' maritime security systems. In December 2002, adoption of the new code — the International Ship and Port Facility Security Code (ISPS Code) — was made mandatory through the International Convention for the Safety of Life at Sea (SOLAS), of which Australia is a signatory.

The Code, which entered into force on July 2004, covers: Cargo vessels over 500 gross tonnes on international voyages, port facilities serving ships on international voyages, passenger ships and mobile offshore drilling units.[72]

It requires ships and port facilities to carry out security assessments, after which ships are required to create ship security plans, appoint ship security officers and company security officers. Ships are also required to carry certain onboard equipment.[73] Port facility requirements will include port facility security plans and port facility security officers. Port facilities are also obliged to keep certain security equipment.[74]

However, the main problem with the new security measures introduced by the IMO is that although most shipping nations are members and therefore signatories of the SOLAS Convention, the IMO has in the past had trouble enforcing its regulations. This is especially true in the case of states that have on their shipping registers flags of convenience vessels. These states lack the resources or people with sufficient expertise to enforce the standards that are acceptable to the shipping community at large. The irony is that it is the flags of convenience vessels that probably pose the biggest security threat to Australian ports.

In fact in the majority of cases one could argue that although security plans may be in place and security officers designated, the unfortunate reality is that it is often crewmembers of a fairly low rank and who have limited training that will implement the Code.

One weakness is that the ISPS Code only covers ships and port facilities (which are defined as "the interface between the ships and the port"[75]), so does not require facilities further along the supply chain or the suppliers of the goods to adopt any new security measures.

The Code also only recommends what "security equipment" should be kept onboard ships and at port facilities and does not evaluate if these equipment, for example, a hand-held radio, will significantly improve maritime security.

Many in the maritime transport industry believe that existing security measures already in place in ports will go some way to meeting the new ISPS requirements. This, and the information above, shows quite clearly that the fulfilment of the requirements of the ISPS Code by Australia will not significantly alter the future situation with regards to the threat from maritime terrorism.

It would seem from the vulnerabilities that exist in the maritime transport sector and the terrorist groups operating in the area that a maritime terrorist attack against an Australian vessel or commercial port is a real possibility and has been for some time.

There are a number of reasons for this. Firstly, an attack directed against any Australian interests would be in line with the long-declared aims of the terrorist groups in the area. Al Qaeda, JI and the ASG have not only declared their aims to be to target Westerners and Western interests but have in the past carried out attacks against these targets. An attack against an Australian port or ship would therefore fulfil the terrorists' aims.

Secondly, Al Qaeda, JI, ASG, GAM and the MILF have shown their interest in targeting maritime infrastructure and shipping, as they have either attacked such targets before or intelligence sources have revealed their plans to do so.

Thirdly, most of the terrorist groups in the area certainly have the capability to carry out an attack against an Australian port or vessel. It is possible to draw this conclusion because the terrorist groups in question have either carried out an attack before, or would be able to easily obtain the equipment and materials necessary to conduct an attack. If the tactics of the LTTE are anything to go by, all that is needed is an explosive laden speedboat.

Fourthly, Australian maritime commercial shipping and ports are not only attractive targets because they are Western but also because an attack against the maritime industry has the potential to do immense damage in a number of different ways. It has the potential to fulfil a terrorists' most basic aim — to create terror. Not only that, the targets — commercial ports and vessels — are relatively unprotected.

If terrorists gained entry to a container on board a vessel, which due to the seals used would be relatively easy, they could either hide on board ready to execute an attack against the vessel or smuggle dangerous substances or explosives into Australia. As was noted earlier, Al Qaeda has attempted to hide one of its members on board a container ship in the past. Although that time Al Qaeda was unsuccessful, it is quite possible that the group has smuggled its members overseas in that way before. Also, due to the lack of security checks at boarding stations of cruise ships and ferries, terrorists could easily board the vessel carrying explosives. In fact, in 1999, a US Customs inspector "during routine questioning of a passenger travelling on a vehicle ferry from Victoria, B.C., to Port Angeles, Washington, discovered an Algerian named Ahmend Ressam with a mini-bomb factory stuffed into the trunk of his rented Chrysler".[76]

In another worrying case last year, in what has been called a "telling... 'experiment' that exposed the gaping holes in America's port security",[77] ABC News borrowed 15 pounds of depleted uranium from an environmental group, packed it in a container with wooden horse carts and terra cotta vases and successfully shipped it from Turkey to New York. Despite the fact that the container of depleted uranium was clearly marked, it made its journey undetected.[78] If it can be done by ABC News, surely there is a possibility that it could be done by a terrorist group.

Shipping containers have even been likened to "modern-day Trojan (sea)horses ... Slow-moving cruise missiles which load up at the port of origin, meander their way through the littorals and propel across the pelagic commons towards their target destination at some distant port, often changing platforms at transhipment hubs on route".[79]

The vulnerability of an Australian ship in transit through the narrow waterways of the Malacca Straits has already been discussed. If we combine this information with the high rates of success seen by pirates in their attempts to illegally board ships, it seems likely that a group of terrorists could take over an Australian merchant vessel. Just recently pirates boarded a chemical tanker in the Strait of Malacca, captured the crew and began navigating the vessel.[80] If the pirates had in fact been terrorists the results could have been devastating.

Freighters carrying large cargos of chemicals or petroleum would be particularly attractive to maritime terrorists. According the Director of Terrorism Studies at the Australian National University's Strategic and Defence Studies Centre, Clive Williams: "Terrorists could feasibly take over a cargo ship and use it as a weapon against military vessels or civilian infrastructure such as bridges ... A seized ship could be used to cause large scale pollution".[81]

There is also the possibility of terrorists boarding Australian commercial vessels while appearing to be legitimate crewmembers. This seems highly probable given how many maritime certificate fraud cases take place in the Philippines and Indonesia, where the terrorist groups are known to have bases.

Another reason why maritime terrorism is a real possibility is the attraction of the cargo on the freighters in Southeast Asia. For example, the fertiliser ammonium nitrate which is transported in bulk overseas and can be used as a powerful explosive. However, a more attractive target might be vessels carrying nuclear waste. One of the most important routes for the carriage of nuclear materials at sea is to and from Europe and Japan. The ships have on occasions passed close to Australia. The devastation that would be caused if terrorists hijacked one of these vessels and released the radioactive waste into Australian waters would be massive.

In conclusion, although the unpredictability of terrorism makes it hard to carry out accurate risk assessments, from the evidence presented above, the threat from maritime terrorism must be taken seriously. Australian commercial ports and shipping are at risk from maritime terrorism.

On the other hand, perhaps the threat is not as great as the information above would suggest. The fact that maritime terrorist attacks only make up 2 percent of all terrorist attacks worldwide should be considered. Also, Australian commercial shipping and ports have not yet been a target of a maritime terrorist attack and law enforcement officials continue to be successful in foiling planned maritime attacks in Southeast Asia. For example, early in 2002 Singapore intelligence disrupted an Al Qaeda plot to attack a US ship in the region.

However, if any lesson should be learnt from the attacks of 11 September 2001, it should be that just because it has not been done before, does not mean it is not possible. As D.J. Shackleton of the Royal Australian Navy Sea Power Centre correctly remarks: "One could suggest many scenarios, equally alarming and equally credible — or incredible. But, however far-fetched, we need to consider them".[82]

In order to make a proper estimation of the extent to which maritime terrorism poses a threat to Australian commercial shipping and ports, it is necessary to consider a number of events and developments which have taken place recently which appear to have increased the threat from maritime terrorism. The most significant of these is the 9/11 attacks. This catastrophic event not only set new precedents for terrorism in general but also led to a number of developments that have increased the threat of maritime terrorism.

The mass casualties that were the result of the 9/11 attacks show that terrorists today are willing to carry out strikes against targets that will result in a large number of civilian deaths. It has often been argued in studies of terrorist groups and their tactics that they wish to gain the maximum media coverage with the minimum of deaths. The main reason for this was thought to be that terrorists did not want to alienate themselves from the masses, which they felt they represented. Post-9/11 this theory has lost its credibility. If terrorists are now more than ever willing to carry out mass casualty attacks, then ports, which are often located near highly populated areas and have cruise ships carrying hundreds of people aboard docked at their piers, are now more at risk. One example is Sydney Port, which is located very near the Sydney Opera House and Harbour Bridge; famous Australian tourist destinations.

The 9/11 attacks showed the world that the technical sophistication, the amount of planning and the dedication that the Al Qaeda network is capable of is far greater than previous estimates. According to David Claridge of Janusian Securities Ltd: "Al Qaeda has shown themselves to be able to learn from previous attacks".[83] Also, Al Qaeda is believed to be investing in improving its maritime attack capabilities. If it shares its expertise with the other terrorist groups in the area, the situation could be even more worrying. It now seems even more within the capabilities of Al Qaeda and its associate groups in Southeast Asia to carry out a maritime terrorist attack.

Following 9/11, governments around the world, including Australia, tightened aviation security considerably. They also tightened security around their embassies abroad. This improved security around the more traditional *hard* targets will, according to security experts, lead to terrorist groups "aiming at *soft* targets, which have an impact on tourism, trade and commerce".[84] Thus, maritime targets are under an increased threat.

An increase in attacks on so-called *soft* targets is already starting to be seen. The Bali nightclub bombing, the attack on the French super-tanker, the *Limburg*, and the Marriott Hotel bombing are all examples of this. Al Qaeda has specifically expressed a wish to target "economic lifelines"[85]; therefore, the Australian maritime industry — one of Australia's "economic lifelines" — is under more threat from maritime terrorism than ever before.

Another reason why Australia is potentially under more threat from maritime terrorism now than it was in the past is that Al Qaeda's base of operations has shifted to Southeast Asia following the destruction of its network in Afghanistan. Although Al Qaeda and the other terrorist groups examined in this study have been operating in the region for some time, the bombing of the Bali nightclub emphasised their increased presence in the region and their willingness to carry out attacks against Western *soft* targets on Australia's doorstep.

Australia's commercial shipping and ports are particularly at risk from a maritime terrorist attack because of Australia's early involvement in the war on terrorism. Australia's close alliance with the United States, now more than ever, puts it in the firing line of terrorism. Also, Australia's increasing use of flags of convenience vessels leaves it more than ever before open to a terrorist attack. Flags of convenience vessels have been caught in the past ferrying terrorists, weapons and explosives for Al Qaeda. Thus, Australia's ports are potentially more vulnerable than they have ever been.

It has also been argued by terrorism experts that the success of the attack on the *USS Cole* and the intense media coverage it generated set a precedent for maritime terrorism, increasing the likelihood that more maritime terrorist attacks will be carried out in the future. According to intelligence sources "the success of the *Cole* attack ... prompted more terrorist groups to express an interest — and a few to invest — in maritime attack capabilities".[86]

The new trend of suicide bombing, which was first seen in the 9/11 attacks and subsequently in the Bali nightclub bombing, has considerably enlarged the potential scenarios that a terrorist attack can take. The terrorists' capabilities are no longer limited by having to have an escape route; therefore, the potential targets of terrorists are now more vulnerable. It would also appear that most security currently in place around possible targets is rendered largely useless against an attack by a suicide bomber(s).

Finally, it could be argued that in an era of reduced state sponsorship of terrorist groups, terrorists may turn increasingly to maritime attacks in order to generate funds for their activities. The success of the pirates in Southeast Asia may also influence this trend.

Not only will maritime terrorist attacks be more likely to be attempted, but the probability of the attack being successful is also likely to increase. This is due to two factors. Firstly, according to the IMB, there has been "a marked increase in successful boarding by pirates combined with a drop in the number of attempted attacks suggest[ing] that many ships were complacent about the need for additional precautionary measures".[87] If the terrorists tapped the pirates' expertise, which many terrorist experts have argued is very possible, the consequences would be an "increase the probability of success for a terror attack on a targeted ship".[88]

Secondly, improvements in marine technology are taking place all the time and the most up-to-date equipment is well within the purchasing power of Al Qaeda. According to Vijay Sakhuja, a maritime security analyst:

> Dual use technologies such as the Global Positioning System (GPS), satellite communications systems, seaport scooters, scuba diving equipment and mini-submarines are either being added to the inventory list of maritime terrorists or will be done so in the near future ... Already, terrorists are going beyond the crude employment of an explosive laden speedboat to the use of long-range rocket launchers and armour piercing weapons.[89]

The use of increasingly sophisticated equipment by the Southeast Asian terrorists and in particular those within the Al Qaeda network will further weaken any present security in the maritime industry and will result in a higher rate of success for their maritime terrorist attacks.

The full extent of the threat from maritime terrorism against Australian commercial shipping and ports will never truly be known until such an attack is carried out, as was the case with the 9/11 attacks. However, the evidence presented above should not be ignored. It shows that the threat from maritime terrorism, and the likelihood that an attack will be successfully carried out against the Australian maritime industry, has increased substantially in recent years.

Potential Consequences for Australia of a Maritime Terrorist Attack

Terrorist attacks are by definition very difficult to predict and the scale of any such attack will vary considerably from case to case. Thus, the consequences of a terrorist attack will also vary considerably, making them difficult to estimate. Therefore, "attempts to quantify the ... impact of a theoretical attack are bound to be vague and deal *in orders of magnitude* rather than in precise sums".[90] However, the consequences of a maritime terrorist attack can be roughly divided into three categories: human casualties, economic and environmental.

The human costs of a maritime terrorist attack are likely to be low if the target is a single commercial freighter, but potentially much higher if an attack is carried out against a cruise ship docked at a major commercial port such as Sydney or Melbourne. If this was the case, death tolls in the thousands could be expected.

The economic consequences of a maritime terrorist attack are very hard to calculate. The reason being that "like most economic activity, trade is much more susceptible to unquantifiable psychological factors than we often like to think. Above all though, it cannot flourish where there is no confidence in the security environment within which commerce must operate".[91] A good example of this is the attack on the *Limburg*, which although it was only an attack on a single vessel, had a profound economic impact on the Yemeni maritime industry:

> Immediately following the attack, underwriters tripled insurance premiums for vessels calling on Yemeni ports. These premiums ... led some lines to cut Yemen from their schedules and/or switch to ports in neighbouring counties ... Yemeni terminals had seen throughput plummet ... and had to lay off workers. Local sources claim as many as 3000 people have lost their employment and government estimated losses stemming from the attack are USD 15 million per month. Assuming that these losses are sustained over a 6-month period, they would account for nearly 1% of Yemen's 2001 GDP.[92]

The Southeast Asian shipping industries are already suffering from the sharp rise in piracy in the late 1990s. Thus, a terrorist attack in the Strait of Malacca would considerably add to the already existing perception that the region is insecure. If a maritime terrorist attack caused the closure of the Sunda and Lombok Straits, Australian ships would be forced to reroute around the Indonesian archipelago. This would raise freight rates, putting severe pressure on the Australian economy. So too would the closure of one of Australia's major ports following a terrorist attack. One consequence would be that manufacturers would face increased warehousing costs due to the backlog of exports that would be created if a port was closed for several days.

The possible environmental consequences of a maritime terrorist attack could also be very severe. If terrorists hijacked an oil tanker or a freighter carrying toxic chemicals and released its cargo off the coast of Australia it would devastate the marine environment and could cause the contamination of Australia's waterways. Australia's tourist industry, which is largely based around coastal resorts, would also suffer.

Counter-Measures and Risk Treatment Options

It is beyond the scope of this chapter to provide a full discussion of the counter-measures and risk treatment options that would decrease the threat from maritime terrorism. However, a few preliminary suggestions will be made.

The problem with increasing the security of the maritime transport industry is that the smooth and efficient flow of trade and cargo may well be disrupted. A cost–benefit exercise would help policy-makers to impose the correct levels of security. However, "the threat of terrorism ... comprises so many unknown variables that traditional benefit–cost analysis is rendered nearly impossible".[93]

Rather than increasing the security wall around the maritime transport industry, risk treatment options should be directed against the threat itself. In other words, the terrorist groups and their networks in Southeast Asia need to be neutralised before they even have a chance to plan a maritime terrorist attack. To do this the countries of Southeast Asia must invest much more in "high-grade counter-terrorist intelligence".[94]

More importantly, the states of Southeast Asia must cooperate in their fight against terrorism. Maritime terrorism is a global phenomenon; therefore, the only way it will be combated is through increased multilateral cooperation. To combat maritime terrorism, all the Southeast Asian states should sign the IMO's 1988 Convention on the Suppression of Unlawful Acts against the Safety of Maritime Navigation: "Ratification of the convention gives signatory governments the power to prosecute people caught in their own territorial waters for acts of piracy committed under another countries jurisdiction".[95] In Asia, only Japan, Singapore and China are signatories to this convention.

Finally, the long-term response should address the social environment that provides the support base and source of recruitment for the terrorist groups in the area. This can only be done through improvements in education and the standard of living in Southeast Asia.

Conclusions

The devastating attack in the United States on 11 September 2001 clearly demonstrated two things. Firstly, a terrorist's next move is very hard to predict. Secondly, terrorists should never be underestimated. However fantastical some of the possible scenarios of a terrorist attack may be, they must be treated as though they may one day become a reality. Most importantly, we cannot afford to wait for the terrorist attack to become a reality before we become aware of the weaknesses in our defence. The events of 9/11 made this only too clear. We must respond quickly to new developments and trends. The fact that the UK government is only now doing drills for an attack on the underground is indicative of this failure. Ten years have passed since an incident of this kind took place in Tokyo.

Terrorists have moved on. They are looking for new targets, and maritime transport could be part of their new agenda. The risks need to be assessed.

Australian commercial ports and shipping are suffering from weaknesses inherent in the international maritime transport industry's infrastructure. Its preoccupation with the principle of "*just enough — just in time*" and a free-flowing system, has left it vulnerable to breaches in its security. This chapter also finds that within easy striking distance of Australia are a number of groups that have the declared aim of targeting Western economic interests, and have demonstrated their capability to carry out such attacks.

The threat of maritime terrorism has existed for a number of years. However, recently there have been a number of events and developments, that when examined, point to the fact that the threat from maritime terrorism against Australian commercial ports and shipping has increased. The most significant event was the 9/11 attack and the precedent it set for a new scale of terrorist offensive. This, in addition to the Bali nightclub bombing, confirmed that a new brand of global terror had arrived in Southeast Asia. The most significant development seen in recent years that has affected the extent to which maritime terrorism poses a threat to Australia is the *hardening* of land targets following 9/11. The "soft underbelly" of the maritime industry is now, by default, one of the new targets of this global terror.

Notes

1. S. Quentin, "Shipping Activities: Targets of Maritime Terrorism", *MIRMAL* 2, 2003, p. 1.
2. "Co-operation for Law & Order At Sea", *CSCAP Memorandum* 5, 2001, p. 24.
3. A. Young and M. J. Valencia, "Piracy, Terrorism Threats Overlap", *Washington Times*, 12 March 2003, p. 3.
4. "Art. 101, United Nations Convention on the Law of the Sea", available online at http://www.un.org/Depts/los/convention_agreements/convention_overview_convention.htm.
5. "Co-operation for Law & Order At Sea", p. 14.
6. Ibid.
7. C.C. Salinas, "Improving Maritime Security in the APEC Region", *FASA*, 2002, p. 5.

8. P. Chalk, "Threats to the Maritime Environments: Piracy and Terrorism", *RAND*, 28 October 2002, p. 9.

9. R. Gunaratna, "The Asymmetric Threat from Maritime Terrorism", *Jane's Intelligence Review*, available online at http://www.jfs.janes.com/public/jfs/additional_info.shtml.

10. Ibid.

11. Maritime Transport Committee, "Security in Maritime Transport: Risk Factors and Economic Impact", *OECD/OCDE*, 2003, p. 14.

12. Gunaratna, "The Asymmetric Threat from Maritime Terrorism".

13. R. Gunaratna, "Trends in Maritime Terrorism — The Sri Lankan Case", *Lanka Outlook*, 1998, p. 4.

14. Hoffman, "Rethinking Terrorism & Counterterrorism Since 9/11", p. 303.

15. M. Ressa, "Terrorism's New Frontline", *CNN.com*, 7 November 2002. Also available online at http://edition.cnn.com/2002/WORLD/asiapcf/southeast/10/29/asia.html.

16. I. Lim, "Not Yet All Aboard... But Already All At Sea Over Container Security Initiative", *Institute of Defence and Strategic Studies*, 2002, p. 2.

17. T.T. Guingoa, "Opening Remarks", *ASEAN-EU Experts' Group Meeting on Maritime Security*, Manila, 2002, p. 1.

18. R. Holleran, "What if Asia's Terrorists Join Hands?" *South China Morning Post*, 17 May 2003, p. 1.

19. L.S. Kong, "Opening Address", *Maritime Security Seminar*, 5 May 2003. Available online at http://216.239.37.104/search?q=cache:KTek_yDtwuIJ:www.mpa.gov.sg/homepage/pressreleases/030505b.pdf++2003+International+maritime+and+port+security+conference&hl=en&ie=UTF-8.

20. K. Akimoto, "Re-routing Options and Consequences", *Australian Maritime Affairs*, 10, 2003, pp. 113–128.

21. "Treasures within the South China Sea", *German Industry & Commerce*, 3/02, p. 4.

22. N. Brew, "Ripples from 9/11: the US Container Security Initiative and its Implications for Australia", *Current Issues Brief*, 28, 2003, p. 3.

23. M. Richardson, "Australia Takes Steps to Halt Illegal Immigrants", *Herald Tribune*. Available online at http://www.iht.com/IHT/MR/99/mro51899.html.

24. Fred Brenchley, "Troubled Waters", *The Bulletin*, 23 April 2003. Available online at http://bulletin.ninemsn.com.au/bulletin/eddesk.nsf/All/C552A0F1A789676ECA256D0E0079BED5.

25. Brew, "Ripples from 9/11: the US Container Security Initiative and its Implications for Australia", p. 3.

26. "Australian Sea Freight 2000–01", *Information Paper 48*, Bureau of Transport & Regional Economics. Available online at http://www.btre.gov.au/docs/ip48/index.html.

27. Sydney Ports. Available online at http://www.Sydneyports.com/au/port-factilities/main.asp?pageid=156.

28. Maritime Transport Committee, "Security in Maritime Transport: Risk Factors and Economic Impact", p. 4.
29. J.Z. Hecker, "Port Security", *United States General Accounting Office*, 2002, p. 6.
30. Brew, "Ripples from 9/11: the US Container Security Initiative and its Implications for Australia", p. 5.
31. "Shipper Nation", *The Baltic Asia-Pacific Shipping 2003*. Available online at http://www.stroudgate.net/aps/articles/027.html.
32. J. Saunders, "Marine Vulnerability and the Terrorist Threat", *International Maritime Bureau*, 2003, p. 4.
33. Maritime Transport Committee, "Security in Maritime Transport: Risk Factors and Economic Impact", p. 23.
34. "IMB calls for clamp-down on fake documents", Available online at http://www.iccwbo.org.
35. Maritime Transport Committee, "Security in Maritime Transport: Risk Factors and Economic Impact", p. 10.
36. "The Ships that Died of Shame", 14 January 2003. Available online at http://www.smh.com.au/articles/2003/01/13/1041990234408.htm.
37. "Shipper Nation".
38. R. Gunaratna, *Inside Al Qaeda* (London: Hurst & Company, 2002), p. 1.
39. K. Bradsher, "Warnings From Al Qaeda Stir Fear That Terrorists May Attack Oil Tankers", *South East Asia Security*, 12 December 2002, p. 1.
40. "Al Qaeda", *National Security Australia*. Available online at http://www.nationalsecurity.gov.au/www/nationalsecurityhome.nsf/Web+Pages/A58E9224C81B4A44CA256D35000C9BC2?OpenDocument.
41. Gunaratna, *Inside Al Qaeda*, p. 10.
42. "Al Qaeda", *National Security Australia*.
43. Gunaratna, *Inside Al Qaeda*, p. 11.
44. Ibid., p. 12.
45. G. Holloway, "Spy Boss Warns of Terror Strike", *CNN.com*, 13 August 2003. Available online at http://edition.cnn.com/2003/WORLD/asiapcf/auspac/08/12/australia.terrorism/.
46. Gunaratna, *Inside Al Qaeda*, p. 174.
47. L.K. Siang, "Al Qaeda Threat in Malaysia — Time for Truth and Frankness", *DAP Malaysia Article*, 31 October 2002. Available online at http://www.malaysia.net/dap/lks1910.htm.
48. J. Mintz, "15 Freighters Believed to Be Linked To Al Qaeda", *Washington Post*, 31 December 2002, p. 1.
49. J. Saunders, "Marine Vulnerability and the Terrorist Threat", p. 4.
50. F.A. Rahim, "Terrorism Experts Warn Al Qaeda May Target Cruise Liners", *Channe lNews Asia*, 18 October 2002. Available online at http://www.channelnewsasia.com/stories/singaporelocalnews/view.htm.

51. Gunaratna, *Inside Al Qaeda*, p. 200.
52. "Terror Alert For Ships", *CBS News*, 22 November 2002. Available online at http://www.cbsnews.com/stories/2002/11/13/attack/main529166.htm.
53. "Investigators leave Indonesia to Question Suspected JI Chief", *ABC Radio Australia News*, 20 August 2003. Available online at http://www.abc.net.au/ra/newstories/RANewsStories_928692.htm.
54. "Massive Blast at Jakarta Embassy", *BBC News*, World Edition. Available online at http://news.bbc.co.uk.
55. "Moro Islamic Liberation Front", *International Policy Institute for Counter-terrorism*. Available online at http://www.ict.org.il/inter_ter/orgdet. cfm?orgid=92.
56. "Police Link MILF Bomb Suspect to Al Qaeda", *The Nation Newspaper*, 27 May 2003. Available online at http://www.inq7.net/nat/2003/may/27/nat_5-1.htm.
57. Ibid.
58. "Abu Sayyaf Group", *National Security Australia*. Available online at http://www.nationalsecurity.gov.au/www/nationalsecurityhome.nsf/Web+Pages/EE03462FCADDEAC8CA256D35000D8BF1?OpenDocument.
59. Ibid.
60. M. Baker, "Manila told to step up war on terror", *The Age*, 12 April 2004. Available online at http://www.theage.com.au/articles/2004/04/12/1081621892235.html?from=storyrhs&oneclick=true.
61. Rupert Herbert-Burns and L. Zucker, "Drawing the Line between Piracy and Maritime Terrorism", *Janes Intelligence Review*, 1 September 2004, p. 4.
62. Ibid., p. 6.
63. Ibid., p. 3.
64. "Killings by Pirates on the Rise", *BBC News*, 26 July 2004. Available online at http://news.bbc.co.uk/2/hi/asia-pacific/3925277.stm.
65. "Threats to the Maritime Environments: Piracy and Terrorism", p. 4.
66. Ibid., p. 4.
67. Salinas, "Improving Maritime Security in the APEC Region", p. 5.
68. R. Holleran, "Sea Piracy Raises Watch for Terrorists Links", *The Japan Times*, 18 May 2003.
69. P. Westmore, "Defence: Navy League Endorses Coastwatch, Rejects Coast Guard", *News Weekly*, 17 November 2001. Available online at http://www.newsweekly.com.au/articles/2001/Nov17_coastwatch.html.
70. Ibid.
71. S. Chaffer, "Call for Coast Guard in Wake of Drug Haul", *Maritime Union of Australia News*, 22 April 2003. Available online at http://www.mua.org.au/news/general/drughaul.html.
72. "Safeguarding Australia", *AAPMA News,*12 August 2003. Available online at http://www.aapma.au/news/120803.php3.

73. "SOLAS: International Ship & Port Facility Security Code", p. 3.
74. Ibid.
75. "Safeguarding Australia".
76. B.N. Meeks, "FBI: Al Qaeda Interested in Ferries", *MSNBC News*, 31 July 2003. Available online at http://www.msnbc.com/news/946574.asp?0bl+-0&cpl=1.
77. Lim, "Not Yet All Aboard ... But Already All At Sea Over Container Security Initiative", p. 2.
78. Ibid., p. 2.
79. Ibid., p. 4.
80. J. Brandon, "Terrorism on the High Seas", *Herald Tribune*, 5 June 2003, p. 1.
81. Brew, "Ripples from 9/11: the US Container Security Initiative and its Implications for Australia", p. 3.
82. D. Shackleton, "Opening Address", *International SLOC Conference*, 2001, p. 3.
83. Ressa, "Terrorism's New Frontline".
84. Rahim, "Terrorism Experts Warn Al Qaeda May Target Cruise Liners", *Channel News Asia*. Available online at http://www.channelnewsasia.com/stories/singaporelocalnews/view.htm.
85. Bradsher, "Warnings From Al Qaeda Stir Fear That Terrorists May Attack Oil Tankers", p. 1.
86. Gunaratna, "The Asymmetric Threat from Maritime Terrorism".
87. "High Seas Terrorism Alert in Piracy Report", *The World Business Organisation*, 29 January 2003. Available online at http://www.iccwbo.org/home/news_archives/2003/stories/piracy%20_report_2002.asp.
88. Ong, "Pre-empting Maritime Terrorism in Southeast Asia", p. 2.
89. Ibid., p. 3.
90. Maritime Transport Committee, "Security in Maritime Transport: Risk Factors and Economic Impact", p. 22.
91. Shackleton, "Opening Address", p. 2.
92. Maritime Transport Committee, "Security in Maritime Transport: Risk Factors and Economic Impact", p. 17.
93. Ibid., p. 22.
94. R. Gunaratna, *Inside Al Qaeda*, p. 235.
95. N. Ronzitti, *Piracy and International Law* (London: Martinus Nijhoff publishers, 1990), p. 21.

III. *Prospects for Regional Cooperation*

Chapter 9

Legal Implications of the Proliferation Security Initiative

Robert Beckman

Introduction

The terrorist attacks in the United States on September 11, 2001, shocked not only the United States, but also the entire international community. Since the September 2001 incident the United States has led a two-pronged approach to obtain international cooperation to deal with the threat of maritime terrorism. First, it has worked patiently to encourage the relevant international organisations such as the UN Security Council and the International Maritime Organisation (IMO) to take action that requires member states to impose new measures to deal with the threat of maritime terrorism. Second, it has used its power and influence to get cooperation from other states through bilateral agreements and the establishment of "coalitions of the willing".

In this chapter, I will outline the actions and measures that have been initiated by the United States to deal with the transport of weapons of mass destruction (WMD) by sea. I will focus on the Proliferation Security Initiative, which is an effort by the United States to deal with the issue of the proliferation of WMD through the establishment of a coalition of willing partners, outside of the institutions and regimes. I will also discuss the efforts by the

United States to work with the UN Security Council and the IMO to change the legal regime governing the proliferation and transport of WMD. This analysis will include the proposed protocol to the 1988 Convention for the Suppression of Unlawful Acts Against the Safety of Maritime Navigation.[1]

US Proliferation Security Initiative

The Proliferation Security Initiative (PSI) is an initiative of the United States to establish a coalition of willing partners to respond to the growing challenge posed by the proliferation of WMD. Like the Container Security Initiative (CSI), it is an attempt by the United States to create a framework for international cooperation to deal with the threat posed by WMD outside the international organisations and international treaties that regulate the proliferation of WMD.

The PSI was announced by US President George Bush in Poland on 31 May 2003, just prior to the G8 Summit. President Bush stated:

> When weapons of mass destruction or their components are in transit, we must have the means and authority to seize them. So today I announce a new effort to fight proliferation called the Proliferation Security Initiative. The United States and a number of our close allies, including Poland, have begun working on new agreements to search planes and ships carrying suspect cargo and to seize illegal weapons or missile technologies. Over time, we will extend this partnership as broadly as possible to keep the world's most destructive weapons away from our shores and out of the hands of our common enemies.[2]

The statement by President Bush suggests that new international agreements would be created that would allow the United States and its allies to search planes and ships carrying suspect cargo and seize illegal weapons or missile technologies. However, as the PSI has developed, it has not been based upon the development of new international agreements, but on the development of cooperative arrangements among participating states regarding the interdiction of ships suspected of carrying WMD.

The United States began working with ten other countries in 2003 to develop a set of principles that would identify practical steps to interdict shipments of WMD flowing to or from "state or non-state actors of proliferation concern". The ten countries were Australia, France, Germany, Italy, Japan, the Netherlands, Poland, Portugal, Spain and the United Kingdom.[3] At a meeting in Brisbane in September, 2003, the ten original participating countries agreed that North Korea and Iran were of particular proliferation concern.

At the meeting in September, 2003, the participating states also agreed to a "Statement of Interdiction Principles".[4] The ten original participating countries were later joined by five new participating countries — Canada, Denmark, Norway, Singapore and Turkey.

Interdiction Principles and the Law of the Sea

Questions have been raised as to whether some of the actions called for in the Statement of Interdiction Principles are consistent with existing rules of international law. Of particular concern was whether the principles with respect to interdiction at sea are consistent with the provisions of 1982 UNCLOS.

In the Statement of Interdiction Principles, participating states agreed to take certain specific actions in support of interdiction efforts regarding cargoes of WMD, to the extent their national legal authorities permit and *consistent with their obligations under international law and frameworks*. Some of the specific actions set out in the principles are consistent with international law as set out in 1982 UNCLOS. However, others actions set out in the principles must be qualified or interpreted in a manner that is consistent with the provisions in 1982 UNCLOS.

The actions set out in the interdiction principles with respect to vessels flying the flag of participating states are entirely consistent with the provisions in 1982 UNCLOS. In the Interdiction Principles, states agree, on their own initiative, to board and search any suspect vessels flying their flag in their internal waters or territorial seas or in areas beyond the territorial seas of any state. This is consistent with the principles governing the law of the sea. States have a right to board and search vessels in their internal waters and territorial sea which are flying their flag because the sovereignty of a state extends to its internal waters and to its territorial sea and a state's laws apply on ships flying their flag. In addition, states have a right to board and search vessels flying their flag beyond the territorial seas of any state because flag states have exclusive jurisdiction over acts aboard ships in such areas.[5]

The interdiction principles also provide that a participating state should seriously consider giving other states consent to board and search vessels flying its flag under appropriate circumstances. Given that the flag state has exclusive jurisdiction over vessels flying its flag outside the territorial sea of any state, it is consistent with 1982 UNCLOS for flag states to give such consent.

One of the goals of the United States under the PSI seems to be to enter into bilateral agreements with major flag states that give the United States permission to board and search vessels flying their flag when such vessels are suspected of carrying WMD. The first such boarding agreement was signed by the United States and Liberia on 11 February 2004.[6] The boarding agreement provides the United States authority to board vessels flying the flag of Liberia if they are suspected of carrying illicit shipments of WMD. Liberia has the world's second largest ship registry. According to the United States, this boarding agreement is an important step in further operationalising the PSI and strengthening the mechanisms that the United States has at its disposal to interdict suspect WMD-related cargoes. On 12 May 2004, the United States and Panama signed the bilateral Panama–United States PSI Ship-Boarding Agreement. Panama is the world's largest ship registry. Now that the United States has bilateral ship-boarding agreements with the world's two largest ship registries, almost 50 percent of the total commercial ships in dead weight tonnage are subject to the rapid consent procedures for boarding, search and seizure by United States forces.[7]

The interdiction principles also provide that participating states should take action regarding vessels in their ports and internal waters as well as vessels entering or leaving their ports or internal waters. Participating states agree to stop and/or search vessels in their ports or internal waters when such vessels are reasonably suspected of carrying such cargoes to or from states or non-state actors of proliferation concern. Participating states also agree to enforce conditions on suspect vessels entering or leaving their ports and internal waters. Such conditions might include a requirement that such vessels be subject to boarding and search prior to entry. Although there is no provision in 1982 UNCLOS directly on this point, such actions would be consistent with principles of customary international law. Ports and internal waters are within the territorial sovereignty of a state, and states may impose conditions on vessels in its ports and internal waters and on vessels in its territorial sea that intend to enter its ports or internal waters.

The most controversial actions set out in the interdiction principles concern actions of coastal states with regard to vessels in their territorial sea or contiguous zone, and with regard to vessels entering or leaving its territorial sea. These are controversial because under 1982 UNCLOS the vessels of all states have a *right of innocent passage* through the territorial sea of all states.[8] Passage is innocent so long as it is not prejudicial to the peace, good order or security of the coastal state. It is difficult to argue that the mere passage of a vessel containing WMD through the territorial sea of a coastal state is prejudicial to its peace, good order or security, given the fact that military vessels carrying nuclear weapons have a right of innocent passage through the territorial sea of the coastal state.

Furthermore, special passage rules for the vessels of all states apply in straits used for international navigation that fall within the territorial sea of the littoral states. The vessels of all states have the right of transit passage through straits used for international navigation, and such right cannot be impeded or suspended by the littoral states.[9] The right of transit passage is an even broader right than the right of innocent passage.

Therefore, states that are party to the 1982 UNCLOS are not likely to interfere with the vessels exercising the right of transit passage through a strait used for international navigation or the right of innocent passage through the territorial sea. Instead, they are likely to take the position that any action taken with respect to such vessels must be *consistent with their obligations under international law* as set out in 1982 UNCLOS. However, it would be legal for the coastal state to board and search a suspect vessel passing through its territorial sea if the flag state of the suspect vessel expressly authorised or requested such action by the coastal state.

There is one other circumstance in which it may be legal for a coastal state to board and search a suspect vessel in its contiguous zone or territorial sea. If a suspect vessel was on a route that indicated that it was intending to bring WMD into the territory of the coastal state in violation of its customs laws and regulations, such vessel would not have a right of innocent passage. It could be boarded and searched by the authorities of the coastal state in its territorial sea. Similarly, it could be boarded and searched in the contiguous zone, which is a zone adjacent to the territorial sea in which the coastal state has special powers to enforce certain of its domestic laws, including its customs laws.[10]

The PSI and the International Legal System

The United States has argued that the PSI builds on efforts by the international community in existing treaties and regimes to prevent the proliferation of WMD. It has pointed out that the PSI is consistent with and a step which implements the Statement of the President of the UN Security Council in January 1992, when he stated that the proliferation of all WMD constitutes a threat to international peace and security. They also argue that the PSI is justified because of the threat and danger posed should WMD fall into the hands of rogue states or terrorist organisations.[11]

Critics of the United States can argue that the PSI is another example of the United States using its military power to establish an international framework for creating and enforcing norms outside the framework of existing international conventions and international institutions. They point out that the existing legal regimes governing nuclear non-proliferation do not contain any provisions authorising member states of the UN to enforce the principles of non-proliferation through the interdiction of vessels carrying WMD. They argue that this is not an example of multilateralism because multilaterism is action within the framework of the relevant international institutions to build upon and develop existing international legal regimes and conventions to meet new problems. By contrast, the PSI, like the US invasion of Iraq, is another example of the superpower using its influence to create a "coalition of the willing" to act outside of existing international legal regimes and conventions. This, they argue, is a threat to the existing international legal order.[12]

The Under-Secretary-General for Disarmament Affairs of the United Nations has characterised the present situation as a crisis of enforcement of international norms established by existing international institutions and regimes. He stated that unless this crisis is resolved, the global norms for non-proliferation will suffer, and the world will move ever closer to a security system based exclusively on considerations of self-help and military means.[13]

The problem faced by the United States is that the interdiction of a ship on the high seas that is suspected of carrying WMD in violation of non-proliferation principles would be a prima facie breach of international law. Article 92(2) of UNCLOS expressly provides that:

> Ships shall sail under the flag of one State only and, *save in exceptional cases provided for in international treaties or in this Convention*, shall be subject to its exclusive jurisdiction on the high seas.

The interdiction of a ship suspected of carrying WMD would be lawful if it is expressly provided for in an international treaty. It would also be lawful if the UN Security Council authorised the interdiction through the exercise of its enforcement powers under Chapter VII of the UN Charter. The former would be binding only on states that are parties to the international treaty. The latter would be binding on all members of the United Nations.[14]

UN Security Council Resolution 1540 of 28 April 2004

In September 2003, President Bush asked the United Nations Security Council to adopt a new anti-proliferation resolution that called upon all members of the UN to criminalise the proliferation of WMD, to enact strict controls consistent with international standards and to secure any and all such materials within their own borders.[15]

On 28 April 2004, the UN Security Council unanimously adopted Resolution 1540 on preventing proliferation of WMD. Invoking its enforcement powers under Chapter VII of the UN Charter, it affirmed that the proliferation of nuclear, chemical and biological weapons constitutes a threat to international peace and security. Under the resolution all members of the United Nations are legally bound to establish domestic controls including legislative measures to prevent the proliferation of WMD, in particular for terrorist purposes.[16]

The resolution calls upon all States, in accordance with their national legal authorities and legislation *and consistent with international law*, to take cooperative action to prevent illicit trafficking in WMD. It fills a gap in the international legal regime governing non-proliferation. Significantly, however, the resolution, at the request of the delegation from China, contains no reference to interdiction.[17] Furthermore, the statements from United Kingdom and Indian delegations made it clear that the resolution did not authorise use of force or enforcement action against any State or non-State actors in the territory of another country, and that any enforcement action would require a new decision of the Security Council.[18]

Given that the Security Council resolution does not authorise the interdiction of vessels on the high seas, this resolution does not seem to legitimise the boarding and search of suspect vessels by the United States and other states participating in the PSI.

Proposal for a New Protocol to the 1988 SUA Convention

In October 2001, one month after the September 11th incident, the Legal Committee of the IMO decided to review the 1988 Convention for the Suppression of Unlawful Acts Against the Safety of Maritime Navigation (SUA Convention) and its Protocol in the wake of the terrorist attack on the United States. The Legal Committee agreed to include the review of the SUA Convention as a priority item in its work programme.[19]

In April 2002, the Legal Committee agreed to establish a Correspondence Group led by the United States with the short-term aim of developing a working paper on the scope of possible amendments for consideration at the 85th session of the Committee. The longer aim was to draft a new protocol to the SUA Convention.[20]

On 17 August 2002, the delegation of the United States, as lead country for the intersessional Correspondence Group, introduced document LEG 85/4 containing draft amendments to the SUA Convention and Protocol, together with related documents.[21] Among the most important amendments proposed by the United States are the following: (1) the addition of seven new offences into article 3 of the SUA convention, four of which are concerned with activities taking place on the ship or directed towards the ship that involve a terrorist purpose; (2) new provisions permitting the boarding and search of a suspect ship by law enforcement officials of another state when such ship is in international waters (located seaward of any State's territorial sea) and is reasonably suspected of being involved in, or reasonably believed to be the target of, acts prohibited in article 3 of the SUA Convention.

The Legal Committee had a preliminary discussion of the proposed amendments at its 85th session from 21 to 25 October 2002. Concern was expressed by some delegations to some of the US proposals, especially the new provisions on the boarding and search of a suspected ship. The US draft was described as a "work in progress" and the discussion was described as a preliminary exchange of views. It was decided that it was premature to establish an intersessional working group, but it was decided to continue the work of the correspondence group. It was emphasised that the objective must be to develop a draft instrument that would attract wide ratification.[22]

The intersessional working group has continued to work on a revised draft protocol over the past 2 years. It has received comments and suggestions from 64 states and eight organisations. The two articles that have been the subject of major debate and disagreement are article 3 bis, which sets out new offences to be added to the Convention, and article 8 bis on boarding provisions.

Article 3 bis on new offences has been through numerous drafts. Article 3 bis is intended to add new offences that bring the Convention up to date to deal with maritime terrorism in light of the September 11 incident. The current draft provides that there is an offence if a person unlawfully and intentionally:

> (a) when the purpose of the act, by its nature or context, is to intimidate a population, or to compel a Government or an international organisation to do or to abstain from doing any act:
>
> > (i) uses against or on a ship or discharges from a ship any explosive, radiological material or prohibited weapon in a manner that causes or is likely to cause, on or off the ship, serious injury or damage, or

(ii) discharges, from a ship, oil, liquefied natural gas, or other like substance in such quantity or concentration, that causes or is likely to cause serious injury or damage, or

(iii) uses a ship in a manner that causes or is likely to cause serious injury or damage.[23]

The most controversial of the new offences in Article 3 bis relate to the issue of whether the SUA Protocol should make it an offence to transport on board a ship any WMD. It appears that the United States recommended the inclusion of this provision because of its concern for the proliferation of WMD. However, some states have objected to the inclusion of this paragraph because it created offences relating to the non-proliferation of WMD that were not directly linked to terrorism. Some states have stated that they do not consider the IMO to be the competent forum for dealing with non-proliferation issues and they do not consider the SUA Convention to be the proper instrument to deal with non-proliferation issues.[24]

Art 8 bis on boarding has also been very controversial because it permits the boarding and search of vessels in international waters (beyond the limits of the territorial sea) if such vessels are reasonably suspected to be involved in offences under the SUA Convention. This enforcement measure is new, as the SUA Convention contains no provisions allowing the boarding and search of vessels. The new boarding provision would create an express exception to the general principle of the law of the sea that ships on the high seas are subject to the exclusive jurisdiction of the flag state. Concerns have been expressed that such a provision would take the SUA Convention to a new level. Fears have also been expressed that the boarding and search provisions might be subject to abuse.[25]

Many states have accepted the need for such a provision, but they have insisted that it be narrowly drafted, and contain detailed safeguards to prevent abuse. As a result, article 8 bis has been through numerous drafts and substantial revisions, as the United States as the head of the intersessional correspondence group has attempted to meet the concerns expressed by states. Article 8 bis is an attempt to balance the interests of the flag state in controlling its vessel and the interests of the boarding state in investigating acts of maritime terrorism.

The current draft provides that if law enforcement officers of a state party encounter a ship in international waters which they believe has been or is about to be involved in the commission of an offence under the Convention, they may request the flag state to authorise them to take appropriate measures, including boarding and search. The major difficulty is caused by problem of the so-called "flags of convenience", that is, states that register ships but do not carry out their obligations or responsibilities seriously, as it may not be possible to contact the appropriate authorities in such states within a reasonable amount of time. To deal with this problem, the draft provision provides that if the authorities in the flag state do not respond within 4 hours to a request from law enforcement officers to take appropriate measures, the law enforcement officers may proceed to board and search the suspect ship. This provision providing for "tacit authorization" to board and search if there is no objection within 4 hours has generated much discussion and debate.[26]

Article 8 bis has also generated much discussion on whether the current draft contains sufficient safeguards to prevent abuse, to limit the possible use of force, to provide for the safety and human rights of the passengers and crew, etc.[27]

Draft SUA Protocol and the International Legal System

The United States believes that the threat of maritime terrorism after the September 11 incident presents new dangers that demand new solutions and further development of the rules of international law. It has taken the position that its objectives can be realised through a new protocol to the SUA Convention if new offences are created and new enforcement powers are legitimised. The United States believes it is essential that its law enforcement officers have the power of interdiction to board and search vessels in international waters if persons on such vessels have been or will be involved in offences under the SUA Convention. It is trying its best to convince the international community to create new exceptions to the existing rules governing the law of the sea as set out in 1982 UNCLOS. This is an example of the superpower taking a multilateral approach, to work with existing international institutions to adapt and change the rules of international law to meet the threat of maritime terrorism.

Where the United States seems to be running into the most difficulty in the negotiations on the proposed new protocol to the SUA Convention is with its proposal to make the transport of WMD an offence. This is because many states believe that the IMO is not the appropriate institution to deal with the enforcement of non-proliferation treaties. Given this development, it is understandable that the United States is also pursuing other approaches to dealing with the problem through the PSI and through the UN Security Council.

If the SUA Convention were amended to provide for the boarding and search of vessels that are transporting WMD on the high seas, it would be an express exception to the principle of exclusive jurisdiction of the flag state on the high seas. However, since treaties are binding only on states that have become parties to them, the United States and participating states would only be able to search vessels suspected of transporting WMD if both the boarding state and the flag state were parties to the SUA Protocol.

In summary, in the absence of a binding Security Council resolution authorising the interdiction of vessels suspected of transporting WMD, the interdiction of such vessels on the high seas without the consent of the flag state would be a prima facie breach of international law.

Conclusion

The PSI is an example of an initiative taken by the United States to enhance international cooperation to strengthen maritime security by establishing a "coalition of the willing" to take measures outside of the international institutions and regimes to deal with the issue of proliferation of WMD by countries of concern. In its implementation the PSI will arguably be limited by the rules of international law, including the UN Charter and 1982 UNCLOS.

The United States has worked with the UN Security Council to create a new international norm declaring that the proliferation of WMD is a threat to international peace and security. It is also working with the IMO to adopt a new protocol to the 1988 SUA Convention, which would make it a criminal offence to transport WMD by sea. However, the United States has not been successful in creating a new rule that would permit the interdiction of vessels on the high seas if such vessels are suspected of carrying WMD in contravention of the international conventions on non-proliferation.

The United States has worked within the rules set out in 1982 UNCLOS to make it easier to board and search vessels suspected of carrying WMD. First, it has entered into bilateral agreements with major flag states to obtain authorisation in advance to board and search vessels flying their flag on the high seas if such vessels are suspected of transporting WMD. Second, it has been working with its partners in the PSI to obtain their cooperation in boarding and searching vessels suspected of carrying WMD. So long as these cooperative efforts are consistent with the rules set out in 1982 UNCLOS, they do not represent a threat to the existing international legal order.

Notes

1. The SUA Convention entered into force on 1 March 1992. As of 31 April 2004, 104 states are parties.
2. Remarks by the President to the People of Poland, Wawel Royal Castle, Krakow, Poland. Available online at http://www.whitehouse.gov/news/releases/2003/05/20030531-3.html.
3. See US State Dept web page. http://www.state.gov/t/np/c10390.htm.
4. Ibid. Also available online at http://www.state.gov/t/np/c12207.htm.
5. United Nations Convention on the Law of the Sea, Articles 2, 92.
6. See http://www.state.gov/r/pa/prs/ps/2004/29338.htm.
7. US State Department, Daily Press Briefing, 12 May 2004. Available online at http://www.state.gov/r/pa/prs/dpb/2004/32428pf.htm.
8. UNCLOS, Art 19.
9. UNCLOS, Art 38.
10. UNCLOS, Art 33.
11. Baker Spring, "Harnessing the Power of Nations for Arms Control: The Proliferation Security Initiative and Coalitions of the Willing", *Backgrounder*, No. 1737, The Heritage Foundation, 18 March 2004.
12. Articles critical of the PSI include "The Proliferation Security Initiative: The Legal Challenge", *Bipartisan Security Group Policy Brief*, September 2003. Available online at http://www.gsinstitute.org/gsi/pubs/09_03_psi_brief.pdf.
13. Address by Nobuyasu Abe, "Non-Proliferation and the Challenge of Compliance", *Second Moscow International Non-Proliferation Conference*, 19 September 2003. Available online at http://www.un.org/Depts/dda/speech/12Jan2000.htm.
14. Under International Law treaties are binding only on parties. Under Article 25 of the UN Charter, decisions of the Security Council under Chapter VII are binding on all members of the United Nations.
15. Address to the UN General Assembly, 23 September 2003. Available online at http://www.whitehouse.gov/news/releases/2003/09/20030923-4.html.
16. UN Security Council Resolution 1540, 28 April 2004. Available online at http://www.state.gov/t/np/rls/other/31990.htm.
17. Statement of Chinese representative Wang Guangya, 22 April 2004. Reprinted in Wang Guangya, "Security Council Members Express 'Doubts' about UN Draft Resolution on Weapons of Mass Destruction", *Disarmament Documentation*, 22 April 2004. Available online at www.acronym.org.uk/docs/0404/doc03.htm.
18. Statements of Adam Thomson of the United Kingdom and Vijay K. Nambiar of India, Ibid.
19. IMO Legal Committee, 83rd Session, 8–12 October 2001. A summary of the work of the Legal Committee is available on the IMO Home Page under Committees. See website http://www.imo.org.

20. IMO Legal Committee, 84th Session, 22–26 April 2002.

21. IMO Legal Committee, 85th Session, 21–25 October 2002.

22. IMO Legal Committee, 86th Session, 28 April–2 May 2003.

23. Article 3 bis, LEG 88/3, Annex 1, 13 February 2004.

24. Report of the Legal Committee on the Work of its Eighty-Seventh Session, pages 14–20, LEG 87/17, 23 October 2003.

25. Ibid.

26. Article 8 bis, paragraph 3, LEG 88/3, Annex I, 13 February 2004.

27. Report of Legal Committee, supra note 31.

Chapter 10

Political Implications of the Proliferation Security Initiative

Seema Gahlaut

Introduction

The Proliferation Security Initiative (PSI) is an initiative to develop political commitments and practical cooperation to help impede and stop the flow of weapons of mass destruction (WMD), their systems and related materials to and from states and non-state actors of concern. It was launched by President Bush in May 2003 as a practical response to the growing challenge posed by the worldwide spread of WMD, and their delivery systems and related materials. The Statement of Interdiction Principles (SOP) was agreed upon among the initial 11 PSI countries on 4 September 2003.[1] These principles are: to establish a more coordinated and effective basis through which to impede and stop shipments of WMD, delivery systems and related materials flowing to and from states and non-state actors of proliferation concern, consistent with national legal authorities and relevant international law and frameworks.

According to the supporters of PSI, despite near universal commitments to non-proliferation, arms control and disarmament, some countries have reneged on promises not to develop, acquire or transfer WMD. Therefore, the new international environment "urgently demands creativity and commitment" to fashion effective responses to the problem of enforcement of international treaties. PSI is justified as fulfilling just these aims: it "reflects the reality that proliferators are actively and aggressively seeking WMD, using techniques that frequently thwart export controls and enforcement measures".[2] Accordingly, the "PSI is part of an overall counter-proliferation effort intended to apply intelligence, diplomatic, law enforcement and other tools at our disposal to prevent transfers of WMD-related items to countries and entities of concern".[3]

The Need for PSI

Supporters usually cite the following events to make a case that PSI is needed to bolster the functioning of existing non-proliferation treaties and regimes:

- For the first time in 35 years, a state has renounced the non-proliferation treaty (North Korea).
- Revelations that two other states have been found to have more advanced nuclear activities than anyone thought (Iran and Libya).
- Revelations about a transnational supply network centred in a nuclear-capable state (AQ Khan network and Pakistan).
- Patchy intelligence has suggested linkages between nuclear, nuclear-capable and nuclear-wannabee states (China–Pakistan–North Korea/Libya/Iran).
- Weaknesses in export controls of supplier countries have become obvious (United Kingdom, France, Germany, Netherlands).
- Unsecured materials and technologies (Russia).
- Newer locations of proliferation chains have been identified, which operate without the knowledge of national governments (Malaysia, South Africa).
- Exploitation of transshipment points by such networks has come to light (Singapore, UAE, Thailand and Central Asia).

The supporters of PSI say that it is a crucial innovation and all responsible states in the international community should support it. This is because PSI demonstrates to proliferators and to any state or non-state actors which support proliferation activities that the international community is prepared and ready to act to deter and stop trafficking in WMD. Moreover, PSI is conceived of as an activity, not an organisation — allowing for flexible levels of cooperation from relevant states. Despite many misgivings about its true

Table 1   Timeline of PSI development

31 May 2003	Announcement of the PSI by President Bush	Krakow, Poland
12 June 2003	First meeting of the PSI	Madrid, Spain
9–10 July 2003	Second meeting of the PSI	Brisbane, Australia
3–4 September 2003	Third meeting of the PSI	Paris, France
9–10 October 2003	Fourth meeting of the PSI	London, UK
4–5 March 2004	Fifth meeting of the PSI	Lisbon, Portugal
June 2004	Anniversary and global meeting of the PSI	Krakow, Poland

purpose, scope and methods, PSI has grown rapidly in membership within a year of its inception (from 7 to 11 to 15). Indeed, as a Canadian official outlined recently, PSI now "faces an institutional challenge: how do we acknowledge those states — now more than 60 — that support the PSI and who can and want to contribute?"[4] (see Table 1).

This chapter assesses whether PSI, despite its many legal and political shortcomings, and despite the current opposition to it, is likely to survive beyond its current phase of hyperactivity. The chapter will use the case of the multilateral export control regimes[5] — which share many of the weaknesses of PSI — to make the case that PSI's chances for survival are very good. The four regimes in question are the Nuclear Suppliers' Group, the Missile Technology Control Regime, the Australia Group and the Wassenaar Arrangement — which are collectively referred to as Multilateral Export Control Arrangements or MECA (see Table 2 for brief descriptions and Appendix A for a fuller description of each).[6]

The chapter begins with a section summarising and examining the main weaknesses of PSI, which, according to critics, will challenge its functioning and longevity. The second section provides a brief theoretical discussion regarding the factors crucial for the establishment and sustenance of regimes. The third section examines the rationale and structure of PSI within the context of informal, non-treaty-based regimes. The fourth section compares and contrasts PSI with a set of informal regimes (the multilateral export control regimes or MECA). Finally, the conclusion highlights some of the political implications of PSI for the international community.

Table 2 Informal agreements to prevent proliferation: four multilateral export control arrangements (MECA)

Agreement name	Established	Members (2004)	Technology it controls
Nuclear Suppliers Group (NSG)	1975	44 [7] + EU	Nuclear materials and related dual-use technology and equipment[8]
Australia Group (AG)	1985	38 [9] + EU	Chemical weapon precursors, plant, animal and human pathogens, and related dual-use technology and equipment
Missle Technology Control Regime (MTCR)	1987	34	Ballistic missiles and related technology and equipment[10]
Wassenaar Arrangement (WA)	1995	33	Conventional weapons and sensitive dual-use goods and technlogies

Problems with PSI

Critics have identified at least three major weaknesses or problems in the structure and functioning of the PSI.

First, critics contend that PSI's operations are likely to violate the established international legal treaties and conventions like the UN Convention on the Law of the Sea (UNCLOS) and even the non-proliferation treaties that it purports to enforce, such as the Nuclear Non-proliferation Treaty (NPT), the Chemical Weapons Convention (CWC) and the Biological and Toxin Weapons Convention (BTWC). PSI interdictions might violate the long-established international law on the right of ships to "innocent passage"[11] within other nation's territorial waters and the inviolability of international waters and airspace. The problems here include two different types of scenarios: infringement of sovereignty of a non-member state when PSI interdictions might occur in its territorial waters without its consent and infringement of the sovereignty of the non-member flag state when PSI interdictions may occur on the high seas, without the consent of the flag state. There are also related concerns that interdictions of shipments of dual-use materials will violate the trade and technology cooperation principles within several non-proliferation treaties that allow member states to trade such materials so long as these are intended for peaceful civilian uses. Conventional weapons, moreover, are freely traded among states unless international sanctions clearly forbid trade with one state party or another.

PSI members have sought to allay the concerns about territorial sovereignty by ensuring that all of PSI plenary statements emphasise the commitment to act "consistent with national legal authorities and relevant international law and frameworks, including the UN Security Council". But this has not reduced the concern among critics that the possibility of infringement of sovereignty in territorial waters remains.

Beyond this, however, PSI members have moved to minimise the possibility of infringement of sovereignty on high seas. Three of the states that are the most popular choice as flags-of-convenience states — Panama, Liberia and Marshall Islands — have signed bilateral agreements with the United States allowing US agents to board ships flying their flags and search them for WMD shipments, based on suspicion. Other PSI members are likely to draw up similar bilateral agreements with these three states as well — ensuring that a series of bilateral agreements will, operationally, work like a multilateral agreement when required. Similar bilateral agreements and understandings with a series of relevant coastal states are expected to minimise concerns about illegal interdictions in territorial waters of such states. PSI members have currently found no way to legitimize their interdictions vis-à-vis non-proliferation treaties, except to claim that interdictions will be primarily targeted against terrorist groups, unauthorised shipments and end-users suspected of being involved in developing WMD. There is, for instance, little effort to specify how PSI will deal with shipments of WMD-relevant materials going to the non-NPT states or such shipments going to allies of PSI states.[12]

Second, critics point out that PSI is an informal agreement among a small group of self-selected countries, who appear to be more interested in safeguarding their own commercial and security interests rather than in upholding international or regional security. At issue here is the contention that PSI is likely to operate like a judge, jury and executioner — chasing and punishing those that PSI itself judges to be guilty. There are also concerns that such judgements will be passed on the basis of the national security and economic interests of the PSI members rather than on the basis of some objective criteria. Selective enforcement, in other words, will allow PSI to operate like a posse rather than as a legally authorised, impartial body of enforcers of non-proliferation principles.

These possibilities and charges cannot be denied. PSI has been formed by a core group of mainly Western, industrialised states who believe that the international non-proliferation principles have received no more than lip service from a majority of their adherents. They also believe that decisions on monitoring, tracking and interdicting specific proliferation activities have become too politicised in the international organisations — to the extent that clearly dangerous proliferators are allowed to go unchecked while the international community engages in endless debates about equity and sovereignty principles. However, there has been some attempt by the PSI to recruit non-Western states as members — Japan, South Korea, Singapore, Russia have all been co-opted and efforts are on to recruit others such as China. Besides these states, PSI members claim that at least 60 other states from around the world have promised support for PSI activities in their neighbourhoods. When Japan held "Team Samurai" during 26–28 October 2004, Thailand, the Philippines and Cambodia (as well as New Zealand) showed up to watch a PSI exercise for the first time. And Singapore will host a similar exercise in August 2005.[13]

In sum, while the questions remain, more states appear willing to overlook those possible inconsistencies in PSI operations.

Third, critics argue that PSI has no clear legally acceptable means to define and identify dual-use technologies that it will target for interdiction. Nor does it have a similarly definable and acceptable list of target states and entities whose involvement in a trade is supposed to trigger an interdiction. These arguments also draw sustenance from the larger critique of non-proliferation efforts: that controls on trade and transfers of technology are an indirect means for developed states to deny developing states the economic and security benefits of scientific and technological developments.

This charge is likely to stick — no matter how PSI members choose to operationalise their definition of proliferation. No international treaty provides a list of dual-use items that are banned from trade between their members — their injunctions are only against trade and transfers of WMD.[14] The export control requirements of these treaties merely include a commitment by the members that they will not help anyone develop or produce WMDs — which is usually interpreted to mean that unless the exporting country knows for sure that the recipient is developing WMDs, there is no culpability or violation of this principle.

Given the paucity of control lists among international non-proliferation treaties, PSI members are likely to use the target list of entities and control lists of items that have been developed by the four multilateral export control arrangements (NSG, AG, MTCR and WA) — which, while clarifying the substantive issue, raise more legitimacy questions because these arrangements are themselves like PSI in structure and functioning. They are informal, non-treaty based groupings of self-selected states that have developed the control lists based on their own criteria and definitions of WMD-relevant dual-use items! Again, the perception of whether using the MECA lists is the right thing to do will depend on one's overall threat assessment. Those who object on legal grounds base their judgement on the unfairness of legitimising non-treaty-based agreements in international practice. Those who find it acceptable, on the other hand, base their judgement on the assessment that the international non-proliferation regime has gaps that need to be urgently filled — even if it means using non-treaty-based agreements.

The above discussion summarises the various objections to PSI and outlines some of the ways in which PSI members have sought to answer or deflect such objections. The overall thrust of the criticisms relates to the objectionable way in which a few states got together and in a seemingly arbitrary fashion, they have been using their political, economic and military power to define the objective and operational principles of this new regime. Such a critique implicitly assumes that regimes ought to be broad-based, serve the interests of the larger international community and draw their legitimacy from strict adherence to existing international treaty laws. It is, therefore, useful to look at some of the processes, identified in the academic literature, by which security regimes get established.

How do regimes get established?

According to structural realist scholars, the self-help system of international relations makes the achievement of security a high stakes enterprise.[15] This ensures that international regimes are rare in the security realm. The hegemonic stability theorists, while sharing the structural realists' assumption of anarchy and power politics, acknowledge the reality of numerous regimes in the international system but continue to see them as epiphenomena of existing power relationships.[16] Therefore, for such theorists, the emergence of regimes can be explained via power-based factors, such as hegemonic leadership. A hegemonic power uses a range of policies, from benign ones such as economic incentives, to coercive ones such as economic and military sanctions to force other states to join a regime.[17] A hegemonic power may also use socialisation to induce minor powers to accept and embrace particular norms that it articulates.[18] Regimes persist as long as the hegemonic power is able to enforce rules and regulations and compel violators to follow the regime norms.

Liberal institutionalist scholars, on the other hand, consider norms as a source of state behaviour — regimes arise because they solve collective action problems and serve several regulatory functions. They reduce verification costs and simplify decisions while punishing violators.[19]

Constructivist scholars add to this mix by postulating that norms are independent factors that, once internalised, can shape state identities and interests. National security policies and national interests are "not just out there waiting to be discovered, they are constructed through social interactions", especially through international organisations.[20]

Policy debate on the legitimacy and utility of the international non-proliferation regime, and of its various components, appears to follow similar lines of argument. States/perspectives that see the non-proliferation regime as inherently unfair tend to portray it exclusively as a creation and a tool of the powerful states. The creators and ardent supporters of the regime, on their part, tend to portray it exclusively as an entity embodying the functional and moral aspirations of the entire international community. Those who see the subjectivity in the implementation of the regime tend to focus on the seemingly sinister attempt by a few to define international norms to their advantage and corner the market for morality through such definitions. Those who see the merits of sustained cooperation, on the other hand, tend to see such attempts at defining international norms as a public good — which engenders habits of thinking and working cooperatively. Even a cursory examination of the origins and development of the various components of the international non-proliferation regime suggests that the truth lies somewhere in between. While the role of major powers is often necessary, it may not be sufficient — the regime has to fulfil some needs of its weaker members.[21] Similarly, norms are not always an instrument for brainwashing of the weak by the strong — they can also, overtime, constrain the stronger states.

Almost 20 years ago, in an approach that appears to synthesise the realist focus on power and the institutionalist focus on functionality, Robert Jervis identified several systemic conditions that are necessary for the emergence of security regimes.[22] These conditions are: (1) major powers "want to establish" regimes, (2) states "must believe that others share the value of mutual security and cooperation", (3) no state "believes that security is best provided for by expansion", and (4) "war and individualistic pursuit of security must be seen as costly".

Following this, it is not surprising that PSI came to be established due to a convergence of interests and perspectives among a small group of major powers. As discussed before, these states agreed on the urgency to strengthen enforcement of existing non-proliferation treaties and were equally pessimistic about the chances of this happening through formal and extended dialogue among treaty members. As PSI has increased its membership during the past one year of its existence, clearly, more states have bought into this idea either for tactical or strategic reasons. Moreover, if around 60 states are ready to give PSI conditional cooperation, it would suggest that despite their particular misgivings about PSI's operations, they support the broad objectives underlying it. In other words, there is some amount of agreement among PSI participants and supporters that PSI enhances their mutual security, and that cooperation within it is (at least) a marginally better way of pursuing their individual national interests on this issue. In sum, while the establishment of PSI does not reflect ideals of international community building and does not fulfil expectations regarding the crucial role of international law in regime formation, it does reflect the political reality that regimes get formed when the interests of major powers coincide.

Spectrum of Legalisation across International Regimes

Most of the criticisms of PSI tend to focus on the fact that it is a non-treaty-based organisation, informal in structure, with loosely defined parameters for activity in support of non-proliferation. This seems to assume that international regimes, in order to be acceptable, need to be based in the established international law, should be formal and clearly defined. Yet a cursory survey of existing international regimes would indicate that the current international system supports a wide variety of regimes that differ along the continuum of legalisation. Scholars distinguish between regimes that represent "hard law" versus those that represent "soft law" agreements. Duncan and Snidal, for instance, argue that "international actors choose to order their relations through international law and design treaties and other legal arrangements to solve specific substantive and political problems.... international actors choose softer forms of legalised governance when those forms offer superior institutional solutions".[23]

By using hard law to order their relations, international actors reduce transactions costs, strengthen the credibility of their commitments, expand their available political strategies and resolve problems of incomplete contracting. Doing so, however, also entails significant costs: hard law restricts actors' behaviour and even their sovereignty. Soft law offers many of the advantages of hard law, avoids some of the costs of hard law and has certain independent advantages of its own.[24] For instance, it is often easier to achieve than hard legalisation especially when the actors are states that are jealous of their autonomy and when the issues at hand challenge state sovereignty. Soft law offers more effective ways to deal with uncertainty, especially when it initiates processes that allow actors to learn about the impact of agreements over time. It facilitates compromise, and thus mutually beneficial cooperation, between actors with different interests and values, different time horizons and discount rates, and different degrees of power.

By this token, PSI would appear to be a logical response of states that are concerned about enforcing non-proliferation norms but are not certain of the actual impact and effectiveness of adopting the strategy of interdictions. They also appear to have different economic, security and technological interests and are unsure about how these might evolve in the future, especially with reference to interdiction of shipments to and from different neighbouring (or distant) states. In this sense, a series of bilateral agreements with a range of coastal and flag states appears to be a more cost-effective way of proceeding rather than starting multilateral negotiations on a formal (hard law) instrument to define and legitimise interdictions. Similarly, the possibility that PSI can have non-member supporters, who need not cooperate in all interdiction efforts in their region, allows for variable participation and level of support — which may change over time or across issue-areas.

Similarities Between PSI and MECA[25]

The four Multilateral Export Control Arrangements (NSG, MTCR, AG and WA), hereafter referred to as the MECA, are the non-formal components of the broader non-proliferation regime. They share several similarities with the PSI.

Both the MECA and the PSI owe their origins to consensus among a small group of members around the need for a tool that can deal with some of their common concerns. The participants share impatience with the shortcomings of the existing non-proliferation treaties. They believe that the treaties, while necessary, have not proved to be sufficient for curtailing proliferation, and that they need to improve enforcement. They believe that the agreement will provide them some measure of security against common identifiable threats, by "giving teeth" to the norms embodied in the treaties. The participants of the MECA and the PSI also do not have major problems about accepting the leadership of a hegemon (United States).

Just like the PSI today, the MECA have faced criticism from a larger number of opponents based on common assessment that at best they are cartels that are united around common *commercial* considerations masquerading behind the non-proliferation concerns, or at worst, they are vigilante groups that use their superior military and economic resources to impose their will on the rest of the states. The basic problem with these institutions, therefore, is that the members of MECA and PSI act capriciously in their own self-interest. However, it is interesting to note that despite little change in their basic mandate and character, the MECA have won over several former critics.[26]

An additional set of concerns about the MECA and the PSI is that their targets are subjectively defined, that they are not truly international because their membership is restricted[27] and nor are they a legitimate regime because their actions go beyond the scope of established international law. The MECA seek to deny dual-use technologies to states that they deem a proliferation concern — regardless of whether these states are signatories of particular non-proliferation treaties and have been abiding by them.[28] In sum, according to critics, groups like the MECA and the PSI pose a threat to the established international legal order.

Differences Between PSI and MECA

Despite the similarities in their aims and modus operandi, there are several crucial differences between the MECA and the PSI.

First, the MECA were established in secret, and continued to be secretive about their aims and methods until recently. In contrast, the PSI Statement of Principles[29] was shared with the general public very soon after its inception. Secondly, the MECA were hesitant in drawing linkages with treaties that they sought to uphold. PSI's focus, on the other hand, has been on drawing explicit linkages with the non-proliferation treaties, conventions and statements.

MECA have generally justified their actions based primarily on national regulations. PSI focus has been on the search for appropriate authority in both existing national laws and international legal conventions. The Statement of Principles, for instance, stresses that members will "take specific actions in support of interdiction efforts regarding cargoes of WMD, their delivery systems, or related materials, to the extent their national legal authorities permit and consistent with their obligations under international law and frameworks".

Table 3   Finding the means to work with international treaties: PSI operational experts meetings

9–10 July 2003	Brisbane, Australia
30 July 2003	London, United Kingdom
3–4 September 2003	Paris, France
8–10 October 2003	London, United Kingdom
16–17 December 2003	Washington, DC, United States
16–17 April 2004	Ottawa, Canada
5–6 August 2004	Oslo, Norway
30 November–2 December 2004	Sydney, Australia

Source: PSI Calendar of Events 2004, http://www.state.gov/t/np/c12684.htm.

Another PSI strategy has been to make existing laws work where they can, and make amendments to these where the existing laws and PSI's needs diverged. Among the non-plenary meetings of PSI, called the Operational Experts Group Meetings (see Table 3), some were explicitly devoted to finding ways to use existing treaty laws to legitimize PSI interdictions, and to identifying gaps in the existing laws that need to be filled via amendments, in order to allow PSI to achieve its basic goals.[30]

Third, the MECA did not actively seek either members or partners until very recently. Indeed, much of the early lives of each of the MECA were spent in consolidating the agreement among the original participants. There was also a lot of sensitivity to criticisms from the non-members, and membership in the MECA was not often publicised. PSI, in contrast, has been seeking all types of supporters by active outreach, and is allowing cooperating states to maintain flexibility in the level of support they provide (including case-by-case support in interdiction).[31]

Fourth, the MECA have only recently begun to focus on cooperation with relevant enforcement agencies in the member states. PSI, from its very inception, has identified such cooperation as essential to its operations. The PSI plenary meetings provide a political point of contact whereas the experts on various relevant issue-areas of enforcement meet separately to work on the nuts and bolts issues to foster better coordination on the ground. Beyond the exercises listed in Table 4, operational experts of PSI members will continue to refine the schedule of interdiction training exercises through the remainder of 2004 and 2005.

Fifth, despite all their institutional and legal shortcomings, the MECA have been able to establish themselves as widely accepted points of reference in

Table 4 Practicing joint operations: interception and interdiction exercises by PSI members

10–13 September 2003	Exercise PACIFIC PROTECTOR: Australia-led maritime exercise conducted in the Coral Sea
8–10 October 2003	Air CPX: United Kingdom-led air interception command post (tabletop) exercise conducted in London, UK
13–17 October 2003	Exercise SANSO 03: Spain-led maritime exercise conducted in the Western Mediterranean
25–27 November 2003	Exercise BASILIC 03: France-led maritime exercise conducted in the Western Mediterranean
11–17 January 2004	Exercise SEA SABER: United States-led maritime exercise conducted in the Arabian Sea, USA
19 February 2004	Exercise AIR BRAKE 03: Italian-led air interception exercise conducted over Italy (Trapani)
31 March– 1 April 2004	Exercise HAWKEYE: Germany-led customs exercise conducted in Germany (Frankfurt Airport)
19–22 April 2004	Exercise CLEVER SENTINEL: Italy-led maritime exercise conducted in the Mediterranean
19–21 April 2004	Exercise SAFE BORDERS: Poland-led ground interdiction exercise conducted in Poland (vicinity Wroclaw)
23–24 June 2004	Exercise APSE 04: France-led simulated air interception exercise
3–4 August 2004	Shipping Container Security Workshop, Copenhagen, Denmark
27 September– 1 October 2004	US-hosted PSI gaming exercise, Naval War College, Newport, RI
25–27 October 2004	Exercise TEAM SAMURAI: led by Japan
8–18 November 2004	US-led Caribbean maritime "chokepoint" exercise

Source: PSI Calendar of Events 2004, http://www.state.gov/t/np/c12684.htm.

the international discussions regarding non-proliferation. Members and non-members refer to control lists of the MECA and the standards/guidelines set by them, to establish that they are in compliance with international non-proliferation norms. This bodes well for the PSI, especially since the PSI appears to have deliberately set out to overcome many of the political and institutional shortcomings of the MECA. PSI is not only widening its support base by encouraging membership and cooperation by all willing states, but it is also deepening the commitment and capabilities of its existing members by focusing on regular high level plenaries, joint expert meetings and exercises.

Finally, the PSI is operating in a different international environment where no state is likely to come out in support of activities that PSI is supposedly targeting: terrorism, unauthorised uses of dual-use materials and black marketing in dangerous materials. This voluntary non-opposition to the broad mission of PSI in the international community is now further reinforced by UNSC Resolution 1540, which requires all states to strengthen national export controls and to criminalise export control violations by any natural and legal entity within their borders.[32] Together, these three factors, the conscious strategy of PSI members to overcome the criticisms faced by similar institutions in an earlier era, the fast-paced institutional development of PSI and the supportive international environment, are likely to account for the success and survivability of the PSI in the near future.[33]

Political Implications of PSI

PSI demonstrates to proliferators and to any state or non-state actor that supports proliferation activities that at least a part of the international community is prepared and ready to act to deter and stop trafficking in WMD technologies. Such a formulation suggests several changes in the operative political environment of the PSI.

Before the Persian Gulf War I in the early 1990s revealed Saddam Hussain's success at assembling a nascent WMD programme, the international community was apt to emphasise the sovereignty principle when opposing "unilateral" action by a few members. Since that time, and particularly after 9/11, mainstream opinion has accorded some legitimacy to the argument that it is the international duty to intervene and prevent proliferation[34] — especially when the security stakes are considered sufficiently high. There is growing realisation in the international discourse that treaty and non-treaty efforts to control the proliferation of WMDs are not, and can never hope to be, fool proof.[35] Therefore, when established measures fail to deter trafficking in WMD-relevant materials and technologies, few in the international community would openly oppose measures to intercept sensitive items that have been successful in evading the web of national and international regulations and procedures.

In the earlier period, the opposition to informal groupings and non-proliferation efforts claimed that anti-proliferation efforts (like MECAs) stymied developing countries' efforts to develop technologically and economically. Now the opposition claims only that anti-proliferation efforts (like PSI) may impinge on their right to trade freely — especially if they are applied indiscriminately (i.e. on the high seas or without support of the littoral states). The reality of non-state actors (individuals, groups, networks, businesses) operating on the margins of national systems has made it harder for state actors (governments) to assert that such actors/activities should not be stopped. There is a related realisation that national governments do not often have the resources to unilaterally monitor, intercept and convict the transnational networks of non-state actors — bilateral and multilateral cooperation is crucial to such tasks. The remaining concern, however, is that *legitimate* trade by their citizens should not be hampered. If PSI can demonstrate that it seeks to, and will, operate with this caveat in mind, there can be few legal grounds to oppose it.

Before the end of the Cold War, the members and the non-members of the anti-proliferation efforts defined their enemies and allies ideologically. Now, both sides are struggling to identify enemies that are amorphous and often include non-state actors (individuals or business entities). The allies, similarly, now include both states and responsible businesses. There is a growing realisation in the international security community that the enemy is not necessarily "out there" but may be comprised of a network of domestic and transnational actors that cooperate based on a mix of motivations: ranging from ideological to economic to local political.[36] The capabilities of national authorities are vastly supplemented by transnational intelligence sharing and coordination in interdicting such actors. PSI offers such an avenue for *conditional* cooperation.[37]

Before, the focus of the international community was on promoting the positive side of technology development by state entities. Now, the major concern is regarding the possible misuses of technology by unauthorised entities. Many states in the developing world face insurgent movements at home or on their peripheries. The possibility that such movements can acquire dangerous capabilities and use it against governments appears to have encouraged more states to look at PSI somewhat favourably.

Earlier, the anti-proliferation efforts saw state actors as the problem. Now, state actors are conceived of as a necessary part of the solution.[38] The passage of UNSC Resolution 1540, moreover, requires all states to ensure that their laws establish penalties for their citizens and businesses for violating

WMD-relevant export controls. The developed states, who have been most concerned about WMD proliferation, have come to the realisation that their earlier focus on state-actors as the locus of technology controls, denials and sanctions is becoming both outdated and impractical. Indeed, state actors can be the most easily identifiable, monitored and sanctioned end-users of sensitive technologies. It is when the technologies go to the non-state actors that monitoring and end-use verification is difficult and it is consequently harder to pin the responsibility for diversion to dangerous uses.[39] In all such cases, external suppliers of technologies need the support of state actors to enforce the agreement of verifiable end uses. PSI is thus a means for the technology suppliers to elicit such cooperation from recipient states.

In sum, the opposition to, and critique of, the PSI is likely to be limited to discussing its shortcomings as per the established legal texts. Even within this limited space, the only legitimate objections that countries are likely to raise appear to be in the realm of application in particular instances, such as interdiction in high seas or in the territorial waters of a littoral state that is neither a member not a cooperative partner. In the latter case, there is a further political constraint on the right of such a littoral state to refuse cooperation: if PSI members are providing actionable intelligence about activities of a citizen/entity of the littoral state, that state cannot plead ignorance and therefore cannot avoid taking some action to demonstrate that it does not condone such an activity. The only leeway would be on the mode of response — it could act on its own or in tandem with the PSI states. Indeed, as a recent analysis suggests:

> . . . it is getting much harder for countries to duck their anti-proliferation obligations entirely. By October 28th, all governments were due to make a first report to the UN detailing their national legislation on trafficking-prevention, on export controls and on how dangerous weapons-related materials are secured. Those who miss the deadline, or have inadequate controls, can expect pointed questions from a special committee, backed by UN-hired experts.[40]

This situation is quite possible because safety and security concerns are now explicitly articulated as widely accepted limitations when it comes to trade and transport of hazardous materials and contraband. Whether it is hazardous material or contraband, the commonly accepted formulation is that the ultimate responsibility for the proper end-use of these substances lies with the "authorising entity" — usually a government, or an authorised intermediary, usually a business. No state would like to be on record as defending the right of free trade as being above the internationally shared concerns about terrorism (or terrorists getting access to dangerous materials and technologies). Likewise, few legitimate businesses would like to be branded as aiding and abetting terrorists.

The prevailing political context, therefore, offers few means to the opponents of PSI. Indeed, PSI is "best understood as a set of partnerships that establishes the basis for cooperation on specific activities, when the need arises. It does not create formal 'obligations' for participating states, but does represent a political commitment to establish 'best practices' to stop proliferation-related shipments".[41] Given this focus on political commitment rather than legal obligation, PSI has raised the bar of action for its critics: states that fail to act against a particular targeted activity have to choose from among several equally unpalatable choices. In the event that a proliferation-relevant shipment is in their territory or on their ships, failure to act would mean that those states are either morally supportive of the activity or are complicit in it. Alternatively, it would suggest that their national anti-proliferation policies suffer from legal limitations or just plain incompetence.

Notes

1. These were Australia, France, Germany, Italy, Japan, the Netherlands, Poland, Portugal, Spain, the United Kingdom and the United States. By January 2004, these 11 were joined by Canada, Denmark, Norway, Singapore and Turkey.
2. *Proliferation Security Initiative Frequently Asked Questions (FAQ)*, Fact Sheet, Bureau of Nonproliferation, US Department of State, 24 May 2004. Available at http://www.state.gov/t/np/rls/fs/32725pf.htm.
3. *The Proliferation Security Initiative*, Fact Sheet, Bureau of Nonproliferation, US Department of State, Washington, DC, 28 July 2004. Available at http://www.state.gov/t/np/rls/other/34726.htm.
4. Remarks by James Wright at the Operational Experts Working Group meeting, 16–17 April 2004, Ottawa, Canada. Available at http://www.dfait-maeci.gc.ca/arms/psi3-en.asp.
5. These export control regimes were similarly informal, *ad hoc* and worked on extra-legal principles to control the supply of WMD technologies.
6. It is important to note here that these regimes refer to themselves as "arrangements" because they are self-consciously informal agreements among member states, and do not have the status of formal, international treaty regimes.
7. Estonia, Lithuania, Malta and the People's Republic of China were admitted as the newest members, effective June 2004. European Union is an Observer at the NSG.

8. NSG Trigger list includes the equipment and material relevant for nuclear weapons development and its Dual-Use Guidelines contain an additional 65 items that have uses in nuclear power reactors and related technologies.

9. Estonia, Latvia, Lithuania, Malta and Slovenia joined in 2004. EU is an Observer at the AG.

10. Category I of MTCR control list includes complete systems and subsystems capable of carrying a payload of 500 kg over a range of at least 300 km and specially designed production facilities for such systems. Category II includes missile-related components such as propellants, avionics equipment and other items used for the production of Category I systems.

11. This is the subject of Article 19 of the Law of the Sea Convention, which states that ships may pass through territorial waters so long as their passage does not jeopardise "the peace, good order or security of the coastal state".

12. For instance, how would PSI states treat WMD-relevant dual-use shipments to India, Pakistan and Israel — when these are being legally exported from non-PSI states? Given the traditionally close relationship between United States and Israel, and the growing US dependence on Pakistan, would PSI interdict suspect shipments to Israel and Pakistan?

13. "Counter-proliferation in Asia: No Place to Hide, Maybe", *The Economist*, 28 October 2004 (print edition).

14. The Zangger Committee, composed of supplier states within the NPT, has a "trigger list" of items that require the importing state to accept international safeguards on facilities where they will be used. The various lists of the CWC, similarly, ban very few items for export — those in Schedule 1. There are no bans of export of Schedule 2 & 3 among members, only end-use certification and post-shipment verification requirements. Of course, Schedule 2 items may not be exported to non-CWC states. The BWC has no such list, and there are no treaties that ban the sales of advanced conventional weapons or missiles.

15. For the realist view on anarchy and its effects, see K.N. Waltz, *Theory of International Politics* (New York: Random House, 1979), and J.M. Greico, "Anarchy and the Limits of Cooperation: A Realist Critique of the Newest Liberal Institutionalism", *International Organization*, 42(3), 1998, pp. 485–507. For another perspective on why security cooperation is difficult to achieve, see C. Lipson, "International Cooperation in Economic and Security Affairs", *World Politics*, 37(1), 1984, pp. 1–23.

16. S. Strange, "Cave! Hic Dragones: A Critique of Regime Analysis", in S.D. Krasner, ed., *International Regimes* (Ithaca, NY: Cornell University Press, 1983).

17. H. Mueller, "The Role of Hegemonies and Alliances", in R.C. Karp, ed., *Security without Nuclear Weapons* (Oxford: Oxford University Press, 1992).

18. G.J. Ikenberry and C.A. Kupchan, "Socialization and Hegemonic Power", *International Organization*, 44(3), 1990, pp. 283–316.

19. A.A. Stein, *Why Nations Cooperate: Circumstance and Choice in International Relations* (Ithaca, NY: Cornell University Press, 1990). See also M.W. Zacher and B.A. Sutton, *Governing Global Networks* (Cambridge: Cambridge University Press, 1996).

20. M. Finnemore, *National Interests in International Society* (Ithaca, NY: Cornell University Press, 1996), p. 2. See also A. Wendt, "Anarchy is What States Make of It: The Social Construction of Power Politics", *International Organization*, 46(2), 1994, pp. 391–425; P.J. Katzenstein, ed., *The Culture of National Security: Norms and Identity in World Politics* (New York: Columbia University Press, 1996); and G. Chafetz, "The End of the Cold War and the Future of Nuclear Proliferation: An Alternative to the Neorealist Perspective", *Security Studies*, 2(3–4),1993, pp. 127–158.

21. See an excellent analysis of why the NPT has survived despite its obvious unfairness in T.V. Paul, "Systemic Conditions and Security Cooperation: Explaining the Persistence of the Nuclear Non-Proliferation Regime", *Cambridge Review of International Affairs,* 16(1), 2003, pp. 135–155.

22. R. Jervis, "Security Regimes", in S.D. Krasner (ed.), *International Regimes* (Ithaca, NY: Cornell University Press, 1983); pp. 176–178.

23. Kenneth W. Abbott and Duncan Snidal, "Hard and Soft Law in International Governance", *International Organization* 54, 3, Summer 2000, pp. 421–456.

24. Ibid.

25. This (and the following) section borrows from, and expands upon an earlier article on the similarities and institutional/tactical differences between the MECAs and the PSI. See Seema Gahlaut, "PSI Will Parallel The Multilateral Export Control Regimes", *The Monitor*, Vol. 10, No. 1, Spring 2004, pp. 12–16. Available at http://www.uga.edu/cits/documents/pdf/monitor/monitor_sp_2004.pdf.

26. Argentina, Brazil, South Africa and China have all become members in one or more of these agreements. India appears to be interested in joining as well.

27. Membership in these groups is closed to other states unless the existing members allow it.

28. The AG, for instance, would deny dual-use chemicals and related technology to states it considers dangerous, whether or not these states have signed the CWC and are abiding by their obligations under the CWC. The NSG, similarly, has gone beyond the NPT requirement of facility-specific safeguards. NSG decided in 1992 to make fullscope safeguards a condition for all nuclear exports, whether the recipient is in the NPT or not. WA denies exports of arms to regions where it deems that a "destabilising accumulation" may occur — and the fact that this determination is often subjective is visible by looking at the recipients of arms from WA members.

29. Available at http://www.state.gov/t/np/c12207.htm.

30. Remarks by James Wright at the sixth Operational Experts Working Group Meeting, 16–17 April 2004, Ottawa, Canada. URL http://www.dfait-maeci.gc.ca/arms/psi3-en.asp. Eight such meetings have taken place so far.

31. Liberia (in February 2004), Panama (in May 2004) and Marshall Islands (2004) have agreed to cooperate with the United States in PSI-interdictions. These countries account for a majority of the world's shipping registries. Cooperation from Panama and Liberia alone would mean that nearly 15 percent of the world's roughly 50,000 large cargo ships are now subject to being boarded and inspected on short notice. Judith Miller, "Panama Joins Accord to Stem Ships' Transport of Illicit Arms", *The New York Times*, 11 May 2004. Available at http://www.nytimes.com/2004/05/11/international/americas/11ship.html.

32. For more on the implications of this resolution, see Cassady Craft, *Challenges of UNSCR 1540: Questions about International Export Controls*, CITS Issue Brief #002. Available at http://www.uga.edu/cits/documents/pdf/Briefs/CITSBrief_002.pdf.

33. This is especially relevant since many opponents of the PSI see it as a misguided brain-child of the current Bush administration. This led some critics to expect that PSI would wither away if and when a new non-Republican administration comes to power in the United States. The factors outlined here suggest otherwise.

34. Lee Feinstein and Anne-Marie Slaughter, "A Duty to Prevent", *Foreign Affairs*, January/February 2004.

35. "Current Controls Not Enough to Keep WMD Out of Terrorists' Hands, Leaders Say", *Global Security Newswire*, 29 September 2004. Available at http://www.nti.org/d%5Fnewswire/issues/2004/9/28/a13e1daf%2D97cb%2D4fa6%2Dab21%2Db9f212d5c21.html.

36. The challenge, as one European official put it, is how to identify "the bad guys in a good country".

37. "Ultimately, the United States wants states to establish the practical basis to cooperate on interdiction efforts. It may well be that a state that indicates interest in the PSI is never asked to help on interdictions, simply because a case requiring that state's help does not arise. However, states should be ready for quick and effective action in the event that they can be helpful in preventing a shipment of proliferation concern". *Proliferation Security Initiative Frequently Asked Questions (FAQ)*, 24 May 2004. Available at http://www.state.gov/t/np/rls/fs/32725pf.htm.

38. This is evident from the emphasis of MECA members on development and strengthening of national export control policies around the world. United States, Japan and the United Kingdom, for instance, have been offering assistance and outreach to countries around the world to help them establish robust laws and procedures to regulate their dual-use trade. The UNSC resolution 1540 makes it mandatory for all states to have such domestic laws.

39. Since 1984, US dual-use exports to Indian end-users, for instance, required a guarantee by the *government* of India that the items would be used for authorised purposes and will not be re-transferred or re-exported. Similarly, India requires that

when Schedule 3 chemicals are exported by Indian businesses, the end-use/end-user certificate has to be signed by the concerned (government) authority of the recipient (importing) country.

40. "Counter-proliferation in Asia: No Place to Hide, Maybe", *The Economist*, 28 October 2004 (print edition).
41. *The Proliferation Security Initiative*, Fact Sheet, Bureau of Nonproliferation, US Department of State, Washington, DC, 28 July 2004. Available at http://www.state.gov/t/np/rls/other/34726.htm.

Annex A: Multilateral Export Control Regimes

The Nuclear Suppliers Group (NSG) is an informal agreement comprised of 44 states, more than half of whom are nuclear technology suppliers. It establishes common guidelines governing nuclear transfers in an effort to ensure that civilian nuclear trade does not contribute to nuclear weapons acquisition. The International Atomic Energy Agency (IAEA) first published the NSG guidelines on nuclear export in 1978. Prompted by the common concern about Iraq's clandestine efforts to acquire weapons of mass destruction, in 1992 the NSG established additional guidelines for transfers of nuclear-related dual-use equipment, material and technology. Its control list includes nuclear material, nuclear reactors and related equipment, non-nuclear material for reactors, plant and equipment for the reprocessing, enrichment and conversion of nuclear material and for fuel fabrication and heavy water production, and technology associated with each of the above items. Final interpretation and implementation of these lists is left to the national discretion of participating states. Members voluntarily adhere to the guidelines, and share information on nuclear proliferation concerns. Recently, NSG members have begun to consider proposals for responding to the threat posed by nuclear terrorism.

The Australia Group (AG) is an informal agreement comprised of 38 states that was established in 1984 at the Australian initiative, as a response to evidence about chemical weapons use in the Iran–Iraq War. Its aim is to allow exporting or transshipping countries to minimise the risk of assisting chemical and biological weapon (CBW) proliferation. Fifteen states met initially in Brussels, but later decided to meet annually in Paris. The Group's actions are viewed as complementary measures in support of the 1925 Geneva Protocol, the 1972 Biological and Toxins Weapons Convention and the 1993 Chemical Weapons Convention. The Group has no charter or constitution. It operates by consensus. Its control list includes chemical weapons precursors, human, animal and plant pathogens, as well as equipment that may be used in production of chemical and biological weapons. Final interpretation and implementation of these lists is left to the national discretion of participating states. Members voluntarily adhere to the guidelines, and share information on missile proliferation concerns.

The Missile Technology Control Regime (MTCR) is an informal agreement among 34 states that was established in 1987. Members share the goals of non-proliferation of unmanned delivery systems for weapons of mass destruction and to coordinate national export licensing efforts aimed at preventing their proliferation. It controls exports of missiles (and related technology) whose performance in terms of payload and range exceeds stated parameters. There are two categories of items controlled. Category I includes complete systems and subsystems capable of carrying a payload of 500 kg over a range of at least 300 km and specially designed production facilities for such systems. Category II includes missile-related components such as propellants, avionics equipment and other items used for the production of Category I systems. Final interpretation and implementation of these lists is left to the national discretion of participating states.

The Wassenaar Arrangement (WA) is an informal agreement among 34 states established in 1995 to control transfers of conventional weapons and sensitive dual-use goods and technologies. It replaced the Cold War export control mechanism, COCOM, which sought to deny the Soviet Union and its allies military-related articles. WA was designed to promote transparency, an exchange of views and information, and greater responsibility in preventing destabilising accumulations of advanced conventional weapons and dual-use technologies. The institution has no list of target countries or restricted entities, although it does (since December 2001) target "terrorist groups and organisations, as well as individual terrorists". There are, however, agreed lists of items: a munitions list that consists of the same basic categories of major weapons systems as the UN Register on Conventional Weapons; and a dual-use technology list that is broken into two tiers. Tier 1, the basic list, is made up of sensitive items and technologies; and tier 2 consists of very sensitive items that are subject to more stringent monitoring. Final interpretation and implementation of these lists is left to the national discretion of participating states. There is a small Secretariat located in Vienna, and there are several expert and technical working group meetings held each year in addition to the plenary in December.

(*Source*: Adapted from Appendix 1, *Road Map to Reform: Strengthening Multilateral Export Controls*, Report, Center for International Trade and Security, Athens, Georgia, November 2004. URL http://www.uga.edu/cits/.)

Chapter 11

New Initiatives for Maritime Cooperation

Stanley B. Weeks

Introduction

During the first decade after the end of the Cold War, efforts to enhance regional maritime security focussed on various types of maritime confidence and security building measures. Progress in recent years in improving transparency, particularly in various bilateral contexts, has been particularly noteworthy. However, in the coming months and years, we must increase our focus on more extensive Asia-Pacific maritime cooperation, to deal with the growing threats posed by maritime terrorism (and its close relation, maritime piracy). This is particularly true as the trend continues of greater East Asian dependence on the sea lanes for transport of oil, gas and trade products. The UN International Maritime Organisation (IMO) is addressing some elements of maritime security (for ports, containers and ships) against terrorism through global multilateral rules, but scope remains for action by nations in the region to help secure the sea lanes themselves.

Accordingly, Asia-Pacific nations now need to move beyond the previous successful focus on maritime confidence-building measures (often small-scale and bilateral), and emphasise Maritime Operational Cooperation as the ultimate in "Security-Building" against the common new threats of maritime terrorism. Such an emphasis will focus on more coordinated, more multilateral and more interoperable maritime security and patrols for critical regional sea lanes and choke points.

A Decade of Real Progress in Asia-Pacific Maritime Confidence-Building

There has been noteworthy progress over the past decade in implementing various types of maritime confidence-building measures. Progress in this area has generally been steady, while the focus of such measures has largely remained bilateral in nature — a reflection of both subjective national preferences and of the objective vast differences and disparities among nations of the region.

Previous writings[1] categorised the variety of Confidence-Building Measures in three main areas — Declaration Measures (basically statements of intent), Transparency Measures (such as information exchange, dialogues, military-to-military contacts/exchanges, communication, notification, and observation and inspection measures) and Constraint Measures (such as Incidents at Sea Agreements, nuclear-free zones and limits on personnel, equipment and activities).

Of these three major categories of confidence-building measures, in the maritime context, the greatest and most valuable progress has been in Transparency Measures. However, in the first category, Declaratory Measures, in the maritime area there have been both bilateral (PRC, Philippines) and recent multilateral (PRC-ASEAN) South China Sea Code of Conduct initiatives. Although the earlier bilateral declaration seemed of limited effectiveness in calming disputes, at least the recent multilateral declaration has kept in the forefront the need to address such disputes peacefully. Likewise, the third category, Constraint Measures, has seen continued progress on Risk Reduction measures at sea — notably, the US–PRC MMC (Military Maritime Consultative) Agreement, earlier Russia–Japan and Russia–ROK Incidents at Sea (INCSEA) agreements, and less well-known INCSEA-like agreements between Malaysia and Indonesia. Particularly noteworthy is a recent action in the (unofficial, but authoritative) senior Asia-Pacific naval group, the Western Pacific Naval Symposium, to approve an INCSEA-like agreement (CUES) for multilateral naval use among ships unexpectedly encountering ships from other navies at sea.

The major progress in maritime confidence-building has been in the broad category of Transparency Measures. Indeed, if one thinks back just a decade ago, the current advanced state of dialogues, personnel exchanges, ship visits, seminars, communications and even observation measures is truly remarkable. Most noteworthy has been the extent of bilateral military-to-military meetings and dialogues and exchanges of ship visits. Long estranged major regional powers have instituted regular high-level defence and naval consultations, and exchanged ship visits — particularly, PRC–Russia, US–PRC, Japan–ROK, ROK–PRC and Japan–PRC. There have also been increasing naval exchanges between the major ASEAN nations (plus Australia, New Zealand and Canada) and the major Northeast Asian powers (PRC, Russia, Japan and ROK), as well as increasing exchanges between the defence and maritime forces in ASEAN itself. Also, the Indian Navy, isolated for years even from its Russian friends, has now assumed a major role in cooperative regional naval dialogues and exchanges, including exercises with some ASEAN nations and ship visits to Japan and the PRC.

In addition to these burgeoning official ("Track One") naval dialogues and ship visits, the official ASEAN Regional Forum (ARF) has, through its Intersessional Group on CBM meetings, periodically addressed issues of maritime cooperation, initially at a Maritime Experts Meeting in October 1998, which identified and endorsed several measures for maritime cooperation, and subsequently at a Maritime Cooperation meeting in Mumbai in March 2003. At the unofficial ("Track Two") level, regional maritime meetings have been instrumental in identifying confidence-building measures and preparing the way for subsequent official cooperative measures. In this regard, the CSCAP Working Group on Maritime Cooperation has prepared and forwarded to the official ARF co-chairs three CSCAP Memoranda — Guidelines for Regional Maritime Cooperation (December 1999), Cooperation for Law and Order at Sea (2000) and the 2002 memorandum on The Practice of the Law of the Sea in the Asia-Pacific. Another "unofficial" but authoritative forum has been the Western Pacific Naval Symposium (WPNS), with its biennial meetings of heads of navies (and annual workshops) involving all the major navies of the region among its 18 member nations and three observer nations. In addition to the development of the INCSEA-like CUES measure, WPNS has advanced information exchange and interoperability, though the Maritime Information Exchange Database, adoption of Experimental Tactical Publications (EXTACS) for WPNS use, development of an Interoperability Matrix and various exercises and personnel exchange initiatives.

On the other hand, there has been little action among the navies of the Asia-Pacific regarding the more formal transparency measures of notification, observation and inspection, as well in the actual constraint measures to formally limit naval forces and/or activities. However, even here, there has been an increasing invitation of observers to major exercises (e.g. the US invitation of the PRC and other observers to the recent Cobra Gold exercises in Southeast Asia).

Overall, in the area of maritime confidence-building measures, Asia-Pacific naval and other maritime forces should continue and build on the remarkable progress in transparency measures achieved over the past decade. The dialogues and exchanges of these measures provide a good basis for the necessary advancement, to a greater focus on Maritime Operational Cooperation, as "Security-Building" against common new threats of maritime terrorism.

New Threats Posed by Maritime Terrorism

We must now reconsider the requirements for Asia-Pacific maritime cooperation in light of the new threats posed by maritime terrorism (and its close relation, maritime piracy). The initial post-Cold War period of CBMs — focussed on confidence-building for increased transparency through contacts, exchanges and ship visits — has now become almost routine, and must now be leveraged to move to "Security-Building" maritime cooperation in dealing with new threats to vital sea lanes. This is particularly essential since the sea lanes of East Asia are becoming even more critical to the continued economic development and prosperity of regional nations. As Professor Ji Guoxing of the PRC recently noted, Asian oil imports, mostly from the Middle East, will rise from the current 60 percent to 75 percent of total consumption by 2010, with tankers using the Malacca Strait increasing two to three times by 2010 from today's average of 26 tankers daily.[2] Of particular note is China's increasing stake in sea lane security as its oil imports from the Middle East increase rapidly.

Events of the past 2 years have provided the international maritime community a sobering wake-up call on the potential scope of maritime terrorism. The most publicised threats to ships have been from suicide small boats, such as those that damaged the French oil tanker *Limburg* off the coast of Yemen in October 2002, and the destroyer *USS Cole* in Aden port in October 2000. But there are other maritime terrorist threats to ships underway at sea and in port, including aircraft (manned or unmanned), underwater swimmers with explosives or even a terrorist mini-sub. Commercial shipping, including not only merchant ships such as oil and chemical carrying tankers and liquefied natural gas (LNG) carriers, but also passenger ships such as large cruise liners and passenger ferries are vulnerable to terrorist attacks. Beyond the immediate ship targeted by such an attack, the potential costs to the marine environment and to the global oil, shipping and marine insurance markets are very serious.[3] Another possibility is that maritime terrorists could seize a ship and use the ship itself as a weapon, driving it into other ships or into port or commercial facilities (including refineries). Similarly, a cruise ship could be hijacked, with up to thousands of passengers onboard. Oil and gas platforms at sea could be attacked or seized by maritime terrorists, with the loss of hundreds of lives and the creation of an environmental disaster. Maritime terrorists can also use commercial shipping and containers to transport weapons and even personnel — the explosives Al Qaeda used to blow up two US Embassies in East Africa in 1998 arrived by ship in Kenya.

Indeed, the most serious threat of maritime terrorism is from the potential use of commercial shipping and containers as a delivery platform for Weapons of Mass Destruction — a nuclear weapon, a "dirty" bomb with radiological material, or chemical and biological weapons. One approach to counter this threat is the Proliferation Security Initiative (PSI). In the United States alone, there are 361 ports (50 of them major ports), receiving over six million containers each year, only 2 percent of which are inspected by Customs. This is why enhancing security in ports, at home and overseas, has been an initial priority for the United States and for the international maritime community. The UN IMO in London in December 2002 finalised a year's work on new measures requiring ports and ships to have security officers and security plans and to conduct vulnerability assessments, as well as numerous other measures, by 1 July 2004. On a national level, the United States has several initiatives to enhance port security against terrorism — including advance notification requirements for ships, Sea Marshals and the Container Security Initiative for US Customs personnel to assist in the 20 biggest overseas ports to inspect and certify container cargo bound for US ports at its "point of origin".

As this brief summary indicates, the threat of maritime terrorism is broad and growing.[4] (The threat of maritime piracy at sea, often violent, is of course similar in many respects to maritime terrorism and has been a growing concern for over a decade.) A considerable part of the threat of maritime terrorism and piracy must be addressed at the national level, in ports and territorial waters. But other aspects of the maritime terrorist threat can be addressed at the global level by the current work of the IMO, regional shipping organisations and even the recent APEC shipping security initiative, to establish global standards for anti-terrorism security for ports, containers and ships. However, there still remains the real need for enhanced regional cooperation to operate against the terrorist threat against ships underway at sea, particularly in the sea lanes and choke points of the Asia-Pacific region.[5]

Asia-Pacific Maritime Operational Cooperation: Maritime Security Requirements to Counter Today's Maritime Threats

Now is the time to consolidate the gains achieved in maritime confidence-building and transparency over the past decade and move to "security-building" through Maritime Operational Cooperation against the new maritime terrorist threats to critical Asia-Pacific sea lanes and choke points.

Geopolitically, the foundation for greater Maritime Operational Cooperation has been established by three elements: a common threat (in maritime terrorism (and piracy)), a common goal in security for the sea lanes — increasingly essential to provide the oil/gas and trade products on which East Asian economic development and prosperity depend, and adequate basic levels of maritime familiarity and trust to provide a basis for initial maritime cooperation. This basic level of familiarity and trust is thanks largely to the maritime confidence-building measures, especially naval dialogue and visits, of the past decade. In fact, initial elements of Maritime Operational Cooperation can be seen in a variety of recent maritime events in the Asia-Pacific region, including the increasing exercises and cooperation of maritime vessels from Japan and India to help counter piracy in the Southeast Asia region, the coordination of piracy patrols by Indonesia, Malaysia and Singapore, US and Indian naval cooperation (including anti-piracy patrols), and the increasing multilateral character of major regional military exercises such as Cobra Gold and CARAT.

The new emphasis on Asia-Pacific Maritime Operational Cooperation will require efforts that are more focused, coordinated, multilateral and interoperable. Focus is needed to identify where, in the vast distances of sea lanes between the Persian Gulf and Northeast Asia, limited naval (and coast guard) forces should focus their Maritime Operational Cooperation. Since such cooperation would logically consist initially of patrols of sea lanes and choke points that are at greatest threat from maritime terrorists (as well as violent piracy at sea), an initial geographic focus might best be on sea lane patrols (and escorts of particular selected high-value ships) from the Western to the Eastern entrances to the Straits of Malacca. For the long, open distances from the Persian Gulf exit to Sumatra, and then again from the Singapore Straits through the South China Sea to Northeast Asia, it would probably be adequate to initially have just informal agreements on loose coordination of neighbouring nations, supplemented by periodic passages and patrols by nations having longer range naval and coast guard vessels. Of course, both these suggested areas of operational focus will require multilateral maritime forces that coordinate their operations more closely, and are capable of at least basic communications interoperability.

Despite the new geopolitical context of common threat, common concern for sea lane security and (maritime CBM-induced) greater familiarity among regional navies — all of which now argue for a move to Maritime Operational Cooperation in the Pacific — there is a need for regional nations to first find a way to address the details of how (and how much) to formalise this Maritime Operational Cooperation. Despite recent progress, regional historical rivalries and territorial disputes persist, and despite the recent first region-wide security forum in the form of the ARF, the region does not have (nor is it likely to have in the near future) an alliance with an integrated military command structure. It was such a structure in NATO that facilitated the establishment and operation of "standing naval forces", and the lack of such conditions explains why there is still no formal "Standing Naval Force Pacific" in prospect. Yet the proposed Asia-Pacific Maritime Operational Cooperation concept, while not a "standing naval force", can help provide the essential elements of maritime security for critical regional sea lanes and choke points.

The Way Ahead

For the Way Ahead, we might consider four paths that could be used, singly or in combination, to promptly work out the details of how (and how much) to formalise Asia-Pacific Maritime Operational Cooperation. The first path is for the CSCAP Maritime Cooperation Working Group to further develop this as one of its next orders of business, perhaps coordinating with the WPNS. (Indeed, Asia-Pacific Maritime Operational Cooperation is consistent with two of the already proposed WPNS action items — Multilateral Cooperation for SLOC Security (Indonesia) and Naval Force Protection (US).) The second path, then, would be for WPNS to address the modalities of this initiative at its next biennial heads of navies meeting, to be held in Singapore later this year. WPNS has the advantage of "unofficial" but authoritative involvement of all key regional naval leaders — with the disadvantage of infrequent annual meetings, which may not pace the urgency of the current maritime terrorism problem. Another, or more likely a parallel, path would be for the CSCAP Maritime Cooperation Working Group to forward its initial ideas to a future ARF Intersessional Meeting on CBMs. This meeting is at the official (Track One) level, but with delegations headed by diplomatic personnel; so to be most useful in endorsing and advancing ideas for enhanced Maritime Operational Cooperation, an ARF Intersessional Meeting on CBMs should also schedule another Maritime Experts Group meeting like the one it held with its October 1998 meeting. Another parallel path is for regional nations to cooperate and help define their national roles in Maritime Operational Cooperation through the new Regional Maritime Security Initiative (RMSI). In any case, enhanced Asia-Pacific Maritime Operational Cooperation is essential to ensure regional navies have the focus and capabilities to deal with the immediate threats of maritime terrorism and piracy, and are able to ensure security for regional sea lanes — and for the economies of all the regional nations that increasingly depend on these sea lanes.

Notes

1. Charles A. Meconis and Stanley Byron Weeks, *The Armed Forces of the USA in the Asia-Pacific Region* (Australia: Allen & Unwin; UK, US, Canada: I.B. Taurus, 1999), pp. 70–79; Susan Pederson and Stanley Weeks, "A Survey of Confidence-Building Measures", Chapter 15 in Ralph Cossa (ed.), *CSIS Significant Issues Series, Vol. XVII, No. 3, Asia-Pacific Confidence and Security Building Measures,* 1995.
2. Prof. Ji Guoxing, "Maritime Security and International Cooperation — China's Viewpoint", Paper presented for the Ship and Ocean Foundation Conference, Tokyo, 8–9 November 2002.
3. W. Blanch, "Terror Attacks Threaten Gulf's Oil Routes", *Jane's Intelligence Review,* December 2002 and Ellen Hale, "Oil Industry Fears New Attacks", *USA Today,* 2 December 2002, p. 6A.
4. Stanley Weeks, "Maritime Terrorism: Threats and Responses", Paper for International Conference "Geo-Agenda for the Future: Securing the Oceans" of the Ship and Ocean Foundation, Institute for Ocean Policy, Tokyo, Japan, 17–18 October 2003.
5. Ed Cropley, "Asia Eyes Sea Security After Threats, US Warning", *Reuters,* 22 April 2004.

Chapter 12

Maritime "Regime" Building

Sam Bateman

The absence of robust multilateral maritime regimes in Asia reflects political calculations by the nation-states regarding the rewards and risks and losses and benefits of maintaining the status quo versus developing regimes acceptable and beneficial to all sides involved.

(Valencia, "Regional Maritime Regime Building", p. 241)

Introduction

Back in 1991, the eminent British scholar in international security studies, Michael Leifer, wrote a seminal paper on the importance of maritime regime building in East Asia.[1] His paper promoted the ideal of a stable maritime regime in the region with the free and uninterrupted flow of seaborne trade and nations able to pursue their maritime interests and manage their marine resources in accordance with agreed principles of international law and without the risks of tension and conflict.

Now, some 13 years on, we are still far from the ideal of Leifer's stable maritime regime. To some extent, maritime disorder prevails in the region. This includes unregulated pollution of the marine environment, over fishing, marine environmental degradation and widespread illegal activities at sea, including piracy, smuggling and the threat of maritime terrorism. Maritime cooperation is underdeveloped in East Asia and as Mark Valencia has noted, there is an "absence of robust multilateral maritime regimes" in the region.[2]

The 1982 UN Convention on the Law of the Sea (UNCLOS) created a system of oceans management based on national rights and obligations while exhorting countries to cooperate in managing their maritime interests. However, this system is ineffective in East Asia because of overlapping claims to maritime jurisdiction, few agreed maritime boundaries and countries acting largely in their own self-interest. Maritime jurisdiction is a divisive aspect of the politics of the sea in the region. The lack of agreed jurisdiction complicates maritime enforcement, leads to unchecked degradation of the marine environment and facilitates illegal activities at sea, including possible maritime terrorism.

A wide array of scholarly literature has been produced recently on the topic of maritime security. However, the reality is that we are still well away from a widely accepted maritime security regime. The last memorandum from the Council for Security Cooperation in the Asia-Pacific (CSCAP) identified the lack of an effective maritime regime to provide security and certainty for regional supply chains as one of the weakest links in the region's ability to manage the current period of dramatic change in world affairs.[3] In considering maritime regime building in the region, this chapter pays particular attention to the development of a regime to maintain law and order at sea and to provide for the security of shipping and seaborne trade.

Background

The Regional Maritime Security Initiative (RMSI) recently launched by the United States, along with related aspects of the Proliferation Security Initiative (PSI), is the latest attempt to build a maritime security regime in the region. Major elements of the RMSI include increased situational awareness, information sharing, a decision-making architecture and interagency cooperation.[4] The PSI and RMSI are clearly related but they are also different. The RMSI is focussed on maritime transnational threats in the Asia-Pacific region while the PSI is a global effort to stem the proliferation, by any means, of weapons of mass destruction and their delivery systems. The PSI does not address other transnational threats.

The concept of a cooperative maritime security regime has quite a long history going back to the proposal for a Regional Maritime Surveillance and Safety Regime (RMSSAR) for Southeast Asian waters initially suggested by the Institute of Strategic and International Studies (ISIS) in Malaysia in 1990. However, several difficulties were identified with the implementation of this regime, including the lack of any clear commonality of interest between possible member countries, the differences in organisational arrangements for undertaking surveillance in these countries and regional sensitivities to particular issues, including fishing and disputed maritime claims.[5]

The idea of an RMSSAR was re-visited in a paper in 1994,[6] which identified maritime interests of common concern to regional countries and then went on to propose a maritime surveillance, safety and information regime to cover low level maritime security issues, specifically in East Asian waters. Such a regime would:

- help safeguard the peaceful merchant shipping, which is so important to the region;
- assist in creating a table maritime regime to permit exploitation of the marine resources of the region;
- contribute to the preservation of the marine environment; and
- develop a framework of cooperation that could provide the basis for dealing with higher order contingencies that might arise in the future.

Since the mid-1990s, both CSCAP and by the Institute for Ocean Policy at the Ship and Ocean Foundation (SOF) in Japan with its "Securing the Oceans" concept have pursued the concept of a regional maritime security regime. The CSCAP Maritime Cooperation Working Group was raised specifically with terms of reference to *inter alia* "foster maritime cooperation and dialogue among the states of the Asia Pacific and enhance their ability to manage and use the maritime environment without prejudicing the interests of each other" and "contribute to a stable maritime regime in the Asia Pacific which will reduce the risks of maritime conflict".[7] Since its establishment in 1995, the Group has produced several memoranda. CSCAP Memorandum No. 5 dealing with cooperation for law and order at sea is particularly relevant to maritime regime building.[8]

The SOF "Securing the Oceans" concept seeks to apply the principle of comprehensive security in the maritime domain. It includes perspectives of marine environment protection and peaceful uses of the ocean within an integrated system that also provides for law and order at sea and the safety and security of shipping and seaborne trade. Two conferences with papers considering aspects of the concept have been held so far in November 2002[9] and October 2003.[10] Another conference was held in 2004 to develop specific proposals and recommendations.

These current and past experiences with maritime regime building are instructive with regard to what might be possible in the future. "Top down" approaches, such as the RMSI, are seen by some regional countries as rather heavy-handed and being imposed by a major power rather than evolving through a process of negotiation and dialogue that takes into account the interests and sensitivities of all. These approaches are regarded as failing to appreciate cultural considerations and sovereignty concerns in the region. Some regional countries do not accept that the benefits of these regimes outweigh their costs and risks.

On the other hand, "bottom up" approaches demonstrated by the activities of CSCAP and the SOF are "second track" and lack the authority of "first track" forums. Nevertheless, they are useful "building blocks' that might pave the way towards an effective and agreed maritime security regime. On the positive side, most regional countries seem to accept that something needs to be done and have demonstrated willingness to cooperate to achieve the common goal of enhanced maritime security. However, there is uncertainty about how to achieve this goal. This chapter seeks to assist in finding a way through this dilemma. It draws on regime theory to illustrate the difficulties involved and to suggest some ideas on how these might be overcome.

Maritime Regimes

International regimes of various kinds play a prominent part in the management of the oceans and maritime interests. This is true of all areas of human activity where no single decision-making entity holds exclusive power.[11] One has only to look at a map of the East Asian seas to appreciate the multiplicity of decision-making entities concerned with some aspect of the management of these seas, including the prevention of illegal activity at sea. Regimes provide benefits and reduce costs in a way that no single state party acting on its own could achieve.[12] They reduce the risks of "a tragedy of the commons" where in the short term, individuals might gain but in the long term, everyone loses.

International regimes are encountered throughout oceans and security studies. The UNCLOS itself is an international *regime* but there are a host of other maritime *regimes* for shipping, fishing, seabed mining, marine environmental protection, sea dumping, the prevention of ship-sourced pollution and so on. These regimes have involved the development of much international law and the establishment of a variety of international organisations. This is all part of the process of growing international interdependence or *globalisation*. The requirement for maritime regimes for the preservation and protection of the marine environment and the conservation of marine species arises from the character of the maritime environment with migratory and straddling fish stocks, the interconnectivity of marine ecosystems and many common maritime interests.

Vogler has observed that "for many years it would have been possible to speak of a single regime for the oceans, or more correctly the high seas".[13] The classical regime of the oceans was simple with sovereignty of the coastal state extending over a narrow territorial sea beyond which were the *high seas*, where the freedoms of the high seas applied. Navigation and fishing were the two classical uses of the seas and regimes to cover them were technical (e.g. rules for the prevention of collisions at sea in the case of navigation) and relatively straightforward. However, contemporary users of the seas face a variety of "complex rules, norms, principles and decision-making procedures", which when put together in a particular issue area (e.g. maritime security in East Asia) form what international relations scholars refer to as an *international regime*. While these regimes may reflect thinking at the global level, they invariably require implementation at a regional and national levels to be effective.

Different writers define *regime* in different ways, sometimes explicitly and sometimes not. But most are agreed that a regime refers to norms, rules and procedures that regulate particular areas of public policy;[14] or, put somewhat more generally, regulated patterns of practice on which expectations converge.[15] They govern state behaviour in specific areas of international relations.[16] The concept of an international regime is broader than international *organisation* (which tends to involve systematic information gathering, inspection, dispute settlement and enforcement) or *international law*, which includes both formal, written agreements between states, and their customary practice.

Regimes may be imposed. Examples of this are the insistence of major Western powers on the right of innocent passage through territorial seas and enforcement through the Freedom of Navigation (FON) programme implemented by the United States.[17] Similarly, the PSI and the RMSI both have the potential to become imposed regimes. In another sense, however, regimes may also give more power to smaller states through the medium of collective action.[18] As Hasenclever *et al.* noted:

> Regimes can be a source of power themselves. Thus, even structurally weak states can sometimes exert a modicum of influence on the collective policies in an issue-area due to the membership and voting rules of the international organization that administers the regime concerned.[19]

Realists believe that international relations are motivated primarily by the pursuit of national interests by states and tend to see international regimes as expressions of the distribution of power among states. The realist theory of international relations supports the view that states will largely act in their own self-interest but idealist theory allows for states sharing some concept of the common good. The distribution of power and wealth in the international system exerts a strong influence on the behaviour of states, and "might" might eventually become "right". For example, the PSI might eventually become established in the customary practice of states despite widespread concern at present about the legality of some measures under PSI.

On the other hand, idealists believe in the possibility of achieving harmonious international order and see regimes as contributions to that order. Or to put this comparison another way, realists will view the situation in terms of relative gains as between states but idealists will hope for absolute gains where all benefit. Many writers, including the author, share the idealistic view when it comes to the maritime domain and pin some hope on maritime confidence-building and cooperation to build a more stable regional maritime regime.

We frequently talk about regional maritime cooperation and its presumed benefits but we need to explore more fully the relationship between cooperation and maritime regime building. The relationship between maritime cooperation and the creation of maritime regimes has been an issue for the CSCAP Maritime Cooperation Working Group. This Group considered the conceptual basis and frameworks for the initiation and development of regimes at its Fifth Meeting held in November 1998. After some members expressed concern about what the Group could actually achieve, it was decided to concentrate more on *principles for cooperation* rather than expecting to contribute to *regime building*.[20] To some extent, this reflected a view that regime building was essentially a "first track" issue and beyond the aspirations of a "second track" forum. There was also the view that civil maritime regimes should "be built on the basis of accomplishing their core tasks — that is, for their own sake; marine environmental regimes should be expected to contribute to environmental protection, for example, without unrealistic expectations of contributing *somehow* to regional security".[21] In effect, this was a denial of the "building block" approach to regional security cooperation where cooperation and dialogue starts with "softer" issues and moves on to "harder" ones later.

The expectation of the *idealists* in the CSCAP Working Group was that cooperation would eventually lead to a regime. As Valencia has put it, "cooperation is a necessary but not sufficient condition for the formation of a regime" and "regimes are subsets of cooperative behaviour and facilitate it, but cooperation can exist without a regime".[22] This was precisely the expectation of the Working Group that "a web of cooperative arrangements can ultimately lead to the establishment of regimes".[23]

We also encounter some paradoxes with regime building. The most wide-ranging global maritime regime, UNCLOS, provides an agreed legal basis for enclosure of a significant proportion of the "global commons" by extending the areas that can be claimed as territorial seas and continental shelves and leading to the establishment of 200 km Exclusive Economic Zones (EEZs). Thus, UNCLOS actually supports *nationalistic* approaches to managing the maritime domain although it also provides strong support for the need for cooperation between states, particularly in the enclosed and semi-enclosed seas such as those along the coast of East Asia. This conceptual dichotomy is very apparent in the seas of East Asia. It bears quite fundamentally on the prospects for maritime cooperation and regime building in these seas. Such *nationalistic* approaches obviously inhibit the development of effective international regimes.

An important feature of maritime regime building is the notion of *epistemic communities*. These are groups of experts, typically scientists, who not only generate new insights into causal relationships but actively (and often effectively) promote changes in public policy at the national and international levels necessitated by these insights. *Epistemic communities* may be defined as "network[s] of professionals with recognised expertise and competence in a particular domain and an authoritative claim to policy-relevant knowledge within that domain or issue area".[24] Community members share a common understanding of particular problems in their field of research *as well as* an awareness of, and preference for, a set of technical solutions to these problems. Most important, they are not content with the essentially passive role of providers of information who speak out only at the request of decision-makers. Valencia has claimed that an epistemic community exists in the marine policy arena in East Asia and is gaining strength.[25] The CSCAP Maritime Cooperation Working Group might be seen as such a community that has some influence on processes of official regional security cooperation.[26]

The Politics of the Sea

Politics provide the basic rationale for state action and fundamentally underpin the development of regimes. The development of the Law of the Sea, for example, reveals "a persistent interaction between law and politics".[27] While the interests of countries in the sea often coincide, they can also conflict. In the case of a maritime security consideration, the maritime powers support the freedom of navigation through archipelagoes and international straits while the straits states and archipelagic countries believe that unrestricted freedoms of navigation compromise their national security and threaten their marine environment. While the law of the sea provides a mechanism for resolving disputes, these issues inevitably require intense political negotiations.

Historically, the politics of the sea involved a clash of interests between coastal states and maritime *user* states but the situation is now more complex. It is no longer sufficient to think simply of coastal state interests because coastal states might also be straits states, archipelagic states, geographically disadvantaged states, leading shipping or fishing countries, industrialised or developing countries and so on. For example, Singapore is both a straits state and a major maritime *user* state with different interests to its neighbours, Indonesia and Malaysia. Conflicts of interest over marine environmental protection, the exploitation and management of marine resources and maritime boundary delimitation are amply evident in the seas of East Asia.

Differences of view have also emerged in East Asia over the rights and duties of coastal states in their EEZs vis-à-vis those of other states. This is particularly an issue with regard to the rights of other states to conduct certain activities such as military operations, military surveying, intelligence collection and hydrographic surveying in the EEZ of a coastal state without the permission of that state.[28] Some coastal states require that their consent be given to such activities while others, particularly the United States, argue strongly that the activities are part of the freedoms of navigation and overflight. As most of the waters of concern for maritime security in East Asia are within EEZs, this is an important issue for maritime regime building in the region.

There is special sensitivity in East Asia, particularly among Southeast Asian nations, to anything that can be construed as a heavy handed approach to uses of the sea by Western maritime powers. Writing nearly 50 years ago, the Indian historian and diplomat, K.M. Panikkar, coined the expression the "Vasco da Gama Epoch" to describe the discrete epoch of history, beginning with the arrival of Vasco da Gama at Calicut in Southern India in 1498, when the rich cultures and commerce of Asia would be dominated by Western maritime powers.[29] Panikkar believed that this epoch ended with the Second World War and the gaining of independence by former British, Dutch, French and American colonies and territories in Asia. However, it might now be argued that the "Vasco da Gama Epoch" will only end with the departure of all US military from the region. There remains what an American writer has seen as:

> ... an underlying anti-Western sentiment dating to the origins of these states. Asians from China to India ... do not see themselves as living in a post-Cold War era; instead they see the West as trying to maintain its grip on power through its domination of military technology and key economic institutions. Resentment is often below the surface and is tempered by other pragmatic considerations but it is common throughout Asia.[30]

This sensitivity is quite fundamental and should be recognised in building maritime regimes. It is evident in the cool reception by most Southeast Asian countries to the idea of international involvement in anti-piracy operations in the South China Sea and the Malacca and Singapore Straits. Japanese initiatives to use Japan Coast Guard vessels in anti-piracy patrols in the South China Sea were initially received less than warmly and more recently, Malaysia and Indonesia have both rejected the RMSI as a means of countering potential terrorist attacks against international shipping in the Straits of Malacca.[31] Yet, on the other hand, Malaysia is said to be "tired of footing the bill for higher standards of security and navigational aids in the Malacca Straits".[32] There is thus the paradox that some straits and archipelagic states lack the resources to provide security in SLOCs through their waters but are reluctant to accept operational assistance from user states.

Cultural Factors

Different cultural factors are of fundamental importance in regime building. East Asian countries are extraordinarily diverse. They vary greatly in terms of their geographical size, population, GDP, defence capabilities, political systems, culture and tradition. Ball has noted how even threat perceptions and definitions of security vary in the region.[33] The reality is that many regional countries do not attach the same priority to the Global War on Terrorism as does the United States and its allies. Most regional countries have other priorities of economic development and poverty alleviation that have a higher call on national resources than measures to combat what is perceived basically as a threat to Western interests.

There is a strong link between the nation-state and a specific territorial unit that for some regional countries includes their maritime domain. The sea is conceived as an extension of the land by several Asian countries. Indonesia is the main example with the concept of *Wawasan Nusantara* (i.e. the archipelagic outlook) and the notion that the islands and the waters between them are bound together into "a single and unified political, social, cultural, economic and defence and security entity".[34] Indonesia's view of itself is well illustrated by the leadership position it has assumed in Law of the Sea issues in the region, particularly the implementation of the archipelagic state regime, and leadership of the Workshop process that has been taking place over the last decade to resolve conflict in the South China Sea. Indonesia has also assiduously pursued the delimitation of its own maritime boundaries. It is most unlikely to accept assistance from other countries in directly maintaining the security of its archipelagic waters.

South Korea and Japan are two other East Asian countries that spring to mind as ones that regard themselves as *maritime* countries and normally play an active role in regional maritime affairs. They have relatively well developed domestic arrangements for managing their marine affairs and would seek to play a major role in maritime regime building. And now China is busily rebuilding a maritime culture based on the rich maritime traditions of Chinese seafarers.

Countries in East Asia attach great importance to their sovereignty and are unlikely in the foreseeable future to move even remotely to some regional organisation such as the European Community. Sovereignty is a political concept directly tied to the right of a state through its government, to exercise jurisdiction over its people and territory, and of being answerable for that jurisdiction under international law. Strong cultural attitudes are attached to sovereignty and borders — and to concepts of territorial unity — and in this regard the erosion of sovereignty is much less apparent in the region than it might be elsewhere in the world, particularly in Europe. These attitudes extend to the sea and claims to national sovereignty.[35] They inhibit the development of a regional maritime security regime.

Political Frameworks

The European and South Pacific experiences demonstrate the importance of having over-arching political frameworks in place as a fundamental prerequisite of effective maritime regimes at a regional level. These frameworks have facilitated the development in these two regions of a regional approach to issues such as maritime safety and the prevention of ship-sourced marine pollution. More arguably they also extend to maritime security. The Niue Treaty on Fisheries Surveillance and Law Enforcement in the South Pacific provides a legal framework for cooperative fisheries law enforcement at sea, but although it entered into force in 1993, it still falls rather short of being an effective operational regime.

For Southeast Asia, ASEAN has been active in adopting regional measures designed to ensure the sustainable development of coastal and marine areas.[36] However, Valencia has noted that obstacles arise in the region from the primacy of nation-building over cooperation and coordination, "inequities and imbalances in marine endowments" and "conflicting territorial and maritime claims".[37] Payoyo also found a number of institutional inadequacies in the ASEAN context for handling ocean issues, including "the multiplicity of agencies, organs and fora", "the sector-by-sector bias of decision-making", "the absence of systematised coordination between ASEAN institutions and non-ASEAN institutions which operate in the region" and a need for "recognition, expansion and consolidation of so-called 'track two' (non-official, including non-governmental) mechanisms".[38]

Problems and Difficulties

If there are difficulties in the region with establishing regimes for "softer" issues such as fisheries management and marine environmental protection, the problems with establishing a maritime security regime are even more acute. The experience of the United States with having the PSI accepted in the region provides an example of this. There are now 17 full members of the PSI: Australia, Canada, Czech Republic, Denmark, France, Germany, Italy, Japan, the Netherlands, Norway, Poland, Portugal, Singapore, Spain, Turkey, the United Kingdom and the United States although more than 60 countries have signalled their support for the initiative. Only two Asian countries are full members of the PSI and one of these, Japan, appears somewhat less than fully enthusiastic about the initiative. While supporting the principles of the PSI, China remains concerned about the legality and political consequences of the PSI. South Korea is unlikely to support the PSI while the initiative is plainly intended to put pressure on North Korea. Malaysia and Indonesia are both opposed to the operational implementation of the PSI in waters under their national jurisdiction.

The RMSI has been promoted as a regime to provide security against a range of transnational threats not just piracy and terrorism but also drug smuggling and human trafficking. However, so far there has been no mention of environmental threats and illegal, unauthorised and unregulated (IUU) fishing that are also concerns of regional countries and constitute threats to law and order at sea. The RMSI recognises the globalised nature of the modern world that makes it difficult for any one nation to provide single-handedly for its own security broadly defined. If it could be implemented, it would meet most of the requirements of Leifer's stable maritime regime. But to some regional countries, both the RMSI and the PSI are seen as "big sticks" with elements about them of a return to the "Vasco da Gama Epoch".

What Might be Done?

If the region has been rather less than enthusiastic about the PSI and the RMSI, what then can be done about building a stable maritime regime? First, we need to distinguish between the objectives of the RMSI and the PSI that are primarily about threats of interest to the United States and its allies, and the general requirement for stability and law and order at sea. The interests of most regional countries lie more with the general need for good order at sea rather than specifically fighting terrorism. The latest speech by Admiral Fargo[39] about widening the interpretation of transnational threats beyond piracy and terrorism suggests that this distinction is being appreciated by the United States. The concepts of the RMSI in particular need to be sold to regional countries in terms that accord with their national interests. It would be helpful if the initiative could address a wider range of threats, including marine environmental protection, pollution and IUU fishing.[40] In the broadest terms, two approaches are possible. On the one hand, there is the "big stick" approach with a dominant player dictating the terms of the maritime security regime. On the other hand, there is scope for a more "home grown" regional approach, possibly building on the web of bilateral arrangements that already exists.

Secondly, new maritime regimes should be discussed in a range of forums, both "first track" and "second track" to ensure their acceptability. At a "first track" level, both the ASEAN Regional Forum (ARF) and APEC are appropriate at providing the nearest the region has at present to an over-arching political framework. The Western Pacific Naval Symposium, CSCAP and the work by the SOF in Japan are examples of useful forums below the "first track" level. The "building block" approach has utility and when it comes to the maritime domain, we need to be idealists rather than realists!

Thirdly, developed countries need to assist the less developed countries of the region with building their capacity to deal with maritime security threats. This is not at the "sharp end" with the better equipped countries sending their own forces to patrol in high threat areas but rather through assistance with training and resources to build up local infrastructure, establish systems and procedures, and train personnel. The recent initiative by Japan to train personnel from Cambodia, Indonesia, Malaysia, the Philippines and Thailand to prevent the spread of weapons of mass destruction by sea is an excellent example of what is required.[41]

Fourthly, the countries in need of assistance must feel that they are still retaining control over waters under their sovereignty and that they have some influence over the process of maritime regime building through their collective bargaining weight. Perhaps an *ad hoc* workshop of like-minded countries might be useful with identifying issues of common concern and a possible way ahead. Indonesia, with its expertise in Law of the Sea and its experience with coordinating the South China Sea Workshops, may be well placed to take a leading role.

Fifthly, multidisciplinary and multinational education and training in maritime affairs conducted at a regional level would make an important contribution to building regional maritime awareness and an appreciation of the benefits of a collective regime.[42] Maritime awareness is generally lacking in the region at present but is fundamental to the implementation of a stable maritime regime. In 1996, the CSCAP Maritime Cooperation Working Group agreed to a proposal for regular workshops on regional maritime issues.[43] One of the major objectives of these workshops was to develop greater awareness and knowledge of maritime issues within the Asia-Pacific region and their security implications. Such workshops would bring together middle-level practitioners from the many different regional and national agencies involved in the process of building a stable maritime regime and its outcomes. They would help establish an epistemic community of maritime practitioners who share a common understanding of the particular problems of the maritime domain.

Sixthly, we need to acknowledge that some countries might now prefer to use their coast guards in implementing maritime regimes. Coast guard vessels may be more suitable than warships for employment in sensitive areas where there are conflicting claims to maritime jurisdiction and/or political tensions between parties. Regional coast guards are expanding rapidly.[44] Bangladesh, the Philippines and Vietnam have all established coast guards and China, Malaysia and Indonesia are following suit. The anti-piracy operations by the Japan Coast Guard (JCG) in Southeast Asian waters demonstrate the use of coast guards as instruments of foreign policy. Similarly, the JCG has been handling the operational side of Japan's involvement in the PSI rather than the Japanese Maritime Self-Defence Force (JMSDF).

Lastly, we need to ensure that a stable maritime regime is high on the regional political agenda. Countries in East Asia share significant maritime interests but sources of conflict exist at sea largely because of the uncertain strategic environment, the incidence of maritime sovereignty disputes and major jurisdictional problems at sea, especially the lack of agreed maritime boundaries. We need to work on the difficulties that have been identified with maritime regime building and respect the genuine and deeply held concerns of some regional countries. China is an important linchpin in maritime regime building. In the future, China will become the major maritime power in the region and must be fully engaged in the processes of cooperation and dialogue to build a more stable maritime regime.

Notes

1. Michael Leifer, "The Maritime Regime and Regional Security in East Asia", *The Pacific Review*, Vol. 4, No. 2, 1991, pp. 126–136.
2. Mark J. Valencia, "Regional Maritime Regime Building: Prospects in Northeast and Southeast Asia", *Ocean Development and International Law*, Vol. 31, 2000, p. 241.
3. Council for Security Cooperation in the Asia Pacific (CSCAP), *The Weakest Link? Seaborne Trade and the Maritime Regime in the Asia Pacific* (CSCAP Memorandum No. 8, April 2004). Also available online at http://www.cscap.org.
4. ADM Tom Fargo USN, Commander, US Pacific Command, Address to MILOPS Conference in Victoria, British Columbia, 3 May 2004, pp. 3–5. Also available online at http://www.pacom.mil/speeches/sst2004/040503milops.shtml.
5. Desmond Ball and Sam Bateman, "An Australian Perspective on Maritime CSBMs in the Asia-Pacific Region", in Andrew Mack (ed.), *A Peaceful Ocean? Maritime Security in the Pacific in the Post-Cold War Era* (St. Leonards: Allen & Unwin, 1993), pp. 158–185.
6. Captain Russ Swinnerton, RAN and Desmond Ball, "A Regional Regime for Maritime Surveillance, Safety and Information Exchanges", *Maritime Studies*, No. 78, September/October 1994, pp. 1–15.
7. Sam Bateman and Stephen Bates, "Introduction" in Sam Bateman and Stephen Bates (eds.), *Calming the Waters: Initiatives for Asia Pacific Maritime Cooperation* (Canberra Papers on Strategy and Defence No. 114: Strategic and Defence Studies Centre, Australian National University, Autumn 1996), p. 1. The stable maritime regime idea was borrowed from Leifer (see note 1).
8. CSCAP, *Cooperation for Law and Order at Sea* (CSCAP Memorandum No. 5, February 2001).

9. Institute for Ocean Policy, *Proceedings of International Conference on Geo Agenda for the Future Project: Protect the Oceans* (Tokyo: 8 and 9 November 2002).

10. Institute for Ocean Policy, *Proceedings of International Conference on Geo Agenda for the Future Project: Secure the Oceans* (Tokyo: 17 and 18 October 2003).

11. John Vogler, *The Global Commons — A Regime Analysis* (Chichester: John Wiley & Sons, 1995), p. 2.

12. Edward L. Miles, "Implementation of International Regimes: A Typology", in David Vidas and Willy Ostreng eds., *Order for the Oceans at the Turn of the Century* (The Hague: Kluwer Law International, 1999), p. 327.

13. Vogler, *The Global Commons*, p. 71.

14. Ernst B Haas, "Why Collaborate? Issue-linkage and International Regimes", *World Politics*, XXXII (3), April 1980, p. 358.

15. Stephen D. Krasner (ed.), *International Regimes* (Ithaca, NY: Cornell University Press, 1983), p. 2.

16. Andreas Hasenclever, Peter Mayer, and Volker Rittberger, *Theories of International Regimes* (Cambridge: Cambridge University Press, 1997), p. 1.

17. William J. Aceves, "The Freedom of Navigation Program: A Case Study of the Relationship between Law and Politics", *Hastings International and Comparative Law Review*, Vol. 19, No. 2, Winter 1996, pp. 259–326.

18. This might be shown by the way in which small Pacific island countries have entered into regional fisheries agreements with major fishing countries. Edward P. Wolfers, "The Law of the Sea and Security in the South Pacific", *Maritime Studies*, No. 77, July/August 1994, pp. 22–29, and Edward P. Wolfers, "Maritime Cooperation in the South Pacific", *Maritime Studies*, No. 57, March/April 1991, pp. 1–10.

19. Hasenclever *et al.*, *Theories of International Regimes,* p. 108.

20. Sam Bateman, "Report of the Fifth Meeting of the Maritime Cooperation Working Group", in Sam Bateman (ed.), *Maritime Cooperation in the Asia-Pacific Region: Current Situation and Prospects* (Canberra Papers on Strategy and Defence No. 132: Strategic and Defence Studies Centre, Australian National University, Canberra, 1999), p. 170. This was consistent with CSCAP Memorandum No. 4, *Guidelines for Regional Maritime Cooperation*, published in December 1997.

21. Chris Rahman, "Linking Maritime Regimes to Regional Security", in Bateman, *Maritime Cooperation in the Asia-Pacific Region*, p. 95.

22. Valencia, "Regional Maritime Regime Building: Prospects in Northeast and Southeast Asia", p. 225.

23. Bateman, "Report of the Fifth Meeting", p. 170.

24. From Haas cited in Hasenclever *et al.*, *Theories of International Regimes*, p. 149.

25. Valencia, "Regional Maritime Regime Building: Prospects in Northeast and Southeast Asia", p. 229.

26. For more information on CSCAP see Desmond Ball, *The Council for Security Cooperation in the Asia Pacific (CSCAP) — Its Record and its Prospects* (Canberra Papers on Strategy and Defence No. 139: Strategic and Defence Studies Centre, Australian National University, Canberra, October 2000).

27. Aceves, "The Freedom of Navigation Program", p. 259.

28. See discussion in Ship and Ocean Foundation (SOF) and East-West Center (EWC), *The Regime of the Exclusive Economic Zone: Issues and Responses* (A Report of the Tokyo Meeting, 19–20 February 2003, Honolulu, East-West Center, 2003) Also available online at http://www.EastWestCenter.org/res-rp-publicationdetails.asp?pub_ID=1418.

29. K.M. Panikkar, *Asia and Western Dominance: A Survey of the Vasco da Gama Epoch of Asian History* (London: Allen and Unwin, 1959).

30. Paul Bracken, "Asia's Militaries and the New Nuclear Age", *Current History*, Vol. 98, No. 2, December 1999, p. 420.

31. Mark Baker, "Malaysia Puts US in its Place Over Offer to Police Busy Sea Lane", *Sydney Morning Herald*, 6 April 2004, p. 8.

32. *Fairplay Daily Shipping News*, 15 October 1999.

33. Desmond Ball, "Strategic Culture in the Asia-Pacific Region (With Some Implications for Regional Security Cooperation)", Working Paper No. 270, Strategic and Defence Studies Centre, Australian National University, Canberra, April 1993, p. 22.

34. A. Hasnan Habib, "Technology for National Resilience: The Indonesia Perspective", in Desmond Ball and Helen Wilson (eds.), *New Technology: Implications for Regional and Australian Security* (Canberra Papers on Strategy and Defence No. 76: Strategic and Defence Studies Centre, Australian National University, Canberra, 1991), p. 62.

35. Ken Booth, *Law, Force and Diplomacy at Sea* (London: George Allen & Unwin, 1985), p. 40.

36. Peter Bautista Payoyo, "Ocean Governance in the ASEAN Region and the United Nations Convention on the Law of the Sea", *Pacific Review*, Vol. 9, No. 2, 1997, pp. 57–71.

37. Valencia, "Regional Maritime Regime Building: Prospects in Northeast and Southeast Asia", pp. 239–240.

38. Payoyo, "Ocean Governance in the ASEAN Region", pp. 63–64.

39. See note 4.

40. The approach in the SOF's "Securing the Oceans" project would seem to have merit in this regard.

41. "Japan to Train ASEAN Nations to Intercept WMDs at Sea", *Japan Today online*, 5 May 2004.

42. Students from other Asian countries being enrolled in the Japan Coast Guard (JCG) Academy as a contribution to measures to combat piracy is a good example

of multinational education and training. *Kyodo News online*, 25 April 2001. Available online at http://home.kyodo.co.jp.

43. Sam Bateman and R.M. Sunardi, "The Way Ahead", in Sam Bateman and Stephen Bates (eds.), *The Seas Unite: Maritime Cooperation in the Asia Pacific Region* (Canberra Papers on Strategy and Defence No. 118: Strategic and Defence Studies Centre, Australian National University, 1996), pp. 279–280.

44. For a discussion of the development and expansion of coast guards in the region see Sam Bateman, "Coast Guards: New Forces for Regional Order and Security", *Asia Pacific Issues: Analysis from the East-West Center No. 65*, Honolulu, East-West Center, January 2003.

Conclusion

As maritime security in the Asia-Pacific has increased in significance over the last 20 years, a number of concerns, trends and challenges have come to light that need to be examined and addressed. The chapters presented in this study attempt to do just that. This volume captures the changing nature of the concept of maritime security, which has evolved from the narrow focus of traditional military concerns to one which incorporates the problems of terrorism and piracy. The result is a more inclusive study, which, it is hoped, will contribute to the building of a comprehensive maritime security environment for the Asia-Pacific.

The chapters contained in this volume highlight the scope of the challenge and represent a number of different perspectives. However, a consensus is reached by all of the contributors on the need for global and regional cooperation in order to enhance maritime security in the Asia-Pacific. Finding solutions to the challenges faced by the region is becoming increasingly important given that the 21st century is predicted to be the Asia-Pacific century. With the centre for global economic activity shifting its focus to the region and the consequential increase in trade and shipping, coupled with the rise of China, which is set to become a regional hegemon, and the increased focus this will draw from the regional and extra-regional navies, the issue of maritime security in the Asia-Pacific certainly warrants increased attention. Now with the region being labelled as the "second-front" in the war on terror and the attention this has drawn not only to the vulnerabilities of the region's maritime industry but also to the continued, and until recently often neglected problem of piracy, there is even more reason to turn our attention to addressing the challenges faced.

The need for cooperation, on both global and regional scales, is paramount. Whether this is under the aegis of the IMO, APEC, a new maritime regime or as a series of bilateral agreements, for example, PSI, cooperation needs to be enhanced in order to address the main challenges to maritime security in the Asia-Pacific, in the current international environment and in the future.

Maritime Security Challenges in the Asia-Pacific

The threats to maritime security are diverse and considerable in number. From the analyses presented in the preceding chapters, it is certainly clear that these challenges cover many issue areas and involve many factors and forces. In the Asia-Pacific, some of the main areas of concern are: port security, freedom of navigation, security of the sea lanes of communication (SLOC), security from pirate attacks or armed robberies against ships and security from maritime terrorism. However, a number of other issues have been highlighted by the contributors to this volume that need to be taken into consideration. Hideaki Kaneda notes seven factors that have, or have the potential to have, a considerable bearing on the security of the maritime sector:

- the proliferation of weapons of mass destruction and ballistic missiles from North Asia to the other regions of the world;
- the rise of the spectre of international terrorism in the region;
- the rapid build-up of Chinese military power, in particular its naval and air power;
- the confrontational military structure, which originated in the Cold War and still remains in the Korean Peninsula and the Taiwan Strait;
- territorial and ethnic disputes that have plagued the region for decades, most of which centre around conflicting claims to the various resource rich islands in the region;
- the confrontation over oceanic interests, caused mainly by Chinese naval activities;
- and finally, the increase in international and organised illegal activities, in particular the problem of piracy.

The growth of regional navies and the evolving patterns of regional naval interaction, while receiving less attention from the world's media, continue to have a bearing on maritime security. Although currently the US Navy continues to dominate in the maritime arena, the modernisation of the region's navies has been impressive and robust and has the potential to destabilise the region and significantly alter the regional balance of power.

This examination of maritime challenges also necessitates the conclusion that maritime terrorism represents one of the most significant threats to maritime security in the Asia-Pacific. As Catherine Zara Raymond concludes in her paper *Maritime Terrorism, A Risk Assessment: The Australian Example*, the commercial maritime industry's preoccupation with the principle of *"just enough — just in time*" and a free-flowing system has left it vulnerable to breaches in its security. Other contributions on the topic of maritime terrorism reinforce this conclusion. Particular attention is drawn to the vulnerability of container shipping and the possibility of it being used by terrorists to carry out an attack on a port or harbour.

The maritime domain has been labelled as an ideal medium within which, through which and from which terrorists can carry out attacks. Evidence of this is given in the chapter by Rupert Herbert-Burns. He refers to international maritime corporate and business practices as "the corporate veil" and concludes that the maritime industry is characterised by "a range of complex interlocking mechanisms that enable anonymity, the ability to circumvent intrusive forensic audits and the freedom to operate sub-standard vessels crewed by poorly trained and salaried crewmen, many with inaccurate or even forged documentation".

Piracy, whilst having been a problem in the region for many years, has come under increased attention in recent times. This is particularly the case now that the potential and real links between piracy and terrorism are more fully understood. The possibility of terrorists adopting pirate tactics is of major concern not only regionally but also globally, reflecting the high value of the region's waterways in the global economy.

Thus, while traditional maritime security concerns persist in the Asia-Pacific, there has been a rise in the significance of non-traditional security threats and this will have implications in terms of shifting theatres of operation, new challenges for technology, changing maritime roles and the management of information.

A less visible but nonetheless important aspect of maritime security in the Asia-Pacific are the problems associated with maritime boundary and territorial disputes. Peter Cozens states that the Third United Nations Convention on the Law of the Sea (UNCLOS III), while providing a "comprehensive set of principles and rules", in fact "opened a sea of troubles that today manifest as maritime territorial boundary disputes". Of significant concern is the fact that in the Asia-Pacific there are still many maritime boundaries still to be fixed. Not only does this have the potential to cause disputes over, or the exploitation of resources but a lack of agreed boundaries could hamper effective international cooperation thus reducing maritime security. In other words, there is a need to provide jurisdictional clarity and certainty, without this any regime of international cooperation, advocated by many of the contributors to this volume as the most effective way to increase maritime security in the Asia-Pacific, will be rendered ineffective.

The Way Forward

Despite the fact that the Asia-Pacific maritime arena is characterised by a wide array of security challenges and deep-seated problems, it is possible to pick out a consensus of views amongst the contributors regarding the solution or panacea to these ills.

The way forward is believed to be in enhanced cooperation amongst the states concerned. In particular, cooperation that seeks to address a number of issue areas in order to form a comprehensive security environment is seen as the ultimate goal.

Contributors on this topic note that the Asia-Pacific nations need to "move beyond the previously successful focus on maritime confidence-building measures... and start emphasising Maritime Operational Cooperation". In this context, Maritime Operational Cooperation refers in particular to the patrolling of sea lanes and choke points in the Straits of Malacca. Existing groupings like the Western Pacific Naval Symposium could be appropriate forums for facilitating Maritime Operational Cooperation.

Sam Bateman then takes this conclusion one step further and discusses the creation of a comprehensive maritime regime, one that would build upon existing arrangements, and most importantly complement and promote the principles enshrined in the Law of the Sea (UNCLOS). Without the development of a maritime regime, the disorder that to some extent prevails in the region will continue; the overlapping claims to maritime jurisdiction and the prevailing trend for countries to act largely in their own self-interest will remain defining characteristics of the regional maritime system.

There is much less consensus amongst the authors of this volume regarding the topic of US efforts aimed at improving maritime security in the Asia-Pacific, for example, the PSI and RMSI. The creation and promotion of these initiatives by the United States has been criticised as being very much a "top-down" approach, which is seen by some regional countries as rather heavy-handed. They are also somewhat narrow in scope, in that they are primarily concerned with threats to US interests in the region.

Despite the PSI's political and legal shortcomings, in particular that its operations may come into conflict with international law, it is possible to argue that it has its place in the effort to enhance maritime security and that despite the criticisms that it has been met with, it will help to establish "best practices" to stop proliferation-related shipments, thus addressing a significant threat to maritime security in the Asia-Pacific.

It is also important to note that building a comprehensive security environment for the Asia-Pacific will require a more broad and inclusive concept of maritime security, one that includes both traditional and non-traditional security concerns and reflects the individual needs of the states themselves.

Concluding Remarks

This study has highlighted a number of key issues and concerns regarding the maritime security of the Asia-Pacific. The way forward is to further develop the notion of a comprehensive security environment. At present a number of issues are often neglected or overshadowed by the more newsworthy maritime security challenges, for example, the threat of maritime terrorism and piracy. These problems, such as human, drugs and arms trafficking, the exploitation of fisheries resource and pollution, despite being given less attention on the international stage, are of great concern to many of the regional players. Any maritime security initiatives developed for the Asia-Pacific region must take into account the differing priorities and sensitivities of the states concerned, otherwise they will be short-lived.

Cooperation must be enhanced in order to build a comprehensive security environment. The regional countries must begin to move beyond their present stage of engaging in confidence-building measures and begin to cooperate at the operational level. However, any initiatives based on enhancing cooperation in order to increase maritime security in the Asia-Pacific must contend with two issues that lie close to the heart of the region's nations, that is, sovereignty and national interest. While the involvement of the extra-regional powers is important to any measures aimed at building a comprehensive security environment, the desire to prevent a complete internationalisation of the issue of security has been clearly voiced by the regional states. Any cooperative arrangements must therefore contain the "home-grown" element in order to minimise any perceived compromise to the sovereignty of the states concerned.

Despite the fact that any multilateral initiatives aimed at enhancing maritime security in the Asia-Pacific will face a host of challenges, it is in this direction that a safer and more secure maritime region lies. Whether it be in increased intelligence sharing in order to counter the threat of terrorism or the more ambitious formation of a comprehensive maritime regime aimed at securing the safety and security of the region's shipping lanes and water ways, ensuring the maritime security of the Asia-Pacific is now of utmost importance.

Index